D1148759

The Which? Guide to Divorce

About the author

After qualifying as a solicitor, Imogen Clout specialised in family law and worked at a number of different practices in London. She was an early member of the Solicitors Family Law Association and a founder member of the National Stepfamily Association. In 1994 she became a lecturer in Legal Practice at the University of Sheffield. She has written on and taught family law for many years. Imogen Clout is married, with three children.

Acknowledgements

The author and publishers would like to thank Carolyn MacBride of Quinn Martin & Langan and Philip Gilpin of Hewitt & Gilpin for revising the chapters on Scotland and Northern Ireland respectively. Jonquil Lowe revised the sections on pensions.

The Which? Guide to Divorce

Imogen Clout

CONSUMERS' ASSOCIATION

Which? Books are commissioned and researched by
Consumers' Association and published by
Which? Ltd, 2 Marylebone Road, London NW1 4DF
Email address: books@which.net

Distributed by The Penguin Group:
Penguin Books Ltd, 80 Strand, London WC2R 0RL, England

First edition August 1992
Second edition August 1994
Third edition January 1996
Fourth edition May 1997
Fifth edition July 1998
Sixth edition March 2001
Reprinted November 2001
Reprinted July 2002

British Library Cataloguing in Publication Data
A catalogue record for this book is available from the British Library

ISBN 0 85202 847 4

For a full list of *Which?* books, please write to Which? Books, Castlemead,
Gascoyne Way, Hertford X, SG14 1LH or access our web site at
http://www.which.net

Cover and text design by Kysen Creative Consultants

Photoset by Paston PrePress Ltd, Beccles, Suffolk
Printed and bound in Great Britain by Clays Ltd, Bungay, Suffolk

Contents

Part 4: Other parts of the UK

★An asterisk next to the name of an organisation in the text indicates that the address can be found in this section

Introduction

Whatever circumstances are leading you to contemplate divorce, you are likely to feel confused and lost about which way to turn. The various legal, financial and practical issues you have to cope with may seem daunting, especially at a time of turmoil. It is important to recognise, however, that there is no single correct path through the problems that you face: each family is different and has different needs. You need to decide what your priorities are, and what you want your future life to be like. This book shows you the various options open to you, so that you can make sensible choices about what would be best for you and your family.

The costs of divorce can be crippling. One factor that all separating or divorcing couples have in common is that they will have two households, not one, to maintain in future. *The Which? Guide to Divorce* focuses on helping couples to minimise the costs of the divorce process itself in order to free up as much money as possible for the family. This itself can reduce the stress of the situation before, during and after the divorce. The guide suggests how to find a good lawyer – one who knows what he or she is talking about and who will adopt a conciliatory approach in legal proceedings, rather than getting too readily into the boxing ring of litigation and escalating costs. You will need to use your lawyer to your best advantage (not as an expensive emotional prop or a source of basic information), and knowing how the system operates will put you in a better position to do this.

The laws relating to divorce and family life are in a state of flux. The implementation of Part II of the Family Law Act 1996, which had been on hold for several years, will now not happen: as this book went to press the government announced its intention to repeal this part of the Act. It is not clear whether other reforms will be introduced and what form they will take.

Significant changes have occurred and others are about to occur over pensions. For divorce petitions filed since July 1996, parties have been able to apply for an 'earmarking' order so that a spouse without any pension can get a court order giving her or him the right to a share of the spouse's pension on retirement. Earmarking orders have their drawbacks: the pension (which is in effect deferred maintenance) is not paid if the ex-spouse dies or the recipient remarries; and, where the earmarking does succeed, actions by the ex-spouse – such as reducing or stopping contributions to the earmarked scheme – may reduce the amount payable. The valuation of the pension has also proved problematic. But the chief drawback for many will be that a divorcing couple can no longer achieve a clean financial break from each other if a pension is earmarked. An option likely to be much more popular than earmarking is pension-sharing, which came into effect on 1 December 2000. Under this arrangement, the pension-holder's pension is divided up on divorce and the spouse gets a part of it to invest either in the same scheme as the ex-spouse's or in another scheme of her (or his) own.

People getting divorced in the new century will find that the Child Support Agency, rather than the courts, is most likely to be dealing with child support payments wherever there is a dispute. The Agency, set up with the laudable aim of improving the system of child maintenance, has failed to live up to its promise, largely because of the byzantine complexity of the system. In December 1996 a new 'departure system' introduced a little flexibility into the formula to take account of payments which the Agency had to ignore before, such as debts built up while the family was together and childcare costs. This is providing very little relief, but until the Agency substantially improves its own poor record on delay and inaccuracy it will continue to be unpopular. In mid-1997 an independent audit showed that 85 per cent of its assessments were still inaccurate.

In an attempt to reform the whole child support system the government has introduced a series of modifications (see Chapter 6), which are likely to come into force in 2002. These simplify the formula on which maintenance is based and aim to bring all families, not just those on benefit, within the system.

Changes brought into the system by the Children Act 1989 have by and large improved the way that children are treated when their parents divorce. Parents are now encouraged to make their own arrangements for their children following divorce or separation, rather than look to the courts to do this for them. Where conflicts do arise, simpler and more specific court orders can be sought in order to resolve them; moreover, couples do not have to wait until they start the divorce process before applying for a court order about their children. Grandparents can make court applications to see their grandchildren, and the new, more flexible system means that other family members, or even other interested parties, can seek the courts' remedies over children (a filtering process ensures that this really will be in the children's interests). Most important, children's voices are better heard within the system, as it ensures that their wishes and feelings are taken into account where possible along with a range of other factors affecting their welfare.

Further reforms are being introduced that will affect the roles of court welfare officers and guardians *ad litem*, who prepare reports about children for the courts. A new resource, Children and Family Court Advisory and Support Service (CAFCASS), is being established, which may well result in changes in procedure.

Changes relating to mediation are being piloted in some areas, so not all parts of England and Wales are operating the same system. Mediation offers a potentially faster and more cost-effective route through the divorce process, avoiding costly and time-consuming litigation, and allows you to create tailor-made settlements according to your individual and family needs. Its family-oriented approach reduces conflict and improves communication, so is much better for the children too. This book helps you assess whether mediation could help you and your spouse resolve your disputes.

Possibly the biggest overall change affecting divorce will be the influence of the Human Rights Act 1998, which came into force on 2 October 2000. Article 8, which covers the protection of private and family life, Article 14, which covers freedom from discrimination, and Article 12, the right to marry and found a family, may all have an impact on family law. Article 6, the right to a fair trial, may also affect court procedure, which could change family law procedure. As yet it is impossible to predict the changes, but all lawyers should be aware of the Act and alert to the possibilities of using it to protect their clients.

The most immediate effects may be felt in areas where unmarried couples and their families are treated differently from married couples.

This book is divided into three sections. The early part of the book is intended to help you if you are thinking about divorce and want to know what it may entail. This has a chapter on the issues surrounding children and how they will cope with a divorce, which will be helpful to parents. The second section deals with divorce proceedings and matters linked with them, such as money and children. The third section covers other issues that you may need help with, such as domestic violence. A completely new chapter focuses on the concerns of unmarried couples when they split up, even though, strictly speaking, divorce does not apply to such couples. The last two chapters deal with the differences in the law in Scotland and Northern Ireland. A number of useful tables and forms have been incorporated into the book. In addition, the bibliography and the list of relevant organisations at the end of the book may be helpful when you are thinking about or going through a divorce.

On a point of terminology, although throughout the book the term 'he or she' is used when referring to a spouse, in certain chapters (for example, those on money in divorce, and domestic violence) one or other gender is specifically referred to. This reflects what happens in the majority of cases: for example, as it is rare for an ex-wife to pay maintenance to her ex-husband, the pronoun 'he' is used to refer to the payer.

Divorce is never easy, but this guide endeavours to help you through the maze. Remember that there is life after divorce.

Part 1

Before a divorce starts

Chapter 1

The costs of divorce

LEGAL HEALTH WARNING
This could be the most important chapter of the book for you:
please do not be tempted to skip it

Starting off a book about divorce with the issue of costs may seem a little odd, but for many people the problem of finding the money to pay for a divorce presents one of the biggest headaches of all. It is all too easy to 'forget' about the question of costs until your divorce and financial problems are resolved, but then the total sum of legal costs that has built up can come as an unexpected shock and can severely limit your and your spouse's ability to adapt to your future lives apart. This chapter throws light on the complex issue of costs and looks at what steps you can take to keep them low – a constant theme throughout the book.

The issue of costs can create particularly severe problems in a divorce in which one party is determined to mount an expensive legal campaign against the other. Whenever there is a legally fought dispute over the children, or over spousal maintenance or property, both sides will generally have to instruct solicitors (and perhaps barristers too). As a result, two bills will have to be paid at the end of the case.

When you are caught up in the thick of the divorce process, it is easy to forget that the costs of the proceedings are going to come out of the family money. The more you spend on lawyers the less you will have left for yourselves. People involved in acrimonious divorces often talk about fighting for their 'rights', or 'justice', or 'the principle of the thing', forgetting that all this becomes very expensive, and that divorce law is not designed to deliver abstract redress or compensation.

This does not mean that it is necessary to cave in to a spouse who is demanding too much. A good solicitor (see Chapter 3 on where to get legal help) will be able to negotiate strongly on your behalf and can in most cases work out a reasonable settlement with your spouse's solicitor without the added expenses of a full-blown court battle. You may be able to come to a settlement with your spouse either by yourself (see Chapter 2) or with the aid of a mediator (see Chapter 5 for a full explanation of what mediation is, how it works and where to find a mediator), thus saving considerably on legal costs. Using the Child Support Agency (CSA)★ to work out the amount of child support and collect it from your ex-partner can cut down on legal costs too (see the end of this chapter and Chapter 6). But gaining a good understanding of the complex system of legal costs is likely to be very helpful.

In the following pages you will find an explanation of how Community Legal Service (CLS)★ funding (which used to be called legal aid) works, how costs in the proceedings are worked out and how solicitors charge. We also explode the myth about CLS funding meaning *free* legal help: this is only rarely the case.

Costs in matrimonial proceedings

Solicitors' charges

Solicitors charge according to the amount of time they spend on your case. A solicitor will log every single thing that he or she does on your file: answering letters, making telephone calls, seeing you or witnesses (referred to as 'attendances'), reading papers (referred to as 'perusals'), going to court (which includes travelling, waiting and the actual hearing) and putting papers in order ready for trial ('bundling').

Most solicitors charge on an hourly basis. They usually record the time spent on a case in 'units' of five or six minutes each. Making a short telephone call or writing a letter will probably not take as long as this, but the practice is to record them as single units each. If any item of work takes longer than a single unit the time recorded will be rounded **up** to the nearest unit spent. A further figure (generally worked out as a percentage of the bill) may be added as a mark-up for 'care and attention'. This is an extra charge solicitors make if your case has been complex or has had to be dealt with especially quickly.

When you first instruct a solicitor, or are making enquiries about firms of solicitors, you should check the hourly rate of the person who will be acting for you. Make sure you ask whether the figure you are quoted includes VAT. A solicitor's hourly charging rate can be anything from £80 upwards (plus VAT) in a firm outside London; in London it may range from £90 to £180 (plus VAT). Hourly rates of £250 (plus VAT) are not uncommon in some up-market London firms. Solicitors' firms generally have staff who have different levels of legal education and/or experience. Naturally, a partner's hourly charge will be more than that of a trainee or a legal executive.

Time is money when you are using a solicitor. It makes sense therefore to prepare what you need to say or discuss before you telephone or go to an appointment. If you use your solicitor as a counsellor or an emotional prop, or telephone him or her about every small disagreement that you have with your spouse, you will find that the costs mount alarmingly.

Bills of costs in CLS-funded cases are constructed on a slightly different basis. Although in such cases too the time spent on any one piece of work is taken into account, there are usually pre-set hourly rates for some aspects of the work: travelling to court, for instance, is charged at a lower rate than actually appearing before a judge. Also, certain items, such as routine telephone calls, may be charged at flat rates.

Barristers' fees

If your solicitor thinks that your case needs the services of a barrister, either for specialist advice or to represent you in court, you will need to pay a further fee for this. Barristers generally charge on the basis of each piece of work they do: a set amount for a conference, or written advice, or an appearance at court ('a brief fee'). If the hearing at court is likely to continue for more than a day, the fee will be on the basis of so much at the outset and then a fee for each subsequent day. This is quaintly referred to as a 'refresher'.

Your solicitor negotiates the barrister's fee. This can subsequently be reduced by the court or the Legal Services Commission (LSC,★ see below) in a process known as 'assessment' (see below). You should bear in mind that if your case comes to the point of a hearing in court and a barrister is instructed to appear for you, the brief fee will be charged even if the matter is settled by agreement shortly before the hearing and your barrister does not actually have to represent you at the hearing.

Disbursements

This is the name given to the costs and fees that your solicitor will pay out on your behalf during the course of your case. It can include such things as fees for valuations, experts' fees and court fees. If VAT is charged, this has to be passed on to you.

Paying costs privately

If you are paying privately, your solicitor will probably ask you for some money in advance 'on account of costs'. A sum as large as £500 would not be unusual; indeed, £1,000 is probably more realistic. It makes sense to ask for interim bills at regular intervals and to try to keep paying them as you go along. If you do not pay your solicitor's bill, he or she is entitled to say that he or she will do no further work for you until the costs are settled. He or she can also retain your file of papers as security for payments.

Solicitors have clear professional rules about the information that they must give their clients about costs. At the beginning of your relationship you should be given a letter full of information about the way in which costs will be charged and about the firm's complaints procedure. You should be given regular (at least every six months) updates on the level of your costs. You should also be told if the firm increases its charge-out hourly rates. If you have been given an estimate of the likely costs, you should be told if this is going to be exceeded.

When you get a bill from your solicitor you can ask for a breakdown showing all the items that have been charged for. If you feel that the charges are too high, you should discuss the issue with him or her, or with someone more senior in the firm, and you may be able to agree a reduction. If you are dissatisfied with the response you receive, you are entitled to have your bill assessed (see below). Normally, you should do this within one month of the date on the bill. Your solicitor should remind you about this in a form of standard wording on the bill. He or she can sue you if you do not pay.

Affording the bills

You may not be eligible for CLS funding but still find it hard to pay your solicitor's bill. Many solicitors will be happy to let you pay by a regular monthly standing order, if this will help to spread the cost. Some have arrangements with credit-card companies and will let you pay using credit cards.

If you are certain that at the end of the case you will get a settlement out of which you can afford to pay your costs, you may be able to persuade your bank to lend you the money, or your solicitor may be prepared to enter into an agreement with you to be paid on this basis. This is not a 'contingency fee' agreement – your solicitor is not saying that he or she will be paid only *if* you win, or that you agree to pay a percentage of what you get. You will still be liable for the costs if you do not get what you had expected, but they should be charged according to the solicitor's normal rates, as agreed with you at the beginning of the case. The court has approved this type of an agreement provided the client gets proper independent legal advice about its terms before entering into it. If your solicitor proposes such an agreement to you, you should be given a draft of the terms and you should consult another solicitor before you enter into it. You will need to bear in mind the risks involved, and be aware that costs can increase very fast, sometimes in ways you had not expected.

Community Legal Service funding (legal aid)

You need to consider whether you will be eligible for legal aid. This does not mean that you will get your divorce for free (as is explained below), but it will help you meet some of the costs.

Both your capital and income are taken into account when your eligibility for funding is considered. However, capital which is in dispute between you and your spouse is not included in the calculation. If you are not working and have little or no income of your own, you may qualify for funding even if you have quite a lot of capital that you own as a couple. This means that quite often a non-working wife may qualify. If you are in this position, you should look at the eligibility tables in this chapter. It can put you at an advantage if your spouse has to pay privately for his solicitor.

The legal aid system has undergone a recent, radical change. In April 2000 the Legal Services Commission replaced the Legal Aid

Board, which had been responsible for administering the system. The new system is called the Community Legal Service. At the same time the various forms of legal aid were renamed, and the rules about them altered. Even the term 'legal aid' has been replaced and is now officially called CLS funding. However, solicitors are likely to continue to refer to it generally as legal aid.

Another key change is that fewer firms offer legal aid. At one time, any solicitors' firm could offer legal aid to a client. Now, a firm has to be approved by the LSC and have a contract with it to offer CLS funding (in the past such a firm was said to be 'franchised'). If you think that you will be eligible (the rules are set out later in this chapter) you should check whether a firm offers CLS funding when you first make an appointment with it.

When you go to your first appointment with the firm, you should take with you details of your income. If you are in work, take your most recent wage slips; if you are on income support or income-based jobseeker's allowance, take proof of this, like your benefit book. If you get working families' tax credit or disabled person's tax credit, take proof that you receive these. You do not need to take evidence of your spouse's income, as this is not counted if you are divorcing or separating. However, if you are already living with another partner, his or her income will have to be brought into account too, so you will need evidence of that.

If the firm that you go to does offer CLS funding and you are eligible, you will find that different levels of the funding apply to different stages of your divorce process.

First-stage CLS funding

What used to be called Green Form advice (from the colour of the form that the solicitor completed) is now called Legal Help, but you may find that your solicitor still refers to it using the former name. It covers the work that the solicitor will do in an undefended divorce suit. It covers only the divorce itself, not dealing with the financial side of things or with any dispute over children. For those matters there are other forms of CLS funding.

When you see your solicitor at the first meeting he or she will work out whether you qualify for Legal Help. He or she will fill in a form with details of your income and capital. Your disposable capital and disposable income must be under certain limits (see box on how to work these out). These figures are reviewed annually in April. (The LSC publishes an information leaflet about Legal Help called *The Community Legal Service* which contains up-to-date financial limits. Like other leaflets produced by the LSC, it is available from the LSC web site, under the 'Seeking Legal Help?' link, and can be downloaded if you wish.) Your solicitor will be able to tell you immediately whether you are eligible for Legal Help and you will be asked to sign the form with your details to confirm that they are true.

If you are eligible for Legal Help, you will pay nothing to the solicitor and he or she will be able to do up to two hours' work for you, or three hours' worth if you are the petitioner (the person filing for divorce) and you file a petition. Once the time limit is used up the solicitor will have to obtain an extension if there is still further work to do to take the proceedings up to decree absolute, which is the final stage in the divorce. At the end of the case, your solicitor will send the bill to the LSC, which will pay him or her. The rates that he or she is allowed to charge are laid down by law and are periodically reviewed (currently they are £45.50 per hour (£48.25 in London) for contracted firms and £44 per hour (£46.50 per hour in London) for non-contracted firms).

Under the scope of the Legal Help form your solicitor can help with:

- general advice on whether there are grounds for divorce or judicial separation
- advice on questions of domicile; proving the validity of a foreign marriage
- advice on the procedure for getting a divorce
- the drafting of the petition and documents to accompany it
- advice on defending a divorce and the implications of doing so
- help with an application for full CLS funding
- advice on obtaining an injunction
- registration of 'matrimonial home rights' (formerly called 'rights of occupation')
- advice about who will look after the children, about 'parental responsibility', 'residence' and 'contact' orders, and other orders under the Children Act 1989

Table A: Income and capital limits for Legal Help

Capital

You do not have to include anything which is likely to be the subject of a dispute between yourself and your spouse during the course of the divorce and the separation. In practice this means that in most matrimonial cases the capital does not get brought into the calculation at all. However, if you have any property which is yours alone and which you think will not be disputed, this has to be added up.

Add up: the value of your savings, which includes cash, investments, National Savings, money in the bank or building society, and any other valuable assets that you have like antiques or jewellery.

Leave out:
- the value of your house (unless it is worth more than £100,000 after allowing for a mortgage of up to £100,000)
- the value of the house contents (unless they are very valuable), clothing, tools of your trade
- any back-to-work bonus under the Job Seekers Act 1995
- any payments under the Community Care (Direct Payments) Act 1996.

Take away from this total:
- £335 if you have one dependant (if your spouse is still living with you, he or she is a dependant)
- £535 if you have two dependants
- £635 if you have three dependants
- £100 for each extra dependant.

You must have less than £1,000 in capital to qualify for Legal Help.

- advice about spousal maintenance, and arrangements concerning the family home
- guidance on pensions – whether a claim might be made under the new law which provides for pensions to be 'earmarked'
- limited correspondence or discussions with solicitors acting for the other spouse to try to negotiate a settlement.

If you need advice on another legal matter (for example, you might

Income

If you are receiving income support or income-based job seeker's allowance you will qualify for Legal Help automatically provided your capital is not more than £1,000. If you get working families' tax credit or disabled person's tax credit, you will qualify automatically if the amount to be deducted from the maximum tax credit as a result of other income you receive has been worked out at not more than £70 per week.

If you do not qualify automatically, your disposable income is worked out as follows.

Add up: all the income that you have received for the last seven days (including child benefit, if you receive it). **Note:** disability living allowance, attendance allowance, constant attendance allowance, council tax benefit, housing benefit and payments made under the Earnings Top-up Scheme or the Community Care Direct Payment scheme are **not** counted as income.

Take away:
- income tax
- National Insurance
- £29.75 (if you are still living with your spouse)
- £26.60 for each child aged 15 and under
- £31.75 for each child aged 16 or over.

If your disposable income works out to £84 per week or less, you will qualify for Legal Help.

have to deal with a building society over debts and possession proceedings), a new Legal Help form can be completed.

If you are receiving Legal Help, you will not have to pay the court fees for divorce proceedings, which is a considerable saving.

However, if at the end of the divorce you get or keep assets worth more than £2,500 as your matrimonial settlement, you will have to pay back to the LSC what it has paid to your solicitor. This clawback is called the statutory charge (see *The statutory charge* for more details).

Second-stage CLS funding: Approved Family Help and Legal Representation

As has been pointed out, Legal Help does not cover issues to do with the financial aspects of your divorce, or any dispute over children, apart from your solicitor taking initial instructions from you to find out what the position is.

Unless your financial circumstances are very straightforward, or you have sorted them all out before you see the solicitor, you will probably need some legal advice and help with negotiating a settlement. If the financial problems are more complicated, or you are on bad terms with your spouse, you may need to go further and put the matter before the court. To cover the cost of this you can apply for second-stage CLS funding (formerly referred to as 'full legal aid'), which consists of two levels – Approved Family Help, and/or Legal Representation.

This second stage of CLS funding is a recent development and one that solicitors are still getting used to. The first level of it, Approved Family Help, covers advice and negotiation that does not go as far as representation in a contested hearing at the court. This means that it covers issues up to and including the Financial Dispute Resolution appointment at court (see Chapter 12). Approved Family Help can itself take two forms: Help with Mediation, or General Family Help. Help with Mediation has its own particular rules, which are set out below. A General Family Help certificate will be limited to cover up to £1,500 of work. If proceedings go as far as a contested hearing, then the certificate needs to be extended to cover Legal Representation, which is the second level of the second stage of CLS funding. Legal Representation can be granted on an emergency basis; if you need to go straight to court, the certificate will immediately cover Legal Representation.

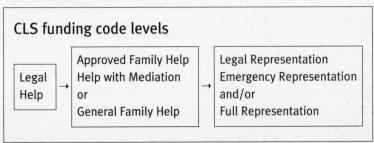

CLS funding code levels

| Legal Help | → | Approved Family Help
Help with Mediation
or
General Family Help | → | Legal Representation
Emergency Representation
and/or
Full Representation |

Help with Mediation

Help with Mediation has its own special rules. It is available only if you are taking part in family mediation or you have successfully reached an agreement with your spouse and need legal advice or support from your solicitor. For example, you may need a solicitor to put your agreement into a legal form so that it can be submitted to the court. You can have help from a solicitor until the work that is done for you reaches a particular charging level (see below).

Issue	Charging level	Hours
Children's issues only	£150	About $2\frac{1}{2}$
Financial issues only	£250	About $4\frac{1}{2}$
Children's and financial issues	£350	About $6\frac{1}{2}$

Uniquely, you do not have to pay the statutory charge (see below) for the work that the solicitor does and the amount that he or she is paid. This is an incentive for using the mediation route to a settlement.

To see if you will qualify for Help with Mediation, look at the way in which eligibility for Legal Help is worked out in Table A. The figures are all the same but the limits are higher. You will qualify if you have £3,000 or less in capital and your disposable income is £180 per week or less.

Mediation pilot scheme

In nearly every area of England and Wales a pilot scheme is in force. (This mediation scheme will probably cease to be a 'pilot' scheme in 2001 and become normal practice.) The effect of this is that you will not be allowed to make an application for Approved Family Help and/ or Legal Representation until you have first been put through a process to see whether your case would be suitable for mediation. If your solicitor is in one of these pilot scheme areas (ask him or her if he or she is), you will first have to attend an appointment at one of the locally approved mediation services. Your spouse will be invited to attend too. At this appointment the mediator will explain how mediation works and explore with you whether you would want or be able to take it further. If your case is not suitable (see below), the mediator will refer you back to your solicitor so that you can apply for further funding.

The pilot scheme recognises that there are some situations that are simply not going to be suitable for mediation: cases where there has been domestic violence, for example, or child-care cases where the local authority is involved. Also, even if you are prepared to use mediation, your spouse may refuse, in which case mediation cannot take place.

This process of trying out mediation inevitably delays the grant of a full certificate of CLS funding, if that is what you are going to need. However, try to make the most of the opportunity. Chapter 5 tells you more about mediation and the possible advantages that it could provide for you.

Applying for Approved Family Help and/or Legal Representation

To apply for Approved Family Help and/or Legal Representation you have to fill in two forms that are much longer than the Family Help one. One form deals with all your financial circumstances, in considerable detail; the other deals with the legal proceedings that you want to take. If you are in work, you will be given a third form to take to your employer so that he or she can confirm your wages. Your solicitor will help you to complete the forms and should check that everything is correctly completed. He or she should also explain to you about the statutory charge (see below) and give you a leaflet about it.

The financial criteria for Help with Mediation (see above) are not the same as those for General Family Help/Legal Representation; it is possible to be eligible for General Family Help/Legal Representation even if you are not eligible for Help With Mediation. If you are receiving income support or income-based job seeker's allowance, you will automatically be eligible for General Family Help/Legal Representation without any inquiry being made into your financial circumstances. If you receive working families' tax credit or disabled person's tax credit, you will have to satisfy only the capital limits. Table B will help you to work out your eligibility.

The forms that you complete are sent off to the LSC, which will work out whether you are entitled to Approved Family Help/Legal Representation. It will consider whether you are entitled on the basis of the merits of the proceedings that you propose to take, and then the forms are passed to the assessment office of the Benefits Agency to check your financial circumstances.

If you qualify for Approved Family Help/Legal Representation, you may be asked to pay nothing, or a contribution towards your legal costs. This may be a one-off payment out of capital, or, more likely, a regular amount each month for as long as the case takes. If you are asked to make a contribution, it is important that you make sure that you pay the amounts regularly. If you miss payments, your certificate will be taken away from you and you may have to pay for all the costs yourself. The payments are made to the LSC; you do not pay your solicitor direct. In due course, as with Legal Help, your solicitor submits his or her bill to the LSC and is paid by it. As has been mentioned in connection with Legal Help, if at the end of the divorce you get or keep assets worth more than £2,500 as your matrimonial settlement, you will have to pay back to the LSC what it has paid to your solicitor. This clawback is called the statutory charge (see *The statutory charge*, below).

If, when you receive the assessment from the LSC, you think that the contribution that you have been asked for is too high and a mistake has been made, you can ask for the amount to be reassessed. But this will take time and delay the granting of your certificate. It is often better to pay the first instalment (see below) and get the certificate issued before asking for the contribution to be reassessed.

It can take some weeks for the LSC to process your application. If you are eligible and you are not being asked to make a contribution, you and your solicitor will hear from the LSC with a copy of your certificate. If you are asked to make a contribution, you will not get the certificate until you have accepted the offer of funding and paid the first instalment. This can hold up your case because a certificate is not retrospective in effect; the LSC will not pay your solicitor for work done on financial matters before the granting of the certificate. If you have Legal Help, then your solicitor may be able to deal with some matters within its scope, but remember that the time the solicitor can charge under Legal Help is restricted and is mostly used up in dealing with just the divorce.

Emergency applications

If you need Legal Representation on an emergency basis – mostly this will be used for domestic violence injunctions – this can be granted. Solicitors in firms that are contracted to do so by the LSC can grant an emergency certificate without applying to the LSC office beforehand. Otherwise the application can generally be made by post/fax and granted the next day. In extreme (and rare) cases, a certificate may be

Table B: Income and capital limits for General Family Help/Legal Representation

If you are receiving income support or income-based job seeker's allowance, you will qualify for funding automatically. Otherwise you will have to comply with the income and capital limits detailed below.

Capital

You do not have to include anything which is likely to be the subject of a dispute between yourself and your spouse during the course of the divorce and the separation. In practice this means that in most matrimonial cases the capital does not get brought into the calculation at all. However, if you have any property which is yours alone and which you think will not be disputed, this has to be added up.

Add up: the value of your savings, which includes, cash, investments, National Savings, money in the bank or building society, and any other valuable assets that you have such as antiques or jewellery.

Leave out:

- the value of your house (unless it is worth more than £100,000 after allowing for a mortgage of £100,000)
- the value of the house contents (unless they are very valuable), clothing, tools of your trade
- any back-to-work bonus under the Job Seekers Act 1995
- any payments under the Community Care (Direct Payments) Act 1996.
- any loans or grants from the social fund.

If you have less than £3,000, you pay no contribution from capital. If you have between £3,000 and £6,750, take £3,000 away from the total to find out the capital contribution: the maximum payment you will have to make will be £3,750.

granted over the telephone. An emergency certificate will cover the first stages of the work that need doing, but in making the application you have to promise to make a full application and complete the forms mentioned above. You also have to promise that if it turns out

If you have over £6,750, you are unlikely to get funding unless your probable costs would be more than your contribution.

Income

Your disposable income is worked out as follows.

Add up: all the income that you have received for the last 12 months (including child benefit, if you receive it). **Note:** disability living allowance, attendance allowance, constant attendance allowance, council tax benefit, housing benefit, payments made under the Earnings Top-up Scheme or the Community Care Direct Payment scheme are **not** counted as income.

Take away: what you have paid in the last 12 months for income tax, National Insurance, superannuation, pension contributions, employment expenses (such as fares to work, trade union membership, reasonable childcare), rent, water rates, council tax, mortgage payments (to a maximum mortgage of £100,000) and any endowment premiums if paid in connection with your mortgage, ground rent, service charges, £5.48 weekly for repairs and household insurance (if you are the householder), and £1,551 (if you are still living with your spouse), £1,387 for each child (or dependant) aged 15 and under, and £1,656 for each child (or dependant) aged 16 or over.

What is left is your **disposable income**. If it is:

- under £2,723, you make no contribution from income
- between £2,723 and £8,067, you will be asked to make a contribution
- over £8,067 you will not be eligible for the funding.

To work out the monthly contribution that you will be asked to pay, take £2,723 away from your figure for disposable income and divide the answer by 36.

If you have a capital contribution to make as well, you will be asked to pay it with the first monthly payment as the initial contribution.

that you are not financially eligible, or you do not accept the offer when it is made to you, you will be liable for all the costs of the case. Normally, a solicitor is very unlikely to make an application for emergency funding unless he or she thinks that you will be financially eligible. It is therefore important to be very accurate about your financial circumstances when you tell the solicitor about them at the outset of your case.

Keeping the LSC informed

Once you get your certificate you must, as has been mentioned above, keep up the instalment payments. You must also keep the LSC informed if:

- there is any change in your financial circumstances
- you stop living with your spouse, or a partner
- you start living with someone as a couple
- you change your address.

You will be reassessed if your disposable income goes up by more than £750 a year, or down by more than £300 a year, or if your capital goes up by more than £750. If your financial position has increased past the point where you would be eligible for funding, your certificate may be discharged (that is, stopped), so that you are then responsible for the costs of your case from that point onwards.

If the LSC decides that you have in some way misled it about your financial position, your certificate can be revoked. This means that it is treated as though it never existed. Your solicitor will then be entitled to seek to recover from you the full amount of costs he or she would have charged on a private basis rather than the reduced fees under the funding certificate.

If you fail to respond to correspondence with the LSC, or fail to meet your monthly repayments, your certificate can be discharged although (unlike the situation where a certificate is revoked) this does not make you liable for the full costs assessed on a private–client basis.

There is a further penalty in the Legal Aid Act 1988: if any person intentionally fails to comply with regulations about information to be furnished by him or her, or in the furnishing of such information knowingly makes any false statement or false representation, he or she will be liable to a fine, or imprisonment for up to three months.

Financial limitations on CLS funding

Just as there are limits on the amount of work your solicitor can do under Legal Help, there are ceilings on the costs for General Family

Help/Legal Representation. For General Family Help your solicitor can do work until his or her costs reach £1,500. If it looks as though the costs will mount higher than this, he or she can apply to the LSC for an extension. He or she will have to justify why this is necessary. A certificate for Legal Representation will also have a financial limit put on it. This will vary depending on what work it covers. The LSC can also put limitations on precisely what sort of legal actions your solicitor can take. Your solicitor should go through the certificate with you and explain any restrictions. Again, if more, or different, action is needed, your solicitor can justify this to the LSC and seek an extension to cover the further work.

Legal fees for someone on CLS funding

If you have Legal Help or a CLS funding certificate you stop being personally responsible for the costs of your case. Your solicitor cannot give you a bill for the work that he or she is doing for you under the certificate or ask you to pay disbursements (that is, costs and fees paid out by him or her on your behalf) for your case. Solicitors are not paid by the LSC at the rates that they charge their private cases. Nor are they paid for all the work that they will do. This may mean that the solicitor will not be paid to attend court on your behalf if there is a barrister instructed for you and so may send a clerk or a trainee instead. This may be worrying for you, but in practical terms the personal presence of your solicitor may make very little difference. You cannot offer to pay an extra amount out of your own pocket for an extra service by your solicitor; he or she is not allowed to be paid by you direct when you have a funding certificate.

Keeping track of costs

As you will not be paying your solicitor direct it is easy to forget that as the case goes on the costs will be mounting. However, even if at this stage they do not impinge on you directly, you need to remember that in due course you will have to face the costs, when the statutory charge (see below) bites. Your solicitor should give you a regular (at least once every six months) update on the running total of your costs. This will have to be an estimate, because the bill will not be finalised until the end, when it is checked by the LSC or the court, but it should give you a realistic idea of how the costs are increasing. It is worth remembering that costs do not tend to mount in a steady progression and can jump up suddenly; some procedures, like applications to court, are cost-intensive because they require a lot of time to be spent.

Your solicitor has a duty to keep an eye on costs for the LSC too – it will not be prepared to fund litigation if it thinks that you are unreasonably escalating the costs. Your solicitor is expected to report to the LSC if he or she thinks that you are not acting reasonably. For example, if your spouse makes an offer to settle the case, your solicitor, and your barrister, if you have one, will advise you on whether you should take it or incur further costs trying to increase the settlement. If you refuse to take their advice, they will have to consider whether to refer the matter to the LSC. This may seem very unfair, but if you were privately paying, you would have to consider whether it was worth the risk of spending more of your money to achieve an outcome that might be uncertain.

The statutory charge

When you sign the forms applying for CLS funding your solicitor should give you two leaflets: *A Practical Guide to Community Legal Service Funding* and *Paying Back the Legal Service Commission: The Statutory Charge* (available from the LSC web site too). Your solicitor should also explain to you how the statutory charge works and answer any questions that you have.

The purpose of the statutory charge is to recoup some of the taxpayers' money that finances the CLS fund. If the contribution that you have paid towards your certificate is more than the costs of the case, you will be entitled to a refund of the difference. More often however, the costs will be more than you have paid. Even if you get an award of costs from the court at the end of your case, this does not mean that your spouse will be ordered to pay for your entire bill. To recover the shortfall, the LSC is allowed first call on any money or property that you 'recover or preserve' (as the Act says) at the end of the case. It does not matter whether this comes to you as a result of a decision by a court or an agreement with your spouse.

The charge will cover all proceedings for which you had funding. So, if your certificate covers an injunction, negotiations about the children, and the financial issues, all the costs for these three things will be rolled up together, even if you recovered or preserved your property in only one aspect of the proceedings.

Maintenance payments do not count as property, and the first £2,500 of any money or property is exempt from the charge. In practice the only chance of keeping any other property out of the scope of the statutory charge would be if you had reached a final agreement about it before the certificate was granted, or it was conceded that it was never a matter of dispute between you and your spouse that you should have it. If this is the case, then it is sensible to tell the LSC about this at the time when you apply for a certificate so that it knows that you are not going to recover or preserve property as a result of the proceedings.

At the end of the case your solicitor is obliged to hold any money or property that you receive from your spouse and pay it first to the LSC, so that it can take the statutory charge out of it before you receive it. If the sum that you have received from your spouse is far more than the projected figure for costs, your solicitor may be permitted to release part of it to you provided he or she retains enough to cover the bill.

The immediate payment of the statutory charge would obviously cause hardship if the property is the home in which you would otherwise be living, or a sum of money intended for the purchase of a home. If this is the case, the charge can be postponed. A charge like a mortgage is put on the house and the money and accrued interest on it is repaid only when the house is sold. Interest (at 8 per cent simple interest per year) is added to the original debt. (If you do not agree to pay the interest, the LSC will not allow the charge to be postponed.) If the house is sold so that another home can be bought with the proceeds of sale, the LSC will generally agree that the charge can be put on the new home, provided the value of the new home is sufficient to cover the debt. If the charge is going to be postponed in this way, it is important that the court order or agreement records that the property is intended to be the home of the funded person, or the money is intended for the purchase of a home for the funded person.

From July 2000 the LSC proposes to send annual statements to people who have charges on their houses. The statements will set out the original amount owed and the amount of interest that has accrued. This will allow you to keep track of what you owe the LSC.

If you do not recover or preserve property at the end of your case, then the charge will not apply. This can happen in cases where there is no capital to be divided, or where there is no interest on which the

LSC can take a charge. The most common example of this is where the couple live in rented accommodation. The settlement or court order may result in the transfer of the tenancy to one party but the tenancy is not something that can be charged with the debt.

Assessment and costs orders

Assessment

Assessment of costs used, confusingly, to be called taxation. (You may still find solicitors calling it by the old name.) Assessment is the process by which the district judge at the county court considers the solicitor's bill and decides whether the charges are fair and reasonable given the circumstances of the particular case. Not all bills have to go through assessment. If you agree that your solicitor's charges are fair you will simply pay them. If your spouse is ordered, or agrees, to pay part of your costs and the figure is agreed with your solicitors, the bill will not be assessed. CLS-funded cases with bills below £500 will be assessed by the LSC and not the court, and if the bill is between £500 and £1,000 your solicitor can opt for the LSC to assess the bill. If a CLS-funded bill is higher than £1,000, it will be assessed by the court. If the figure is challenged, either by you or by your spouse where there is an order for costs against him or her, then the bill will be assessed by the court.

For assessment the bill has to be drawn up in a specially detailed form in chronological order of the steps taken. The costs of drawing up the bill, which is generally done by a specialist called a costs drafts-man, are part of the costs of case. In a CLS-funded case these costs will form part of the statutory charge. Your solicitor then has to submit the bill to the court and the judge goes through it, reducing any item on which he or she thinks there has been an overcharge. The bill is then returned to the solicitor and copies should go to anyone who has challenged the costs. You are entitled to a copy if you have been funded by the LSC. You then have two choices: you can accept the reductions made by the judge or you can challenge them. Typically, the solicitor will want to challenge the reductions by arguing that they should not have been so large. The paying party may want to challenge the reductions by arguing that there should be more of them, or that they should be increased.

If any party is not satisfied with this 'provisional' assessment, he or she can ask for a hearing and the bill is then gone through by the judge with all parties present.

There is a financial risk involved to the paying party if he or she challenges his or her solicitor's bill, because unless he or she succeeds in reducing the bill by at least 20 per cent, he or she runs the risk of the costs of the assessment hearing being ordered against him or her.

Reducing the chances of paying your spouse's costs

You can reduce your potential liability for paying your spouse's costs by making a reasonable offer by letter to settle the financial claims. (This offer, often called a 'Calderbank letter', is discussed in Chapter 12.) If the offer that you make is fair, and your spouse chooses not to accept it and proceeds to a full financial hearing, he or she places him- or herself in a much riskier situation. If the court ultimately makes an order which is similar or less generous than the offer that you made, your spouse may be ordered to pay not only his or her own costs but also a contribution to yours as a penalty for stubbornly increasing costs without merit.

Costs awarded

If you want your spouse to pay at least a part of your legal costs, you must make a request 'for costs' at each stage of the proceedings, whenever orders are sought.

In a divorce, there is usually more than one set of proceedings: apart from the obtaining of the divorce decree, there may be matters of litigation on spousal maintenance, property adjustment or financial applications under the Children Act, all of which run up costs. On applications on any of these proceedings, or any 'interlocutory' (that is, interim) hearings, costs will usually be 'reserved' by the district judge to be dealt with on the final hearing or outcome of your case. At an interim hearing, a party will be ordered to pay the costs only if that party is in some way at fault at that time. At the conclusion of any final hearing, you can or should ask the district judge or judge to make an order for costs; he or she decides there and then whether to make such an order.

If you are asking the court to make an order by consent (that is, in terms agreed by you and your spouse), one of the agreed terms can be in respect of costs.

The court will bear in mind, at a financial hearing, the effect of any order for costs and will be conscious, for example, that such an order will still leave the recipient with a part of the overall bill to meet. Sometimes, the amount of a spouse's share in any property is increased to take account of his or her liability for his or her own costs instead of an order for costs being made against the other spouse.

Where an order for costs is made in favour of a party who is CLS funded against the other spouse who is paying privately, certain rules apply if the certificate was issued after 25 February 1994. According to the rules, the CLS-funded party's solicitors can claim legal fees worked out on private rates against the party ordered to pay the costs and can get back these higher fees from him or her. The CLS-funded spouse will not be affected directly by the fact that his or her solicitor will be able to charge extra fees, but indirectly by a reduction of the family's money 'pot'. (The new rules were brought in to try to stem the numbers of solicitors refusing to take on legal aid cases because of the low hourly legal aid rates.)

If someone who is CLS funded is ordered to pay the other party's costs (this happens, but not that frequently), the certificate does not cover this: the person is likely to have to pay out of his or her own pocket. The court must decide the amount that is reasonable for the CLS-funded person to pay and will usually say that an order for costs cannot be enforced without the court's permission. It may limit the amount of such costs to the equivalent of the person's CLS contributions and make the costs payable by instalments over 12 months.

The costs may be awarded by the court on a standard basis or (the higher level) an indemnity basis.

Unless otherwise specified, an order for costs usually means 'standard' costs. This means that you will recover from the person ordered to pay the costs usually between 60 and 80 per cent of your own bill. The term 'indemnity costs' is used to mean that your bill for legal costs (whether you are CLS funded or not) will be met in full. When an order for costs is made and a figure cannot be agreed, the bill will be assessed. The bill should be sent for assessment within three months of the date of the order for costs.

Costs in different types of proceedings

The issue of costs is fairly complex and confusing, not least now because of the various sets of rules that apply. Different approaches to the question of costs are possible depending on the type of proceedings involved. Set out below are some practical examples.

For the divorce

The petitioner can ask for costs (although this is not usual where the petition is on the basis of two years' separation with consent). If an order for costs is made, the petitioner's solicitor has his or her charges assessed by reference to scales laid down by special rules.

For example, a wife goes to see a solicitor to obtain a simple divorce based on her husband's adultery. She has to settle up with her own solicitor. She obtains an order for costs, assessed on the appropriate scale, at £250, plus court fees. But she has insisted on 'five star' service, requiring the solicitor to come personally to her house, spending many hours discussing the matter, and speaking to him many times on the telephone to find out how the case has been progressing, and her solicitor's bill comes to £2,250, plus court fees. She has to pay the £2,000 difference herself.

For an injunction

Injunction proceedings can run up very substantial costs. The successful applicant should obtain an order for costs against the other spouse. But, in many cases, this may not be worth the paper it is written on, either because the latter disappears or because he or she has no funds.

For residence, contact and other orders

Considerable costs can be run up in disputes over orders made under the Children Act, such as for residence or contact with the children. The fact that one parent obtains an order stating that the children would reside with him or her instead of the other does not necessarily mean that that parent has 'won' in the same sense as would be the case in, for example, a claim for damages for personal injuries, so both parties may be left to bear their own costs. The court is likely to order one party to pay the other's costs only if the former's behaviour during the proceedings has been in some way quite unreasonable, causing unnecessary delays and expense.

Financial matters

Theoretically, the costs of financial cases ought to have been pruned since a court practice direction of January 1995 ordered solicitors to control costs more strictly. The new ancillary relief scheme (see Chapter 12) also has the potential to make costs savings.

The fact that the wife (or, rarely, the husband) obtains an order for spousal maintenance or an order relating to the matrimonial home does not necessarily mean that he or she will be awarded costs, but the impact of costs is likely to be taken into account in making the overall order.

Sometimes a spouse's solicitors will at an early stage make a Calderbank offer (see Chapter 12) to include payment of the other's costs, only up to the date of the financial offer, in order to try to force a settlement. If the latter refuses to negotiate or in any other way unreasonably presses ahead for a court hearing after receiving a sensible offer, he or she puts him- or herself at risk of having to pay not only his or her own costs but also the spouse's costs since the offer was made.

When costs are paid

The theoretical (and usually the practical) position is that the successful party has to pay his or her own solicitor's bill first, and then recover any contribution ordered by the court from the other party. Usually, the solicitor will continue to act by preparing the bill and having it taxed and enforced against the payer.

Sometimes the solicitor may not press his or her client for payment of that part of the costs which are recoverable from the paying party, but that is entirely a matter of the solicitor's benevolence and is based on his or her assessment of the prospect of the other side paying up.

Costs and the Child Support Agency

If you are seeking or will be paying child support, this will usually be dealt with by the Child Support Agency rather than through solicitors and the courts. Fees were charged by the CSA up to April 1995. It then waived its fees for a two-year period, and this period has subsequently been extended. If and when the CSA does reintroduce fees, the rates might be similar to the old rates of £34 for assessing child support and £44 for enforcing payment – both fees payable by each parent. These fees are much lower than legal costs for dealing with maintenance are likely to be, but then unfortunately the CSA does have a reputation for slowness and inaccuracy. (See Chapter 6 for details.)

Chapter 2

Financial planning for divorce

Planning for divorce can be done at any time. It may be something you have been engaged in for some time, waiting just for the right moment to act. On the other hand you may be the spouse who has suddenly (and painfully) been deserted and you cannot see how planning can possibly improve things.

Certainly, in times of emotional crisis it is often difficult to make well-thought-out decisions for the future. In the heat of the moment, when the separation is very recent and the emotional atmosphere charged, it is sometimes best to avoid making long-term decisions, concentrating your energies instead on getting through the next week or even the next day. But as time goes on, the importance of planning for divorce, even if you never wanted the separation to happen, cannot be over-emphasised.

By planning you can frequently help minimise what can be the crippling financial effects of divorce. You can work out in advance how best to divide the income which formerly supported one home but which must now support two. Not only can you clarify your existing financial position but you can also explore how you could improve it: cutting down on outgoings, seeing if there are any ways of increasing your income, minimising the tax consequences of longer-term decisions and perhaps seeing whether you could get any financial help from the state (see later in this chapter and Chapters 6 and 12).

Working out your present financial position

Before you can plan for the future, you need to work out your present financial position. Most of us do not know the details of our finances; we get along from day to day without bothering about the details. But you cannot work out all the financial implications of a split without being fully informed. Sorting out all your financial information will help not only you, it will make instructing your solicitor – if you use one – more efficient, and enable him or her to advise you more effectively.

You need to break down the information into capital assets, income, debts and outgoings. Each is described below.

The following pages set out guidelines for working out a fairly detailed picture of your and your family's current financial position. It is only once you have filled in the detail of what actually happens in the present that you may be able to start making plans for the future. If you can, try to project ahead for the future what your likely income and outgoings might be.

You may not be able to work out all the figures by yourself: your spouse's position may be a blank to you, for example. But you should still fill in as much of the picture as possible.

If you have not been responsible in the past for paying the bills, try to find out how much recent bills have been. Your spouse may be willing to cooperate; otherwise you could contact the utility and telephone companies, and the local authority (about your council tax), and ask them to send you copies of your old bills.

If you still feel at a loss, use these guidelines to prepare a summary of information for your solicitor, who could then help you to sort through them and assist you in planning for the future.

Capital assets

The home

If you own your home:

- what is it worth now? An approximate estimate can be obtained by telephoning two or three local estate agents to ask them for a rough guide of what your property would be worth if you put it on the market now. The estate agents will not usually charge for making informal estimates of your house's worth like this
- when was it bought and for how much?
- how did you arrange your finances to pay for it?
- who put down the deposit, and where did the money come from?

- what substantial improvements have been made to the property since you bought it (for example, central heating)? when? what was the cost and how was it paid for?
- is it in joint names? This is important – if you find that the property is in your spouse's name only, it could be sold without your agreement or knowledge, but you can take steps to prevent this happening by registering your 'matrimonial home rights' – see Chapter 7. If you cannot find out this information, a solicitor will be able to do it for you.

If you own a leasehold property (that is, one with a long lease, usually of 25 years or more):

- what is the ground rent?
- what is the service/maintenance charge (if there is one)?
- how long is the lease?

If you have a mortgage:

- what is the name, address and account/reference number of the building society, bank or other lender?
- how much is outstanding?
- what are the monthly payments?
- when will it be paid off? Ask the building society or other lender for any of these facts if you do not know them
- and if it is of an endowment type, when is the policy due to mature and for how much? What is the current surrender/paid-up value of the policy? Ask the insurance company.

If either you or your spouse owns other properties (for example, a country cottage, villa abroad, time-share, all or part of a parent's home), include its approximate value.

If you rent your home:

- is it rented from a private landlord, the council, a housing association?
- how much rent do you pay (weekly, monthly, quarterly)?
- is there a service/maintenance or management charge? If so, how much?
- what type of tenancy is it?
- in whose name is the tenancy? Check the contract, tenancy agreement or rent book, if you have one.

Car or other vehicle

- Do you own a car? If so what is the make, model, year, value?
- does your spouse own a car? If so, what is the make, model, year, value?
- will you and/or your spouse need a car in the future?
- do you or your spouse have the use of a company car? If so, what model is it and how often is it replaced? What is paid for: car tax? tax on the benefit of having the car? insurance? servicing? repairs? petrol?
- do you and/or your spouse own a motor-bike? caravan? boat?

Pension

- Include details of any occupational pensions, superannuation schemes and personal plans (including, from April 2001, stakeholder schemes) to which you belong
- does the pension scheme or plan provide any benefits for a widower or widow? He or she will probably lose any benefits as a result of divorce
- what is the value of the pension you can expect to receive when you retire? Had you still been married at retirement, your pension may have been viewed as family income rather than yours personally, so your ex-spouse will be losing the right to benefit from it.

Since 1996, courts have been required to take pension rights into account when making orders relating to your finances. Chapter 13 describes the orders the court can make and arrangements you can voluntarily include in a divorce settlement.

When you joined your pension scheme or started your pension plan, you should have been given an explanatory booklet outlining the benefits you are entitled to, the rules, and so on. If you cannot find your copy (and any updates you have been sent in the meantime), ask your employer or pension provider for another.

You should also have been sent regular statements indicating the value of your pension rights to date. If you do not have a recent statement, ask for a new one. There are two types of pension scheme or plan: money purchase and salary-related. The statement from a money-purchase arrangement (which includes all personal pensions and many employers' schemes) will show how much money there is currently in your pension pot and may also show how much pension you might be able to buy with that money. The statement from a salary-related scheme shows how much pension you might get based on your current level of pay.

A court will need to know the value of your pension rights as a single lump sum – called the cash equivalent transfer value (CETV). This is the amount of money your pension scheme would hand over to another scheme if you decided to transfer your pension rights to it. In a money-purchase scheme or plan, the CETV is relatively straight-forward and broadly equals the value of your fund less any transfer charges. In a salary-related scheme, the CETV is more complicated and is the cash sum which, if invested, would provide the pension you have been promised. The scheme actuary has to work out the CETV for a salary-related pension, using assumptions in particular about future stock-market growth.

Once divorce proceedings have started, you or the court can require the pension scheme to provide you with the CETV for your pension rights.

If it is an employer's pension scheme you are looking at, you can get any information about the scheme or your rights from the pensions manager, pension scheme administrator or the scheme trustees, who can usually be contacted via the personnel or human resources department of your employer. If it is a personal pension you are looking at, contact the company providing the plan or your financial adviser if you use one.

For more details about pension arrangements and what happens to them on divorce, see Chapter 13.

Other assets
- Include any joint current accounts or savings accounts you have
- your own savings in building society, bank or National Savings accounts, with details of the account(s) and current balance(s)
- stocks and shares, and unit trusts, with a current valuation of your portfolio
- Personal Equity Plans (PEPs), Tax-Exempt Special Savings Accounts (TESSAs), Individual Savings Accounts (ISAs) or any other type of investment (these may be affected by changes in each year's Budget)
- endowment policies and/or life insurance policies: how much? when do they mature? You could ask the insurance company or

broker for current surrender values and check whether any policy has been written in your spouse's favour

- valuables, such as jewellery, antiques, with estimates of their value and brief details of how and by which of you they were acquired (bought, inherited, gift, etc.).

General contents of the house are rarely realisable, and proposals on how to divide these between you should be considered separately. This is better done after you have reached a general agreement on the broader issues otherwise you may get bogged down in minutiae.

Expectancies and trusts

Are you and/or your spouse likely to come into an inheritance in the foreseeable future? Does either of you have interests under a trust (perhaps as a result of tax planning by you or your parents)? Do you know of any assets that you are likely to receive in the future such as demutualisation payments from a building society or insurance company, or the maturing of an insurance policy?

Income

Employment

If you are self-employed:

- what income have you had for the past three years? Any regular earnings from occasional freelance or part-time work at home should be included
- if you have accounts for the past three years, which would show your expenses as well as your income, you should get these together.

If you are an employee:

- name of employer, nature of job, whether full- or part-time. If you are currently not employed, include details and dates of last employment and qualifications
- normal weekly or monthly earnings – form P60 shows the total amount of pay for income tax purposes including any bonus or commission and what tax and National Insurance payments were made for the previous tax year

- any other relevant information, such as imminent promotion or redundancy, dates of pay reviews
- any fringe benefits, commission or bonuses regularly received, for example, private medical insurance, subsidised loan, expense account, company car (a company car will be treated by the Inland Revenue as 'deeming' extra income, the amount of which will be determined by the year of the model, how many business miles you do and what type of car it is)
- expenses of any clothing and equipment essential for your job
- cost of childminding or nursery school for your child(ren) while you are at work
- details of additional casual or freelance work.

You will also need to look at details of your spouse's income if you know these.

Other maintenance
- Include any maintenance payments made to spouse (or an ex-partner from a previous marriage) and/or to your child(ren)
- children's maintenance payments received from a former husband or wife of yourself or your spouse
- any regular provision to or from someone else, for example, deeds of covenant from grandparents
- maintenance payments you would expect to receive or pay in the future.

Other income
- Include the income from your investment over the past two or three years, for example, dividends, interest on building society account(s)
- future income from investments that you anticipate receiving.

New partner's finances
If you and/or your spouse are cohabiting on a long-term basis with someone else, and/or have plans to marry, you should include what you know of that person's financial circumstances.

Payments from the state
What money do you receive or could you claim from the Department of Social Security (DSS)? For example:

- jobseeker's allowance
- income support
- working families' tax credit
- child benefit, including lone parent benefit
- state pension
- incapacity benefit or other disability benefits.

Debts

Make a list of all the money you owe: for example, tax arrears, what is outstanding under any hire purchase agreement(s), bank overdraft, credit card, other loans. For a loan or credit agreement or other liability that requires payment regularly, note the arrears and the total amount outstanding.

Note who is responsible for each debt – you or your partner or both of you. You are not responsible for each other's individually incurred debts.

Outgoings

Make a list of all your usual outgoings. You do not need to calculate everything precisely to the last penny. But gaining a clearer picture of your current outgoings will help you prepare a budget for your future outgoings.

If you have no idea how much you do spend on what, get a notebook and write down the cost of your shopping as you pay for it, or keep the till receipts for the whole month. If your children are old enough to understand, it may help them to encourage them to make a note as well, so that they get involved with the plans that you are making for the future.

For major recurring bills, such as gas and electricity, make sure that you try to add these together for a period over the last 12 months so that you take into account the seasonal fluctuations before you work out the monthly average.

Remember to take into account any large expenses that are looming in the future, such as major car repairs or kitting out a child in a new school uniform. There may be still larger ones to think about, like re-roofing the house, or replacing the car.

The table below should help you compile your list. Some of the items may well not apply to you, but there are others which it is easy to forget when you first make a list, like the cost of school trips or presents for other children's birthdays.

The list is not intended to be a definitive statement of the expenses that a court will take into account. It is intended to help you remember all the things that you pay out for at present. As has been said before, you may well have to cut back on various expenses and economise for the time being.

When you make a list like this it is important to express everything in terms of weekly or monthly figures, being consistent throughout the list so that you get an accurate picture of what things really cost. If you are working from weekly figures it is important to remember that there are 4.33 weeks in each month; if you simply multiply a weekly figure by 4 you will end up leaving 4 weeks out of your annual total.

List of outgoings

Item	£ per month
Accommodation costs	
Mortgage/rent	£
Endowment policy linked to mortgage	£
Council tax	£
Water rates	£
Electricity	£
Gas	£
Telephone	£
Service charge	£
Ground rent	£
Oil/Solid fuel	£
Household expenses	
Food/housekeeping	£
House insurance	£
Contents insurance	£
Repairs/service contracts	£
TV licence	£
TV/video hire	£
Cleaner	£
Gardener	£
Window cleaner	£
Vet's bills	£
Hire purchase	£
Car	
Insurance	£

Item	£ per month
Road tax	£
Maintenance	£
Petrol	£
Loan for car purchase	£
Children	
School expenses	
Travel to school	£
School dinners	£
Uniform	£
Outings and trips	£
School fees	£
Other school expenses	£
Private lessons	£
Out of school	
Clothes and shoes	£
Nappies	£
Doctor	£
Dentist	£
Optician	£
Cubs/Brownies etc.	£
Childminder/nursery/nanny (gross cost)	£
Hairdressing	£
Books and toys	£
Presents (for other children)	£
Christmas and birthdays	£
Personal expenses	
Clothes and shoes	£
Hairdressing	£
Doctor	£
Dentist	£
Optician	£
Prescription charges	£
Dry cleaning	£
Entertainment	£
Travel to work	£
Lunches at work	£
Holidays (including the children)	£
Legal costs/CLS contribution	£
Subscriptions	£
Other accommodation	
Second home	£
Holiday cottage	£
Other items	£
TOTAL:	£

Once you have a record of what your present expenses are you can start to make projections about what they will be when you split up. Not all items will change. If you have already made plans for a new home, try to make yourself another list with the projected figures for that home. It is helpful too, to do the same exercise for your spouse (as far as you can).

Planning for the break-up

Managing debts

For an increasing number of families, the financial issues involved in divorce are less about dividing up assets than about dealing with the heavy burden of debts and who will or should take them on. Although it may be of little comfort to those in debt, it is a fact that getting into debt has become a common problem. Often, the stresses caused by financial debts can themselves be the cause of the family break-up.

Broadly speaking, a spouse will not be responsible for debts incurred by the other spouse alone. But there are exceptions: a spouse will usually be responsible for the other's unpaid council tax bills and sometimes other outgoings on the home. Spouses also share responsibility for joint debts, say from a joint account, or for joint mortgage repayments or rent.

If your spouse has deserted you, leaving behind high unpaid household bills, the date of separation is important. If your spouse has failed to pay his or her council tax, you must inform the local authority of the date of separation and thus at least cut off your responsibility for paying your spouse's share of the council tax debt accruing after that. Your council tax bill will also be cut if there is now only one adult living in the home. By advising the gas, electricity and telephone companies, you can also get the meters read as near to the separation date as possible and ask for a transfer of the accounts into your own name. This will, obviously, leave you with having to pay future bills and so may not be appropriate, but it can be one way of avoiding responsibility for some previously built-up debts.

If on the other hand you are paying your spouse maintenance, but he or she is not paying the bills, what responsibility do you have for the unpaid bills? The answer lies in what the maintenance is intended to cover. If you make it clear that the maintenance should cover, for example, the payments of electricity and gas bills (and if the amount of maintenance is adequate for this purpose), then you should be relieved of the obligation to pay those bills. Asking the utility companies (for example) to change the accounts into the name of the spouse now living alone in the property clarifies who will be responsible in future.

Working out debt repayments

The first step is to assess the priority of debts with the help of expert counselling (see below). You will probably be advised not simply to pay off the creditor who shouts the loudest. A credit-card company, say, may telephone and write a string of letters in an endeavour to get money from you, but that bill may have to be left, if necessary, to enable you to pay for housing. The credit-card company may take you to court: at worst the court could send in the bailiffs to take away some possessions, but that would be preferable to losing the roof from over your head.

Once you have worked out the total amount of your debt and (preferably with assistance) a list of priorities for repayment, see also whether you can increase your own income – perhaps by getting a part-time job or by applying for welfare benefits to which you may be entitled (see *Financial help from the state*). Look at ways of cutting your own expenditure: by going to markets instead of superstores, say, or by walking or cycling instead of going by car. If you belong to a pension scheme you could ask for your payments to be frozen until you can once more afford them, but check whether you will be financially penalised by making such a decision.

Although it may be tempting to try to avoid your creditors, you may well find that by contacting them and showing that you are willing to try to repay them you can work out a realistic level of repayment. Creditors will very often accept a reduced payment made regularly rather than nothing at all, and will feel happier knowing that you have not fled the country. Also, it will be less expensive for them to agree a repayment with you than to incur extra legal costs in having to take you to court.

As an alternative, you may wish to roll up your debts into one loan and then pay a monthly amount. A problem with this is that the loans advertised for such purposes can charge extortionate rates of interest. Even if your own bank is willing to make you a loan, the interest rates charged may differ little from those charged by credit-card companies. Debt-advice agencies also advise strongly against taking out a loan to help pay off your mortgage repayments (often termed 'distress borrowing'): this only serves to dig you deeper into debt.

If you find it impossible to pay off your debts or to repay a creditor you owe over £750, you could ask the court to make a bankruptcy order. If you take this action yourself it will cost you a deposit of £200 plus court fees. You will thus largely be relieved of the burden of your creditors.

However, once you are made bankrupt, there are limitations: you cannot hold a bank account or obtain credit of over £50, nor be a company director (or a solicitor, for example). Depending on the circumstances, most bankrupts are discharged after two or three years, when they have a clean sheet. But even if you think this is the only way out of your debts, obtain legal advice before going ahead.

Special help and advice about debts

Your best bet for advice and help about debts is likely to be your local Citizens Advice Bureau (CAB), money advice centre or law centre; many of these have special sessions for debt problems. For further advice try contacting the National Debtline,★ the Office of Fair Trading★ and the Council of Mortgage Lenders.★

Many local authorities and some banks have free information leaflets. You can also get help from your solicitor, and Legal Help is available if you are eligible (see Chapter 1).

If you are not in debt

Even if you are not in debt, you may need to take steps to protect your position.

The home

If your home is registered in your spouse's name alone, you need to register a charge on the property to make sure that outsiders are aware of your interest in the home. This will also ensure that your spouse will not be able to sell the home or remortgage it without your consent (see also Chapter 7).

Joint accounts and credit cards

With a joint bank or building-society account on which either of you can draw, there is the risk that the account could be cleared out by one partner without the other knowing about it. To prevent this, the bank or building-society manager should be told to change the arrangement so that cheques can be drawn only with both signatures. Alternatively, you could ask for the account to be frozen (although then neither of you would be able to draw out funds).

Similarly, where each of you has a credit card or cash-withdrawal card for drawing against one account, it is usually wiser, from the main cardholder's point of view, to put a stop on the cards. The card company must be notified and the cards (including, if possible, the other spouse's card) sent back. A new card will then be issued to the main cardholder.

Preventing disposal of assets

If you strongly suspect that your spouse is intending to dispose of assets to try to escape his or her financial obligations, you can ask the court to make an application under Section 37 of the Matrimonial Causes Act to prevent him or her from doing so. You will need to instruct a solicitor (see also Chapter 3). This can be done as an emergency application if necessary, that is, you should not delay if you think that you need to make such an application.

Financial help from the state

When your marriage breaks up and you have separated from your spouse, you may find that you need – and are now eligible for – financial help from the state. This may be a rather off-putting idea; you may have thought that you were not the sort of person who would have to turn to state help at any stage in your life. However, the system is there to help you, whether you think of yourself as working or middle class, and it would be foolish not to take advantage of what is available to you. It may be a vital lifeline at a difficult period in your life.

Over the last few years the benefits system has been changing and the old familiar names, such as supplementary benefit and family income support, have gone. If you have some knowledge of the old system you will need to update it.

Help and advice on benefits is available from your local DSS office, and from the DSS help lines and web site,★ which contains enormous amounts of information with leaflets that you can download.

If you are facing life as a lone parent, you may well be aware that in recent years the government has focused on the problems of single parents and that many measures have been put in place to try to get lone parents back to, or into, work. This should be helpful to you in your new circumstances. Lone parents are offered a 'New Deal'. This provides you with a series of interviews with a personal adviser, who will do his or her best to help you get into work and to explain the benefits system to you. There should also be training courses in your area that you can go on, while still receiving income support, to help you acquire skills that will be useful in the work place. Your local Job Centre should be able to give you information about this (details are also available on the web at www.newdeal.gov.uk).

The types of benefit that you may be eligible to apply for are:

- lone parent benefit
- income support
- jobseeker's allowance
- working families' tax credit
- housing benefit
- council tax benefit
- loans from the social fund.

If you receive jobseeker's allowance, working families' tax credit or income support, you will automatically be entitled to Legal Help (see Chapter 1). It is helpful therefore (though not always possible) to get your benefits position sorted out before you consult a solicitor.

Income support

This benefit replaced supplementary benefit. It is available to lone parents who are looking after children who are under 16. You must be not working, or working less than 16 hours per week.

You can visit, write to or phone your local DSS office and you will be issued with a claim form. You will be asked to attend what is called a 'work-focused interview' with a ONE personal adviser (ONE is the DSS scheme – at present being piloted – to provide a single point of entry into the benefits system). You are obliged to attend this interview if you want to claim benefit. Failure to do so may result in the loss of benefit.

To be eligible for income support, your capital must be worth less than £8,000 (but this does not include the value of your home). The amount that you get depends on your age and on the age of the children living with you, as well as any other income that you have coming into the house.

If you are a lone parent, £15 of your earnings or income will be ignored. The first £3,000 of capital is ignored. If your capital is worth between £3,000.01 and £8,000 (inclusive), what you receive by way of income support will be affected by the assumption that you have a weekly income of £1 for every £250 (or part of £250) over £3,000.

If you are a lone parent in receipt of income support, the Child Support Agency will insist that you make an application for child support via the Agency against the child(ren)'s other parent (see Chapter 6).

You will not receive any of the maintenance that is actually paid by the other parent (unless it is so high that it is more than you would get in benefit), but you can accrue a Child Maintenance Bonus, which allows you to claim a tax-free sum of up to £1,000 when you move off benefit into work. You have to claim this within 28 days of coming off benefit. The amount that you will be able to claim is worked out by taking the number of weeks that you have been on benefit during which maintenance has been due and multiplying it by the amount of maintenance paid, up to a maximum of £5 per week. Or, if the actual amount of maintenance paid is less, the lower figure will be used.

For 2000–1, the maximum income support for a single person over 25 is £52.20 per week. To this, add £26.60 for each child up to the age of 16 (and £31.75 for children aged 16 to 19). A lone-parent family also receives a 'premium' of £15.90 per week.

Income support claimants are also entitled to help with the costs of rent or mortgage, but this has its limitations. If you pay a mortgage, you can have some help with the interest, but not the capital repayments. The amount that you receive depends on when you bought your house. If you bought your house and your present mortgage was taken out before the beginning of October 1995, you will not receive any interest at all for the first eight weeks. Then you get 50 per cent of the interest for a further 18 weeks and only after that 100 per cent of the interest. If you bought your house and took out the mortgage after 1 October 1995, you receive no help at all with the interest until 39 weeks have gone past, but then you get 100 per cent. (If you are aged over 60, the waiting period does not apply.) The maximum mortgage loan taken into account is £100,000. Payments on a loan above that figure will not be met by the DSS. This is only a brief summary of the rules, which are complicated. The DSS publishes a helpful leaflet (IS8), and the benefits office will give you precise advice about your own situation.

If your mortgage does not qualify for help, you may be covered by the terms of an insurance policy. You will need to check the terms of the policy carefully; most cover redundancy but not marriage break-down. Moreover, most policies do not kick in immediately, and may run only for a fixed period, such as two years.

Those who have been lone parents for at least 26 weeks, and who have been claiming income support for at least 26 weeks and then go back to work, can have some extra help called 'lone parent benefit run-on'. You can claim this if the new job is for 16 hours or more each week and the job is expected to last for at least five weeks. The effect is that you go on receiving income support for two weeks after your job has started at the same rate as before.

Jobseeker's allowance

Jobseeker's allowance is another state benefit you may be eligible for. To qualify, you must be unemployed or working on average less than 16 hours per week. If you work part-time and are a lone parent the first £15 of your earnings is disregarded.

To apply, get a claim pack from your local DSS office. This has the claim form in it along with a Jobsearch Plan. You will have to attend an interview and take the forms with you. The interviewer draws up a Jobseeker's Agreement with you.

The rates at which the benefit is paid are the same as for income support and you will qualify for housing benefit and council tax benefit as well. The lone-parent run-on also applies to jobseeker's allowance.

Lone parent benefit

Lone parent benefit, a top-up to child benefit for the eldest child of a lone parent, used to be available to anyone who was getting child benefit in the normal way. This is no longer the case. The top-up is now available only to people who have been getting it since before 6 July 1998, or have been getting income support or jobseeker's allowance since before that date, or who have just come off benefit to start work.

None of these circumstances is likely to apply to you if you are just about to separate, but it is worth bearing in mind that if you go on to benefit, and later start work, you can claim it provided you make the claim within one month of coming off benefit. Child benefit for the eldest child is increased to £17.55 per week at 2000–1 rates.

Working families' tax credit

If you are working 16 hours or more a week and have the responsibility for at least one child you can claim this benefit. You do not have to be a lone parent; it is intended for all families with children where the income is low. Your capital must be no more than £8,000. See Table A to work out whether you are eligible.

You can apply by contacting your local benefits office or Inland Revenue office. Payments can be made directly into your bank account or via the post office, or as tax credits by your employer through your wage packet. The credit will be assessed and paid on a six-monthly basis, so once an award has been made it will be reassessed only at the end of the six-month period even if your circumstances change during the period, unless the change is the last child leaving school.

Working families' tax credit can be an extremely helpful benefit. Payments of child maintenance, whether voluntary or made via the CSA, are disregarded. This can increase the family's income considerably. Families who have a net income of under £11,250 a year will also be entitled to free prescriptions and free dental treatment, but free school meals, which used to be 'passported' with Family Income Supplement, are not available.

Housing benefit

Housing benefit is available if you are living in rented accommodation. If you claim income support or jobseeker's allowance, you can claim housing benefit at the same time via the DSS. Otherwise, you make the claim to your local authority.

If your landlord is the local authority, the amount of rent will be reduced direct. If you pay to a private landlord, the benefit is paid by

Table A: Working families' tax credit

Add together:
- net earnings (gross pay less tax, NI contributions and half any pension contribution) per week
- any maintenance payments that you receive (but not child maintenance)
- child benefit (and lone-parent top-up)
- any 'tariff income' from capital (£1 for each £250 over £3,000, up to £8,000).

This figure will give you the 'applicable amount'.

Then work out for your family the maximum level of working families' tax credit:

Add together:

• adult tax credit	£53.15
• if you work more than 30 hours a week, 30-hour tax credit	£11.25
• child tax credit	
– each child from birth to September following 16th birthday	£25.60
– each child from September following 16th birthday to age 18	£26.35
• child-care tax credit (see below)	
Total = maximum tax credit	£ _____

If your applicable amount is £91.45 or less per week, you will get the maximum tax credit figure. If the applicable amount exceeds £91.45, deduct from the maximum tax credit 55p for each £1 by which applicable amount exceeds £91.45 to work out what you will receive.

Child-care tax credit is available for up to 70 per cent of the eligible child-care costs. The maximum limit is £100 per week for one child and £150 for two or more children. To be eligible, the childcare must be provided by registered childminders, nurseries, out-of-hours school clubs on school premises, or child-care schemes on Crown Property. Since April 2000 the Department for Education and Employment has been accrediting organisations as 'approved providers'.

---

cheque or money order. It is assessed for a period of up to 60 weeks at a time, but may be shorter if your tenancy ends during that period, or if the local authority has other arrangements. The maximum that you can get is 100 per cent of the 'eligible rent', which is not necessarily the amount that you pay to your landlord. You will need to get detailed advice from your local DSS office or from the CAB about the calculation.

If you have more money coming in than the allowances and premiums that you qualify for under DSS regulations, you will receive less housing benefit.

Council tax benefit

You cannot claim council tax benefit if you have more than £16,000 in savings. If you claim income support or jobseeker's allowance, you can claim council tax benefit at the same time. The maximum that you can get is the whole of your council tax bill. If your house is in valuation bands F, G or H, you will have your benefit restricted to the amount payable for a property in band E.

As for housing benefit, if you have more money coming in than the allowances and premiums that you qualify for under DSS regulations, you will receive less council tax benefit.

Loans from the social fund

If you receive income support or jobseeker's allowance, you may be able to get payments from the social fund for items of capital expenditure which would be too large to meet out of your income. There are different kinds of loans. To spread the payment for an exceptional expense you could get a 'budgeting loan'. These are for sums between £30 and £1,000. Any award is reduced by capital over £500. The loan is interest-free but is repayable and is usually made over a period of up to 78 weeks with the repayments coming out of the benefit paid. You could get a 'crisis loan' for expenses in an emergency or as a consequence of a disaster, if there is no other way of meeting the needs. The fund officer at the DSS will want to be satisfied that the loan is the only means of preventing serious damage or serious risk to the health or safety of you or your family.

Social fund loans come out of a fixed budget; if the fund has reached its limit for the year your application may be refused on these grounds alone.

Making plans for the future

By now you could be thoroughly depressed. You will have spent many hours producing meticulous sets of figures and, almost inevitably, they will paint a grim picture. You may wonder how you ever managed to afford living under one roof – let alone how you will juggle two households.

See whether there are any ways you can improve on your financial position – by cutting down on expenditure as well as seeing whether your income can be increased in any way. You could perhaps think of renting out a room to a lodger – under the 'rent a room scheme' you can receive up to £4,250 per year tax free (2000–1 figures). Leaflet IR87 '*Letting your home*' gives further information. It is available from tax offices and from the Inland Revenue's web site.★

Try to consider all the possible scenarios for the future. You strengthen your position by having worked out in detail the likely consequences of plans that you and your spouse may each be putting forward, even if (or particularly if) you are convinced that your spouse's suggestions are ridiculously unrealistic.

In practice, you may have little choice, and what options there are will be fairly stark. Inevitably, you will have to make compromises. It is only by having thought through your priorities that you can mould the eventual compromise into a shape that best suits you and your family. Sometimes professional help from a mediator may be exactly what is needed.

Making plans for the future revolves primarily around accommodation and income.

Where to live

Your first priority, if you have children, will of course be to ensure that they have a roof over their heads. Work out what it would cost you to stay on in your home, and where you could move to if you were to move, and how either option would leave you and your spouse financially.

Factors such as the location of children's schools and being near to helpful friends or willing parents can be important, particularly now that you are going to be on your own.

If you own your home but are likely to have to move, ask two or three local estate agents to tell you what they think it might fetch. There should be no charge for such a valuation if you explain that you may be selling but have not yet decided to. These figures may not be exact (some estate agents tended to undervalue when the housing market was depressed) but they will be a guide. Deduct the likely agent's and conveyancing costs and moving costs (say, about 5 per cent of the house value), plus what you owe on the mortgage, and you are left with the 'net equity'. From that, you would have to pay the costs of setting up a new home or possibly two – one for each of you. Work out what sort of mortgage you and your spouse could each shoulder and then investigate the property market.

If you are in rented accommodation, and indeed even if you are not, investigate the rented sector – private, council and housing association.

This can be a disheartening business at the best of times, but it is only by exploring what might be possible that you can work out what the options are, and the respective advantages and disadvantages of each option.

What to live on

In respect of capital, look at your schedule of assets, having worked out the net equity in the house (if you own it) and the net value of all other realisable assets after meeting outstanding liabilities (including legal fees for the divorce, if you are consulting a solicitor). What is realisable will depend upon your circumstances – cashing in a life insurance policy or selling the car might be foolish in some circumstances but unavoidable in others. Everyday household belongings are rarely realisable and should preferably be linked to need: the parent with the children, for example, is likely to need the washing machine and the majority of the furnishings. The other parent, however, may need to buy, either immediately or in due course, his or her own household equipment and furniture. You may be able to rent some appliances, such as a washing machine, if the capital outlay is too much at first.

Starting off calculating maintenance

If you have dependent children, first work out how much child support might be payable under the formula laid down by the Child Support Acts. This usually has to be the first step because the amount can be precise, whereas other payments tend to be up in the air at this stage. Turn to Chapter 6 to work out how much child support is likely to be payable.

A mother who will be looking after children may be able to claim maintenance for herself to top up her child support. As the Child Support Act 1991 increased the amounts of child support payable, conversely the amount she might expect to receive in her own right has (broadly) tended to decrease.

A wife who does not work outside the home or who is on a low income may also be entitled to spousal maintenance from her husband if he earns enough. Exactly how much he should pay is not easy to quantify as the court will take a number of factors into account. If sufficient income is available, a wife could expect to receive enough to meet her reasonable needs (based on the court's pragmatic 'needs and resources' approach – see Chapter 6) but the court may also expect a wife who is not currently earning to make sensible attempts to support herself financially in the future.

Figures and forecast

Once you have worked out what money will be available, compare the figures with a forecast for the needs of both new households. This may show that one of you has, or both of you have, got nowhere near enough to meeting your projected expenses. Remember that the needs of the children will take priority.

Looking at your incomes, needs and available capital (if any), a decision must be reached on how things can be arranged, but with realistic figures. In many cases, it will just have to be accepted that both of you are going to be very hard up, at least for a while.

Chapter 3

Getting legal advice

At an early stage in your divorce/separation process, you should consider obtaining legal advice about the best course of action for you. While a do-it-yourself divorce is relatively easy if you and your spouse agree that there is to be a divorce and on what basis, you will almost certainly need a solicitor's help if there is little or no common ground between you. Wherever financial arrangements and division of property are at issue, or where there is uncertainty about the children, an initial advisory meeting with a solicitor specialising in divorce problems has much to recommend it, if only to prevent you from giving up rights in ignorance of the law.

If you can sort out your financial affairs as equal partners, between yourselves or with the help of a mediator (see Chapter 5), so much the better – although even then it is wise for you both to ask a solicitor whether the arrangements seem fair, and to ensure that they are framed in a watertight manner so as not to leave you open for future unexpected financial claims and that they do not result in any unnecessary payments of tax.

If you are intending to use mediation as the primary means of sorting out your arrangements comprehensively, ask your solicitor about his or her attitude towards mediation. Some solicitors have now been trained as mediators themselves and are likely to have a more constructive approach towards agreements worked out through mediation, as long as they do not work against your (and the family's) best interests. There are, however, a few, perhaps more old-fashioned, solicitors who may be instinctively anti-mediation and thus may not be helpful in advising you objectively if you do reach arrangements through mediation.

If it is not possible for the two of you to achieve a fair agreement on your own or via a mediator, a solicitor can negotiate on your behalf. It is not usually possible for you and your spouse to instruct the same solicitor as there is a potential conflict of interest between you (although services such as the Cambridge Family and Divorce Centre* can arrange a joint appointment with one solicitor; see Chapter 5).

A solicitor can be of great help, but try to use his or her services efficiently and economically. Ask yourself whether you want to obtain legal advice or want someone to 'fight' for you. Wanting a solicitor to act for you in a contentious way will involve you in expense which may be out of proportion to anything gained. It is also not at all cost-effective to use a solicitor as an emotional support, whatever the temptations.

Time and money are invariably interlinked. The more you use a solicitor's services, the greater the hole that will be cut into your financial budget. What a solicitor can effectively do for you is explained in detail in this chapter. It is of the utmost importance that you consider the question of costs before launching into a major battle. Spending an hour or so (at the very least) with an experienced and competent solicitor to get advice on your legal position is likely to be a worthwhile investment. Of course, how much you want to (or are forced to) involve your solicitor may be constrained by how much you can afford to pay. Explanations and warnings about the problem of costs have already been given. If you have not already done so, read Chapter 1 now.

What a solicitor can do for you

A solicitor should discuss your position dispassionately and advise you from the benefit of his or her experience what is likely to happen about the separation, the divorce (if and when that happens), the children and money matters. Good advice early on may prevent matters becoming complicated, or one party getting less than his or her entitlement, and can generally help to take the heat out of the situation.

Handling your divorce
It is possible to handle an undefended divorce yourself without a solicitor, although it is probably fair to say that it is at least as hard as doing your own conveyancing on your house (and the financial pit-

falls can be worse if something goes wrong). Do-it-yourself divorce packs are widely available but the packs may contain out-of-date forms, so you should double check these with the court. Be wary of taking important steps without legal advice: the packs can give you general but not individual advice, which can be provided only by solicitors or Citizens Advice Bureaux (CABx).

You can also download forms and information leaflets from the Internet. The Court Service★ web page has all the forms that you need together with helpful information leaflets. Your local county court can also supply you with copies of these. It is possible to get your divorce over the Internet,★ though this is not to be recommended unless you are sure that you and your spouse can agree on all the issues and your financial position is simple.

Be particularly wary of the common assumption that getting a divorce means an end to your financial obligations to your ex-spouse – divorce and money matters are considered quite separately by the courts and getting a divorce does not mean an automatic end to your money concerns. In any event, if a divorce petition arrives through your letterbox and you are unsure what to do about it, or if your spouse flatly refuses to cooperate in any way, a solicitor's advice would be useful.

Sorting out problems over children

Protracted litigation over the children can be extremely expensive. Also, it is harmful to the children and you, and rarely produces a satisfactory result. If you cannot come to an agreement by yourselves or through mediation, see if you can arrange a meeting for both of you and your solicitors. A good solicitor will be able to give you sensible advice about the way in which you should deal with the arrangements for the children, and about the attitude that a court would take if you felt that you had to resolve a dispute by going to court. Disputes over children cannot be 'won' or 'lost', and ultimately you are likely to prefer a solution that you reach yourselves, rather than have to accept one imposed upon you by a judge who, however wise and well meaning, does not – and cannot – know you or your children.

Getting a court order for maintenance and division of property

A solicitor will know the appropriate court (see *Which Court? (England and Wales)*) for the particular order you require and the procedure for applying. He or she will be able to advise you on the attitude that the court will take and your prospects of success.

Getting information about finances

You may find that you are faced with a long uphill battle to get financial information out of your spouse. However reasonable you want to be over things, and whatever you do, he or she may refuse to disclose assets.

Withholding information at the early stages does nothing but run up costs and reduce the amount that there is to go round. If you go to see a solicitor, your spouse may then do so too, and may be persuaded to come clean about details of his or her financial situation. You will both need to disclose your finances fully to each other before a proper agreement can be reached.

Getting an agreement about finances

Good solicitors will impress upon both of you the advantages of cooperation and will help you to negotiate an agreement about finances.

If your resources leave very limited room for manoeuvre, fighting it out in court may not be worthwhile. It is pointless getting your solicitor to try to push for more, or less, if the cost of getting it is going to be more than the amount you are asking for. If money disputes go on for months or years, the costs will run into thousands of pounds even where small amounts are in dispute. Even if you are in receipt of Community Legal Service (CLS) funding and do not initially have to pay your solicitor's charges as they arise, you have to do so ultimately under the 'statutory charge' (see Chapter 1).

If you have reached an agreement with your spouse and the issues seem fairly clear cut, it may still be worthwhile considering having one interview with a solicitor to check over the terms of that proposed agreement, particularly if you have reached agreement only about the broad outlines of how you are going to split your finances. Sadly, agreements, especially unwritten, have a habit of unravelling over time unless all their consequences are thought through and the agreements recorded officially. Formalising an agreement need not jeopardise amicable relations with your spouse: indeed, doing so could pave the way for a less painful divorce.

A solicitor may also be able to:

- put an agreement into wording that is clear and will be acceptable to the court
- arrange maintenance and the division of property in a more tax-efficient way
- draw up a 'clean-break' settlement where appropriate (particularly where there are no young children)
- point out things that you may not have thought of: for example, that a wife may be losing substantial widow's pension rights under her husband's pension scheme
- explain how the new pension law works and what changes are in the offing that may affect you
- take into account the effects of any proposed order on welfare benefits entitlements.

A note of warning is relevant at this point. Sometimes couples go to their solicitors with an agreement that they have worked out, and are disappointed when the solicitors – very properly – point out the pitfalls concealed within the agreement as it stands. They then blame the solicitors for 'messing things up'. This is to misunderstand the solicitor's role. Solicitors are trained, and paid, to look for the flaws in agreements and attempt to make them watertight. If you have worked out an agreement without first taking legal advice you may find that you have not taken into account all the long-term legal and practical implications for the future. If your solicitor points them out, he or she is not being unreasonably perverse, but is doing a proper job.

Finding the right solicitor for you

Before you embark on the search for a solicitor, it is worth considering what he or she can and cannot do for you and keeping in mind the criteria that you are going to use to help you make your choice. It may be easiest first to define what your solicitor should **not** be.

Not a hired gun

A solicitor is not (or should not be used as) a hired gun. He or she should be prepared to give you balanced, practical advice, not simply tell you what you want to hear. It is possible that in certain matters you are not right, and your solicitor should retain a degree of professional detachment in your relationship such that he or she can point your error out to you, fairly and sympathetically.

Not a counsellor

A solicitor will give you advice, but he or she is not your counsellor, in the sense of being a therapist. Good solicitors will inevitably have acquired some counselling skills, or even have some counselling training, but that is not their primary function when they are dealing with your divorce. If you need counselling or therapy, you should go to someone who is properly qualified to provide this for you, in a therapeutic environment. Using your solicitor in this way will prove dreadfully expensive and will interfere with what he or she needs to do for you. Your solicitor may well suggest that counselling might help, and may even be able to recommend someone who is skilled in dealing with the area of family breakdown.

Not a friend

Your solicitor is not your friend, though a good solicitor will have a friendly manner and be kind and sympathetic. But resist the temptation to be too intimate in your relationship. There needs to be a certain amount of professional detachment between the two of you, for your good, as much as for the solicitor. Pushing the relationship to friendship will probably result in longer conversations – and greater expense for you. If you have a friend who is a solicitor it may be possible to instruct him or her but you may find that such a friend would prefer not to act for you even though he or she will offer you supportive general advice.

What to look for in a solicitor

What people want in a solicitor varies tremendously – a solicitor who is perfect for one client may not be ideal for another. Before you start looking for one, it is worth thinking about the sort of person that you would like acting for you. You may have certain personal preferences: would you, for example, feel more comfortable with a solicitor of the same gender as you? Would you like him or her to be older than you? Do you want to be steered by your solicitor or do you want to 'boss' him or her?

In addition to these subjective criteria, you should bear in mind the factors that are indications of a good solicitor.

- Clearly, the qualities, both professional and personal, of the solicitor are crucial. It helps if he or she is experienced in matrimonial law, but this is not crucial in a team or department setting where there are experienced staff to turn to if the need arises. Intelligence and thoughtfulness are probably more crucial than experience. A good matrimonial solicitor will be inclined to approach your difficulties with your spouse in a constructive way, exploring whether an amicable solution can be achieved. But this does not mean he or she should be a pushover – your solicitor should be prepared to be tough on your behalf if need be. Be wary, however, of any solicitor who talks in swaggering terms (for example, 'We'll take your husband for every penny he owns'). However hell bent you are on revenge, you must bear in mind that an overly aggressive approach is going to be enormously expensive, and, very often, counter-productive.

- Look at the way in which the solicitor's firm presents itself. Is it reasonably organised and efficient? Does the phone get answered promptly? Does the secretary seem sensible, and take down a proper message? Do you get rung back as promised? Do you know who will take a phone call if the solicitor is not in the office?
- What are the offices like? A lot of solicitors' offices are reasonably scruffy, but if they are downright dirty and depressing and nobody has made any effort to make the waiting room a reasonable place to sit in, does this tell you something about the firm's attitude to its clients?
- Does the solicitor treat you like a human being, or as just a problem to be processed? Are you listened to politely and carefully? Is the office tidy? Does he or she behave in a professional manner (for example, are other clients' papers left out where you can see them; can other clients phone in while the solicitor should be talking to you)?

You should not have to put up with unprofessional behaviour from your solicitor. When you are feeling unhappy because of the state of your marriage it is easy to feel that you just have to take what you find, particularly if you are CLS-funded, but this is not the case and you should not have to accept it.

If you are not happy with your solicitor it is probably best to change to another one early in the case, rather than uneasily enduring the relationship to the point where you feel that you **must** instruct someone else. Even if you are CLS-funded you can change solicitors, but you would need to explain to the Legal Services Commission (LSC) why you were not happy and needed to change, and get the transfer of the certificate agreed.

Finding a solicitor

It may be that a solicitor you have used in the past for some other matter (for example, buying a house) does matrimonial work or has a colleague who does. It might be worth asking and having a preliminary discussion on the telephone. However, if he or she has previously acted for **both** you and your spouse, professional rules say that he or she may not be able to act for you (or your spouse) because of the potential for 'conflict of interest'.

Ask acquaintances who have been divorced whom they used, although you should be wary of recommendations in cases which are very different from your own. It is also worthwhile making enquiries at your local CAB or advice centre or even your local county court (each court keeps a list of solicitors who appear before the court). The Law Society's *Regional Directories* of solicitors practising in the area and showing the categories of the work they undertake are available in CABx, public libraries and court offices throughout the UK. The *Directories* and CABx should also be able to point you in the direction of lawyers who have LSC contracts.

The task of finding a solicitor through *Yellow Pages* and its electronic version, www.yell.co.uk, is relatively easy because in most directories there are special sections for solicitors who are members of the Solicitors Family Law Association (SFLA, see below)★ identified by the SFLA logo, as well as for solicitors who offer CLS funding. Look under the heading 'Solicitors' (usually there is very little listed under 'Divorce').

When you telephone or write to a firm of solicitors asking for an appointment, say that you wish to be advised in connection with your matrimonial difficulties and ask if it has a solicitor specialising in divorce and related financial matters, preferably one who is a member of the SFLA.

The SFLA is in practice a very good source for tracking down a specialist family lawyer. It is an association of about 4,000 matrimonial lawyers in England and Wales who must subscribe to a code of practice (see Appendix II) designed to encourage and assist parties to reach acceptable arrangements for the future in a positive and conciliatory – rather than in an aggressive and litigious – way. This does not mean that an SFLA solicitor will be 'soft'. His or her advice to you and manner of dealing with the various issues that arise will be positive.

You can also ask the administrative secretary of the SFLA for a list of the solicitor members in your region. If there are no SFLA solicitors practising in your area, you can telephone the Records Section of the Law Society of England and Wales,* which can give you the names of three solicitors local to you.

Using the Internet to find a solicitor

Given the increasing use of the Internet as a source of information, readers may wish to find a solicitor through the Net. The usefulness of the Internet in this area is still somewhat limited but improving all the time. Family lawyers have been slow to use the Internet as a means of contacting potential clients via creating their own web sites, but there are some exceptions (some of the addresses listed at the end of this book have their own web sites). Your chances of success in finding a local solicitor on the Internet are closely linked to where you are – London and other major cities are generally better served. You can take advantage of the search facilities offered by the Net by searching for particular keywords – 'divorce', 'family lawyer', 'family media-tion' – ensuring that your search is limited to the UK. You could also type in your locality (for example, Manchester) and see what comes up. Many legal web sites are somewhat 'boring' but at least they should give you an idea of what is on offer at a firm. Others will include full explanations of their services and fees, pictures of solicitors (so you can see what they look like) and sometimes 'update' pages which you can visit to get free information.

Accreditation schemes

Both the Law Society and the SFLA have started accreditation schemes for family lawyers. To be a member of the SFLA scheme a person has to:

- have been a solicitor for at least five years (or a Fellow of the Insti-tute of Legal Executives,* a professional body representing over 22,000 legal executives and trainee legal executives – see *Lawyers who are not solicitors*, below – for the same period)

- pass a special examination
- have worked at least half of his or her working hours over the past three years as a family lawyer
- subscribe to the SFLA code of practice.

The Law Society's Family Law Panel has less exacting standards: solicitors or legal executives have to have been qualified for three years and should have worked as family lawyers for one-third of the total of practice time for the past three years. Panel members also have to pass an examination on family law or demonstrate an acceptable breadth of knowledge.

Neither of these schemes has been going for very long, so while membership may be an indication of competence, the reverse is not the case; plenty of excellent family lawyers will not yet be members of these panels.

Lawyers who are not solicitors

There are many experienced matrimonial lawyers employed by solicitors' firms who are not qualified solicitors. Previously called 'managing clerks', they are now known as 'legal executives', and many of them are Fellows of the Institute of Legal Executives or are working towards qualification as Fellows. (Traditionally their route into the profession was to come straight from school and learn on the job. These days, increasingly, they have degree-level education.) They are likely to be just as competent as the solicitors that they work with, and the same considerations apply to them as to solicitors when you are finding someone suitable to act for you.

Low-priced interview

Until 1993 it was possible to have a fixed-fee interview at a solicitor's firm: half-an-hour's legal advice for £5. Since its abolition no single scheme has replaced it. However, many solicitors do offer a free first interview, or one for a fixed price (although it is likely to be considerably more than £5). Advertisements in *Yellow Pages* will often have this information. You can also ask your local branch of the Law Society if it knows of solicitors in your area who offer a similar service.

The Bar Council's Pro-Bono Unit

With the numbers of people who are potentially financially eligible for CLS funding now shrinking, one possibility of getting legal advice for free is the Bar Council's Pro-Bono Unit.★ The Bar Council★ is the barristers' equivalent of the solicitors' Law Society and runs a scheme whereby barristers (or counsel) offer free legal advice to deserving cases. Normally barristers cannot advise members of the public direct – their clients are the solicitors – but this scheme operates so that barristers can give direct advice. The scheme, which covers many other areas of law too, is limited to those without financial resources who would otherwise be unable to have their case heard. In most cases a solicitor will still need to be involved, but it might be worthwhile enquiring if the Pro–Bono Unit will assist you.

Seeking advice from solicitors

Remember that time is money, so try to use your solicitor's time as efficiently as possible. A succinct letter to him or her setting out what you want to do (your 'instructions') may well be more cost-effective than a long rambling telephone conversation. If you can go prepared for your first interview, so much the better. Some solicitors send a questionnaire to their clients to be completed and returned before the first interview. Otherwise, try to take along with you on your first appointment:

- your marriage certificate
- any correspondence or assessments from the Child Support Agency
- copies of any court orders made in respect of this marriage or any previous marriage – or in respect of your children
- typed or neatly written notes setting out:
    - your name in full, and those of your spouse and children
    - dates of birth of yourself, your spouse and children
    - details of any children in the household who are not children of the marriage
    - your address and (if different) that of your spouse
    - your home and work telephone numbers (and perhaps your email address if you have one)
    - your occupation and that of your spouse
    - your National Insurance number (for CLS applications)
    - names and addresses of the children's schools

- dates of any previous marriage of yourself and/or your spouse and dates of any decrees absolute
- if you have already separated, the date and circumstances of the separation
- a summary of your financial position (include details of your and your spouse's income including welfare benefits; details of the home, its approximate value, and the name and address and mortgage account number of the mortgagee; any other capital assets; and any debts and liabilities – see Chapter 2)
- any correspondence that you might have received from your spouse's solicitor.

To use your solicitor to the best advantage do not hesitate at any time to ask him or her to explain and discuss any points about which you are not clear. It may help to go prepared with notes of what you want to ask and then to take notes of the advice given. Indeed, this is a sensible precaution as otherwise it is all too easy to forget everything your solicitor has told you.

Remember that you can accept or reject advice as you wish. But before you reject advice, make sure that you understand the point.

Using your solicitor's time wisely and cost-effectively means not leaving it to your solicitor to do everything: because of the time basis of costing the bill, the more time he or she spends on the case, the higher the bill will be. Quite a lot can be done by you yourself that will save solicitors' costs, but tell your solicitor first what you plan to do.

Open your own file at home and be organised about keeping correspondence and any relevant documents safe, and keep copies of letters that you send to your solicitor.

You are entitled to be told at any stage how the case is progressing and how much it is costing. Your solicitor should send you a client care letter (see below) at the outset. Remember that you can ask him or her for interim statements of how costs are building up if they are not supplied automatically (firms should do this).

Although it can be tempting to forget about the question of costs, this is an area which you ignore at your peril. Running up hefty bills of costs, whether you are paying privately or have CLS funding, will severely damage the ability of both partners to begin their lives afresh.

Costs are dealt with at length in Chapter 1: read this now if you have not already done so.

Client care code

All solicitors must comply with a client care code, which sets out how clients should be kept informed and advised on who will be handling their case and about costs.

What this means in practice is that at the outset of your case – once you have seen and informed a solicitor that you want him or her to take on your case – you should receive a fairly detailed letter (sometimes called a 'client care' letter) which complies with the code. This might tell you, for example, the name of the person dealing with your case, the name of the head of the department and information about costs. It should also identify the person to complain to in the firm if you think you have got poor service. If your solicitor does *not* send out such a letter, it may be an indication that he or she is not really on the ball – so you may get better service elsewhere.

Complaints about solicitors and barristers

Solicitors

Occasionally the relationship between a client and a solicitor can break down. If you have a real, not an imagined, grievance against your solicitor (for example, if he or she persistently fails to return your telephone calls or to respond to your letters), it may be worthwhile having a word with the person identified in the client care letter as the one to complain to, or the head of the matrimonial department or otherwise the senior partner of the firm (the name on the top of the notepaper). Switching to another solicitor can be an expensive process, as the new person will have to read through all the paperwork that has already been produced: this can itself cause extra delay. So, if a sincere personal intervention can restore a good working relationship with your solicitor, this can often be the best action to take.

If, however, the situation fails to improve, you may wish to complain formally about your solicitor. Address your complaint in writing to the Office for the Supervision of Solicitors (OSS).★ The OSS produces a leaflet called *What to do if you are dissatisfied with your solicitor*, which may be useful, and also operates a helpline.

Once your complaint has been investigated, the next stage, if you are still unhappy, is to write to the Legal Services Ombudsman.★ Appointed under the Courts and Legal Services Act 1990, he or she oversees the handling of complaints against solicitors, barristers and licensed conveyancers.

Barristers

Another possibility is that you may have a complaint against your barrister or counsel, if one is instructed by your solicitor to act on your behalf — say, at a court hearing. Complaints about barristers can be hard to succeed with, but it is a good idea to check with your solicitor first to see if your grounds for grievance are well founded. Many courts carry a leaflet called *How to complain about a barrister* issued by the Bar Council complaints system. You can get hold of this leaflet from the Bar Council.

Other sources of advice and help

Anyone in difficulties over finance, tax, housing, the children, or rights generally, can go for advice to a CAB. All CABx have numerous leaflets and information about local sources of help and services. Their services differ across the UK, but many can provide you with everything from an impartial listener to representation at social security appeal tribunals or advice about money and county court representation. CABx are especially good at providing debt-counselling services. You can find the address of your local branch in the telephone directory.

Chapter 4
Your children

If you, as an individual or as a couple, are considering a divorce and you have children, you need to think carefully about how you tell them and what plans you make for their future. This book is aimed primarily at dealing with the practical financial and legal aspects of divorce, so consult the Bibliography for books that offer more detailed advice on the emotional impact of divorce on children. This chapter gives you some general pointers about sensible ways of handling the situation.

It is important to acknowledge that you are not going to be at your best as parents while the separation and divorce are happening. You are likely to be unhappy and stressed and this is going to make it difficult for you to be rational and even-tempered. You will probably feel that you yourself need looking after, which could make you feel guilty and make it harder for you to be the good parent that you would like to be.

Try to take comfort from the fact that this is a temporary state. Things will change, though it may take some time, and perhaps in a year's time life will be different and will probably be better. You have to get through a bad bit as a family, each looking after each other.

However much you have got to the point of disliking or even hating your spouse, remember the key fact that **you are both going to go on being parents for the rest of your lives**. Your marriage may end, but the parental bond with your children will not. Your children are not going to stop being your children when they get to 18; they will still need you there for their weddings, births, illnesses and crises. Do you and your spouse really want to be in a state of armed truce every time you meet? Do you want your children to be in the position where they can never invite both of you to the same occasion? Do you want to continue to hate each other for the rest of your lives? Somehow you need to find a way of managing to cope with each other in the future.

Many couples, probably most, manage to find a way of doing this. For some it takes quite a while. If you do not find a way, the people that you will hurt most are your children.

Telling the children

The advice on telling the children about your separation or divorce is always that if possible you and your spouse should tell them together and you should do it so that they can ask questions and talk and be hugged and reassured. This may be impossible; if your spouse has left without much warning and you are left with the children you will be faced with their questions and may not be able to arrange this. Try not to tell them just before they go to bed, otherwise they may soon feel abandoned and alone, and lie in bed worrying about what is going to happen.

If the two of you can tell the children together it helps to have worked out what you are going to say and to be in a position to tell them what your plans for the future are. If you have thought about what the contact arrangements will be, you can tell them. If the children are old enough, you can discuss these with them. It is important, however, that they do not feel that they are being asked to take the responsibility for the decisions.

The children's reaction

Even if your relationship with your spouse has reached the point where you feel that you can no longer carry on living together, and the strains have become only too clear to you, you may well find that the prospect of a separation comes as a shock to the children and they are likely to react with disbelief, denial and a frantic attempt to make it not happen.

Most children would rather keep their parents together at all costs, even when they know that they are unhappy together. Moreover, it is quite common for children to blame themselves for what has happened – they conclude that it because they have been naughty that their father or mother has left.

When you break the news to them it is important to stress that it is an adult decision, and that though you do not feel that you can go on being married you still love them very much and are going to go on being their parents. This is a message that you will have to repeat many times. Tempting as it is, especially if you feel that your spouse is to blame, try to keep blame out of it as far as the children are concerned.

Younger children

Younger children may well not understand very much of what is involved, though some may already have encountered other children whose parents are divorced. You will need to explain the situation in words that they can understand, and it is tempting to fudge the issue and not tell the whole truth – say, to suggest that a separation will be for only a little while when you know that it is going to be permanent. It is probably better to be honest at this stage rather than let the children cling to a false hope that will eventually disappoint them.

It is worth remembering that young children tend to associate words such as 'law' and 'courts' with criminal law and prison, so any reference of this kind can be much more alarming than you may have anticipated.

Older children

Older children will be used to being consulted about their wishes in many family decisions. They may be very clear about which parent they want to live with or the sort of contact (access) that they want to have. Try very hard, however, not to let them feel that they are being asked to choose between you and your spouse. It is not fair to burden them with such a choice.

Often older children have fairly complicated social lives of their own and parents need to respect the commitments they already have and factor them in when making plans for the future.

Parents should bear in mind the possibility that older children may wish to live with one parent for a few years and then change to the other.

Adult children

It is tempting to think that once the children have reached the age of 18 and left home a divorce will not affect them very much. Many couples preserve a failing marriage for this reason until the youngest child has gone to university. However, children in their late teens and early twenties can be very badly upset by their parents splitting up. It can be particularly hard for them if the home that they have known disappears while they are away, the bedrooms that they regard as theirs are no longer as they left them, the neighbourhood that they grew up in is lost.

Try to bear in mind that though in the eyes of the law they are adults, they are still likely to be dependent on you. It will be better if you can tell them together, and when they are at home, not while they are away at college, or right at the end of the holiday so that they go back to college to face the shock alone.

What you can do to help

The following is a list (not exhaustive) of suggestions on how to make it easier for your children to deal with the impending separation or divorce.

- Tell the schools as soon as you have told the children, or even in advance. It is bound to affect their school work or behaviour to some extent. If the school knows, staff will be sympathetic and do what they can to help.
- Try to stick to domestic routines as they were, and retain your normal attitude to discipline and behaviour. It is tempting to be super-indulgent to try to make up for the hurt. But children rely on routine and frameworks to reinforce their sense of order in the world. You have already smashed part of their world order; try to keep the rest of it in place.
- You need to talk to the children a lot, but try not to confide in them in the way that you would in an adult friend. They do not need the burden of the intimate detail of your marriage, tempting as it is to justify your side of the story.
- Go on referring to your spouse as you did before (for example, 'mummy' or 'dad'). Do not use terms such as 'Mrs Jones', 'that man', or, more damagingly, 'that bitch, your mother'. Your children can do without this.
- Treats are a good idea, but spoiling is not. Do not start buying expensive presents as compensation, or bribery. Children know when they are being bought and can be quite cold-blooded about exploiting the situation.

- Take advantage of any offer of adult help that you can get. If friends offer to take the children out to let you have a rest, accept gratefully. Life as a single parent is very hard work. It is not an admission of failure to accept help.
- Widen the family circle. It is easy to retreat into your small family world when a divorce hits you. But it can be very claustrophobic and make you more miserable. Instead, try to invite the children's friends home, and get other adults to come round. If you can make your home into an open friendly place, the children will find it easier to adjust to the new situation.
- Children can be greatly helped by adult friends of their own. Grandparents, aunts and uncles, godparents and other family friends (provided they can be persuaded not to take sides) can be very helpful confidants. Your children may find it easier to talk to them than to you. This is not because they do not love you; it is because they feel that they do not want to burden you with their troubles.

What the legal position is

Parental responsibility

Parents who were married to each other when their children were born, or who married after their children were born, automatically have what the Children Act 1989 calls 'parental responsibility'. Parents continue to share this after divorce until the children are 18, whether the children live with them or not.

The Children Act defines parental responsibility as 'all the rights, duties, powers, responsibilities and authority which by law a parent of a child has in relation to the child and his property'. In practice, this means the responsibility and the right to make choices over all the issues that are necessarily involved in bringing up a child, such as:

- where the child will live
- where the child will go to school
- what religious upbringing the child will have
- what medical treatment the child will have.

If you have parental responsibility, you are also able to apply for a passport for the child.

79

If you are living together as parents, the expectation of the law is that you will make joint decisions and exercise your parental responsibility together. Once you are separated you can each (in law) exercise that responsibility without consulting the other, but it obviously makes sense to continue, as far as possible, to discuss matters, such as those listed above, and to try to reach joint decisions. Sometimes, in an emergency, like a medical crisis, you will have to act alone, and you can do this, by law.

The expectation of the Children Act was that, for the most part, parents are capable of deciding matters for their children without the intervention of the courts. Prior to the Act, every divorce where there were children resulted in orders being made for 'custody', 'care and control' and 'access'. This no longer happens, and the old terms have been abolished (even though they are still used in the popular media). If parents can agree arrangements about where the children will live ('residence') and how they will see the parent with whom they do not live ('contact'), the court will not make any order about this. Orders will be made only where parents dispute the arrangements and then only if the existence of the order is felt by the judge to be necessary to keep the parents from further dispute (see Chapter 10 for details about disputes over children).

Residence

You will need to decide where the children are going to make their main home. This is often fairly obvious, with most children staying in the original family home. But other arrangements can be made. If you are going to move them out of their family home, do remember that they will need their own things with them. Children have close and intense relationships with their own possessions. Make sure that they are allowed to take with them whatever they feel they need even if you think that it is junk.

Some families feel that the children can have two 'main' homes and divide their time equally between their parents. If this is your feeling, you need to be absolutely sure that you are not treating the children as an asset that you want to divide equally between you. Children are not commodities. How would you feel if you had to move home every three or four days? Is it likely to be unsettling for them? It is not helpful if you make the decision on the basis of what you feel is 'fair' for you.

Contact

The term 'contact', as used in the Children Act, can mean anything from long overnight visits to telephone calls and letters. There is no single pattern of contact that is laid down or approved in any official way. Each family must make its own arrangements. Whatever you can agree can later be altered to suit changes in, for example, the children's interests or domestic arrangements.

Contact can lead to various problems; the following is a list of tips to help prevent them.

Arrangements for contact

- Regular arrangements (for example, meeting the children every weekend) are best. You know where you stand as parents and the children have a framework that they can rely on – provided everybody sticks to it.
- At the same time, do not be horribly rigid. If there is a special occasion to which your child should go and it clashes with a contact visit, try to be flexible and rearrange it.
- It can be helpful to get a large write-on calendar, and jointly plan the contact times ahead. The children can put stickers on the contact days and this helps them to keep track of their weeks.
- In the early days of a separation, it may not be possible to sort out a regular pattern of contact; both your lives may be in too much upheaval. It may be tempting to say that you will not have contact for a while because you fear that it might disrupt the children too much. In fact, it may be that the contact is going to be more upsetting for you than for the children. Try to start and keep contact; eventually a regular pattern can emerge. The children will need you very much at this time in their lives.
- It is very important to be careful about time-keeping. If you agree to collect or return children at particular times, you should stick to them. Similarly, if the children are being collected from you, you should have them ready at the correct time. Nothing annoys the other parent more than being careless about this. And the children too will be upset if you do not come when they expect you. If something unexpected causes a delay, call and inform the other parent or the children.
- Do not slag the other parent off when you have the children with

you. Also, do not use the children as a way of keeping tabs on what your spouse is doing. Children know when they are being used as spies, and it is unfair to pull their loyalties in two ways.

- Contact is, says the law, the child's right to see the parent, and not the other way about. Do not behave as though the child's time is a possession you are entitled to.
- Telephone calls can be very useful as a way of keeping in touch, but if you are the one phoning the child, try to agree with your spouse about when would be a useful time.
- Try not to turn every contact visit into a wild outing somewhere. Low-key activities, such as drawing, painting and reading together, may be just as pleasurable and valuable for your children. What they want is your time and attention; spending money on them does not compensate for a lack of time or love.
- When children come back from a contact visit they are often cross, fractious and hyped up. It may be tempting for the parent they live with to think that this is because the contact visit is doing them harm – and to try to stop it. But children – as you may remember from the days when you were together with your spouse and the children – are like this at the end of any hectic day. Do not put all the blame on your spouse or on the visit. The children may be a little more upset because the hand-over from one parent to another reminds them of what they have lost, but this does not mean that contact is something traumatic that should be avoided.
- If you are the non-resident parent, it is easy to feel that you have lost, or are losing, your relationship with your children. Of course it is now different, but children are capable of sustaining close and intimate relationships with people that they do not see everyday, and of loving them very much. If you are living a long way away from your children, use the telephone (and e-mail, and even video links). Children love to receive letters, or picture postcards when they are too young to read.
- As children get older they may have very full social calendars of their own. They may be involved in after-school and weekend activities. Somehow, you need to balance all these, and accept that if you have contact visits at the weekend, you will need to take the children to their activities.

If parents cannot agree on contact arrangements

Perhaps surprisingly, most parents do agree the arrangements for their children, and find a way of dealing with contact and residence. This is not to say that it will all be straightforward; there are bound to be extremely tricky times when you quarrel and everybody gets very upset.

Try to focus on the long term. Remember that you both have the children's interests at heart. Make use of mediation if you can to resolve disputes. If all else fails, you may have to use the court, but the court too will try to resolve issues by mediation.

Chapter 10 sets out how the courts will deal with issues over the children.

Chapter 5

Mediation

Couples facing separation and divorce probably have a wider choice of services to help them get through the situation than ever before. This chapter deals with mediation: how separating couples can get skilled help to sort out their disputes over the divorce and all the issues involved in a divorce – money, the home, businesses, debts, pensions, and not least the children – without building up unbearably heavy legal costs. It covers what mediation is (and is not), the types of mediation available, what is likely to happen in the mediation process, who it is likely to work for and how to go about finding a mediator.

Mediation and the Family Law Act 1996

One of the chief intentions of the Family Law Act 1996 was to steer more and more people into mediation to resolve the issues between them in divorce proceedings. Although Part II of the Act will not be implemented, which means that there will be no compulsory meetings at the start of a divorce, the change to Community Legal Service (CLS) funding is already in force. This obliges people seeking CLS funding to explore whether mediation would be a viable alternative to litigation (as described in Chapter 1). The government has indicated that although Part II will be repealed it intends to continue to support and promote mediation.

Ideally, mediation should be a process that neither party feels constrained to go in for – compulsion would ruin the rationale for mediation. The insistence that those obtaining CLS funding under the mediation scheme – see Chapter 1 – should undergo mediation seems to fly in the face of this. Fortunately, mediation services which offer these appointments are conscious of this and are sensitive to the feelings of people who feel unwilling to go through the procedure.

Mediation can take place at any time, even before divorce proceedings have been started. Sometimes it can be of help where the divorce ended years ago but where there are still intractable problems, for example over the children.

Mediation is 'legally privileged', which means that nothing said in the context of the sessions can be used in evidence at court, if, eventually, legal action through the courts has to be taken. Documents disclosing financial information in a mediation are, however, usually treated as 'open', which means that they could be disclosed as evidence if there is a court case over money issues later. Also, any wish not to disclose an address to the partner will be respected. However, there is an important exception to both the confidentiality and privilege attached to mediation: where someone, particularly a child, appears to be suffering or is likely to suffer 'significant harm' (for example, sexual abuse), the mediator may have to stop the mediation process and take steps to protect the child. What steps will be taken in practice may very often form part of the discussion between the mediator and the couple.

What is mediation?

Family mediation has been developing in the USA from the 1960s and emerged in the UK in 1977: it was first used in Bristol in relation to disputes involving children in Bristol County Court. Since then it has grown to become a voluntary process encompassing all issues which arise in the wake of separation or divorce.

Defining mediation is not easy. Dictionary definitions of the word do not capture the complex nature of mediation as practised in family matters. The Code of Practice for Family Mediators, produced by National Family Mediation (NFM)★ and the Family Mediators Association (FMA),★ defines mediation as 'a process in which an impartial third person assists those involved in family breakdown, and in particular separating or divorcing couples, to communicate better with one another and to reach their own agreed and informed decisions about some or all of the issues relating to or arising from the separation, divorce, children, finance or property'. Another, more technical but precise, definition comes from the Family Mediation Code of

Practice produced by the Solicitors Family Law Association (SFLA).*
It describes mediation as a process in which

1.1   a couple or any family members

1.2   whether or not they are legally represented

1.3   and at any time, whether or not there have been legal proceedings

1.4   agree to the appointment of a neutral third party (the mediator)

1.5   who is impartial

1.6   who has no authority to make any decisions with regard to their issues

1.7   which may relate to separation, divorce, children's issues, property and financial questions or any other issues they may raise

1.8   but who helps them reach their own informed decisions

1.9   by negotiated agreement

1.10 without adjudication.

The jargon

First, any potential confusion about the terms that are used here needs dispelling. Although 'mediation' is now the most popular term for describing the process of couples settling their disputes with the aid of an impartial, skilled person, 'conciliation', the term most often used in the past, is still occasionally used. For some people 'conciliation' is interchangeable with 'mediation', but there is an important difference: 'conciliation' is used to describe the court-based process of trying to make parties to a court dispute – usually over the children – settle their differences. The conciliator involved (usually a court welfare officer) may have to report to the court about the outcome of the discussions, so conciliation is not entirely confidential and may involve a degree of coercion which mediation proper should not. Courts without their own conciliation service – and occasionally even those which have it – may suggest a referral to a local mediation agency. If this happens, remember that the decision about whether or not to go is still entirely up to you and that what happens in the sessions will be confidential.

Another confusion can arise over the terminology used. Although the word 'conciliation' sounds like 'reconciliation', the latter means getting couples back together again, which is quite different from both conciliation and mediation. The purpose of mediation is not reconciliation – although a few couples may decide to get back together when they are in mediation, and there is a greater chance of it happening in mediation than in the traditional legal process. It is to enable couples to create their own tailor-made solutions to the issues which inevitably need sorting out in the wake of a separation or divorce. For most couples, therefore, the focus in mediation will be on current and future arrangements to do with each living apart, rather than looking back over the marriage.

Some mediation services deal only with problems relating to the children ('children only mediation'), whereas others deal with all issues (termed 'comprehensive' or 'all-issues' mediation, AIM): whether or not to separate, the children, money, the home, family businesses, pensions and so on. You may therefore need to check what ranges of issues different local services are able to deal with.

Most mediation services also deal with unmarried couples who decide to split up. Here the legal issues are different – unmarried fathers have no automatic legal rights over their children, for example, and there can be no claims for maintenance for an ex-partner in her own right. However, the process is pretty much the same.

This chapter deals with voluntary or out-of-court mediation.

Types of mediation

If you opt for mediation, you will need to decide whether to choose a family mediator with a therapeutic or mental health background (a 'family mediator') or one with a legal background (a 'lawyer mediator'). The former are, generally, mediators who have a background in social work or mental health (like therapists, counsellors, family court welfare officers, or social workers) and are therefore experienced in family problems. The latter are mediators who are experienced family lawyers; their particular skill and expertise is knowing what the law is with regard to family matters and how the courts are likely to deal with cases in divorce. Some services offer co-mediation (see below), where a family mediator and lawyer mediator work together. You should check what experience a mediator has before going to him or her. Advice on how to find a mediator is given later in this chapter.

Family mediators have historically been cheaper than lawyer mediators (for more details on how much mediation costs, see the end of this chapter). Most family mediation services are linked to NFM, and many of them charge fees based on a couple's income or even offer free sessions. Lawyer mediators will almost certainly charge more than family mediators, although some operate discretionary lower rates for low-income families. (See *Free mediation under the pilot scheme* on how you may be able to get free mediation under the pilot mediation scheme.) Because lawyer mediators offer more by way of legal information than family mediators do, it is more meaningful to compare their costs with those incurred by each spouse instructing a solicitor and both solicitors running up heavy costs. Lawyer mediators usually charge similar rates whether they are acting as traditional solicitors for one spouse or as mediators for both together – thus a husband and wife can potentially, by using a lawyer mediator rather than a solicitor, cut their legal costs considerably. Note that each spouse should still get independent legal advice, but because a couple is more likely to reach an agreement faster through a mediator than through separate solicitors, costs savings will be achieved.

There are advantages in having a skilled lawyer assisting in the mediation process: although lawyer mediators do not advise either party individually, they draw on their own experience of family-law cases in first of all piecing together an accurate picture of the family's finances and then in helping the couple work out realistic (and legally acceptable) solutions. Although mediators cannot offer advice, they can give the couple correct, up-to-date information on the rapidly changing law – such as changes in the law on pensions and child support, and in procedure – so their clients can make well-informed choices during mediation. Family mediators often have an arrangement with a local solicitor who will check over the terms of an agreement towards the end of the mediation, but this may be rather late in the day to correct any wrong turnings made in the mediation process. However, an increasing number of NFM services are now using lawyer mediators too, so check with your local service.

The type of mediation service where a pair of mediators – a family mediator and a lawyer mediator – work together, known as co-mediation, was pioneered by the FMA, and is now used in many NFM services as well.

The mediation process

For mediation to work, both partners need to attend. It can be a daunting prospect to face your soon-to-be ex-spouse over a table to discuss what future arrangements should be made, but a skilled mediator, who will always be impartial, will help by managing the process so that both parties can make their views clear. It is the mediator's responsibility to be even-handed, to create a balance between the parties so that they can both negotiate properly over conflicts. Even where a couple are very much in conflict with one another, addressing conflict is common in mediation and the right solutions can often be found. Mediation is very often the most appropriate forum for conflicts to be resolved.

A mediator will not impose his or her own views but will try to help a couple find common ground so that together they can craft arrangements which will work for each of them individually and the family as a whole. Sometimes this process can necessitate a mediator encouraging the more passive partner to put his or her own views forward and ensuring that the more dominant partner stays less verbal. The mediator will establish ground rules to create a more positive framework for working things out. The agreement to mediate, which forms the basis of the terms on which a mediator will act in a mediation, will set out what the partners agree to in the mediation.

Mediation works by setting agendas covering the issues each party wants to discuss – it is up to each of the couple to decide what they need to talk about. The process of mediation is likely to take about five to six sessions, although more or fewer may be necessary. The agenda for the first session could cover, for example, the decision to separate, arrangements for the time being over the children, and payment of bills. Mediations are usually relatively informal, with first names being used. At the first session the mediator will explain what the process of mediation is all about and the terms of the mediation agreement.

As part and parcel of the agreement, in all-issues mediation both spouses must consent to give full disclosure of their finances. Each spouse will fill out a comprehensive form giving details about what he or she earns and any other income, savings, debts, pensions, the home, family business and so on, and supply back-up documents if need be. The forms are then sent to the mediator (usually by at least the third session), who will make a copy for the other partner.

To ensure that both partners are fully aware of the whole picture of the family's finances, the mediator will often put up the figures on a

flipchart. Getting things up on the flipchart in this way helps to identify where more information is needed and clarify which money
matters are issues between the couple. The lengthy (and costly)
process of 'disclosure' in court cases is short-circuited by this method,
because a spouse can often quickly identify if the other is holding back
information and ensure that the figures are corrected. Often, various
alternative arrangements or options are written up on the flipchart.
Each spouse can put forward his or her own options. If he or she gets
stuck, the mediator can help out, so more creative solutions to vexed
problems can be worked through and tested as to how well they will
work in reality.

As and when an agreement is reached, the mediator will prepare a
summary of the agreement for each spouse and his or her solicitors.
The summary contains 'open' information about money matters, but
any agreement reached is 'without prejudice' –that is, it cannot be
made known to the court at a full hearing if the agreement subsequently breaks down. The agreement can then be translated by the
solicitors into court documents – the divorce and a consent order over
finances, for example.

Are solicitors still necessary?

Even if you have gone in for mediation it is still a good idea for you
individually to get legal advice about what rights and responsibilities
you have (so that you can negotiate on an informed basis) and also to
double-check the terms of any agreement made during mediation.
You can check whether the agreement will be watertight, whether
anything has been missed out and whether you are giving away something you should not. Having your own solicitor also means you have
legal back-up in case any urgent legal action needs to be taken – to
prevent a spouse from disposing of assets, for example – or if the mediation does not result in an agreement (in which case you will probably
still have to go to court or your solicitors may be able to negotiate on
your behalf). Thus legal advice is complementary to the mediation
process. But by using a skilled and knowledgeable mediator you
could save thousands of pounds in legal fees by avoiding a full-blown
legal battle.

Mediation and the children

Mediation takes a family-based approach, rather than the adversarial approach adopted in the family courts, where a husband and wife have to be on opposite sides, which is a distinct drawback when it comes to dealing with the children. Parents need to try to work together to sort out how the children will be looked after when the family separates, and the family-based approach of mediation can often help parents cooperate in planning for their children's and their own futures. If the dispute is only over the children, mediation by a family mediator may well be the best option. If problems over arrangements for the children are just a part of broader difficulties over finance generally, mediation involving a lawyer mediator would be a better bet. Try to ensure that comprehensive, or 'all-issues', mediation is available.

The emphasis in mediation is on allowing parents to create solutions which enable them to remain parents in as full a sense as possible. By meeting in a neutral environment in the presence of a non-partisan, experienced professional (or sometimes two professionals) trained in assisting couples to come to realistic agreements, both partners may find that they can at least (and perhaps at last) communicate directly rather than talking at each other or entirely missing each other's points. With the agreement of the parents, the children themselves may occasionally be invited to the mediation, but they should attend only if being there helps them cope with the divorce.

Is mediation appropriate for you?

The potential benefits of mediation are numerous.

- **Control over the outcome** You and your spouse create your own tailor-made solutions to problems involved in the divorce or separation – arrangements which will suit your family, not ones imposed on you by the courts. Solutions worked out in mediation can indeed cover aspects where the court would have no power to make court orders.
- **Speed and cost-effectiveness** The process is speedier – disputes can be resolved in weeks, not months and years – and much more cost-effective. Costs are likely to be measured in at most hundreds, not thousands, of pounds; you may even get mediation for free.

- **Respect for the family** Members of the family can come to value others more. The mediation process can help improve communication between the couple and aid cooperation over the children. The process of divorce can be made more dignified.
- **Confidentiality** The whole discussion in mediation is private and confidential. If you want to ensure privacy and confidentiality over how you and your partner work things out, mediation will be right for you.

Mediation is not necessarily suitable for all couples. A study carried out in 1996 by the SFLA of its clients' views showed that about 30 to 40 per cent of divorcing couples felt mediation could be right for them: others preferred to rely on lawyers acting in the traditional way. Of couples sent to explore the possibility of mediation for CLS funding, about 30 per cent go on to mediation. The uptake may increase further as people become more aware of the benefits of mediation. Couples who have successfully resolved their disputes wisely, efficiently and cost-effectively through mediation certainly need no convincing of its benefits in comparison to costly, time-consuming, antagonistic litigation processes which lead only to pyrrhic victories.

Critics of mediation have argued that it is biased against women, in that a wife may be too eager to agree in mediation to a settlement which gives her less financially than a court would, for the sake of a quiet life. Other studies have refuted this and have demonstrated that couples using all-issues mediation were glad they had used it, that they felt mediation had helped them end the marriage more amicably, that they were more content with child-care arrangements and that their agreements had survived the test of time.

Together with the mediator, you and your partner can decide whether mediation will be right for you as a couple. You should be able to feel safe during mediation, so being scared of a violent partner, say, would make the exercise unworkable. Overall, as a rule of thumb, consider whether you feel that, with expert help, you would be able to negotiate with your spouse with respect for yourself and him or her. If you feel you would too easily give in, or on the other hand if you would definitely try to dominate the process and would refuse to listen, then mediation may not be right for you. However, remember that all sorts of conflicts can be dealt with satisfactorily in mediation – even if you cannot see how there can be a way out of your conflict, a mediator may very well still be able to help you.

If you would like to give it a go, you could always arrange a first appointment with a mediator, go along and then decide whether mediation might work before committing yourself fully to the process. Some mediators offer a free half-hour introduction to mediation for you to have an opportunity to test the water. It is important that you trust the integrity and impartiality of a mediator, so an introductory session could reassure you whether mediation, and in particular your mediator, would offer the right way forward.

One-stop divorce centres

For most divorcing couples, getting help in their divorce may involve visits to several different services. However, the progressive Cambridge Family and Divorce Centre (CFADC)★ may be indicative of the shape of things to come.

The CFADC (which was set up in 1982) offers at a one-stop venue a range of services to couples facing the breakdown of their relationship. The service begins with a form of diagnostic interview, at which a husband or wife separating from his or her partner is assisted in finding out exactly what help is needed. Referrals can then be made to solicitors (with special Law Society permission the CFADC even offers joint information by giving appointments to couples together so both partners do not have to find their own separate solicitor), to one of the Centre's mediators, or to counselling services. Part-time child counsellors are also employed. Where the services identified as needed are not available in-house, referrals can be made to outside agencies. The CFADC does not itself provide legal advice; it merely directs clients to appropriate agencies.

There are now a number of practices, such as the Family Law Consortium★ in London, where solicitors who are also trained as mediators work in conjunction with mediators to offer clients a range of services.

Where to find a mediation service

The first choice to make is whether you want to opt for a lawyer mediator or a family mediator.

If you decide to go for a lawyer mediator, you could contact any of a number of organisations involved in training and recommending lawyer mediators. The best known of these nationwide is the SFLA, whose trained mediators will all be experienced family lawyers who have been practising for at least five years. If you send a stamped addressed envelope to its administrative secretary, you will get a list of lawyer mediators near you.

Other lawyer mediator referral networks are the British Association of Lawyer Mediators (BALM),* and LawGroup UK.* The longest established in the field is the FMA.

Solicitors in some areas are combining forces to make the availability of their mediation services more widely known. You may find local advertising appearing about such a group, but otherwise it is not always easy to find out locally about a mediation service. The heading 'Mediation' has recently started to appear in *Yellow Pages*, although the entries may be restricted or may include cross-references to 'Counselling' or 'Arbitration' (unfortunately nothing ever appears under the heading 'Divorce'). A web site (www.divorce.co.uk) has a useful regional index of mediation services.

The UK College of Family Mediators* was set up by three organisations, the FMA, NFM and Family Mediation Scotland.* Its purpose is to accredit mediation training and set professional standards, and to provide a register of accredited mediators. It publishes the *UK College of Family Mediators Directory and Handbook*, a useful handbook, giving not only up-to-date information on how to get hold of a mediator and details of mediation services but also reference material on the mediation process, taxation and benefits, and changes under the Family Law Act 1996 for example. It is available from many public libraries or from the College.

As an alternative, your local Citizens Advice Bureau (CAB) should also be able to give you the address of your nearest service, or your solicitor can refer you to one.

As with all professional services, it is a good idea to ask for recommendations from trusted friends or acquaintances who may have used a mediator. Bear in mind, however, that as the concept is still relatively little known in the UK, you may not know anyone who has been to mediation already.

How much does mediation cost?

This depends on how long it takes and what type of mediation you opt for. Clearly, the more sessions you have, the more it will cost. Six sessions are typical where there are a number of issues to resolve, fewer sessions are likely if the dispute involves a single issue.

Lawyer mediators
Fees for a lawyer mediator are likely to vary regionally (usually £40 to £60 per person per hour, plus VAT, and more in London). Some mediators have a discretion to reduce fees. Rates charged by FMA co-mediators are similar, and the summary of the agreement reached (or mediation report) may be paid for by the Legal Services Commission (LSC, see below).

Family mediators
Here costs vary. The underlying principle has historically been that such services should be available to all regardless of income. Some schemes charge fees (of about £15 per session), some ask for a contribution dependent on income and others are free.

Free mediation under the pilot scheme
As Chapter 1 made clear, if you qualify for CLS funding for Help with Mediation, you will get funding for your mediation and subsequent advice from a solicitor without making a financial contribution and, crucially, without incurring the statutory charge (see Chapter 1).

Chapter 6

Using the Child Support Agency

This has been the hardest chapter to write in this book because the whole child support system is about to be overhauled radically. At the time of writing, the legislation is still being finalised and is not yet in place. So although this chapter can tell you in theory what the changes are to be, it is not clear when they will all be implemented, which makes it difficult to give readers useful, practical advice.

What this chapter does is describe the ideas of the legislation and the technical terms that it uses; mostly these have not changed. It then deals with the new rules, as they are at present (in their draft form). The last section of the chapter sets out the old rules, which you may already have experienced, as these may still impact on old cases and on current cases until the new procedures are fully operational.

Getting advice about the Child Support Agency

Solicitors, Citizens Advice Bureaux (CABx) and some law centres should be able to offer advice and help about getting or paying child support through the Child Support Agency (CSA).* Many of them have computer programs which will enable them to check a maintenance assessment or calculation, or work out for you what the likely impact of an application to the CSA would be.

Solicitors can offer a limited amount of advice under the Legal Help scheme (see Chapter 1), but they cannot help you complete the application form or even the enquiry form. They would be able to advise you over particular legal points such as paternity, or jurisdiction.

Community Legal Service (CLS) funding is not available to help you challenge a CSA assessment through most of the initial appeal stages: reviewing an assessment or appealing to the Child Support

Appeals tribunal or the Child Support Commissioner. Only if you get past these stages and have to make an application to the court on a point of law will CLS funding be available.

A solicitor can assist you with an application to court under the Legal Help scheme and could help (but not represent) you in the guise of a 'McKenzie friend' (see Glossary) at a CSA tribunal hearing. CLS funding is available for taking a case about paternity to the courts.

The CSA helpline also offers advice, but you may get only general points answered rather than a particular analysis of your circumstances.

The Child Support Act 1991

Background

The Child Support Act 1991 set up the CSA, which started operating in April 1993. It was set up to take over responsibility for child maintenance applications, and the intention was that it should take them out of the hands of the courts. One of the principal aims of the act was to recoup for the Treasury the money that was being paid out through the benefits system to single parents. By pursuing 'absent parents' as the Act called them, and obtaining maintenance from them, it was hoped that single parents would be 'floated off' income support levels.

In order to achieve this, a complicated formula by which the maintenance payable could be calculated was devised. Because the system was set up to take some of the pressure off the income support system, the figures that were used in the maintenance calculation were drawn from the social security allowances. This means that they are revised each year in line with the Department of Social Security (DSS) figures.

The formula has proved to be a problem. It is impossible to work out at a glance what maintenance should be paid; you need to have detailed information about both parties' finances to be able to do this. The possibilities for error are numerous, and the CSA has often itself got the calculations wrong. This is not the place to rehearse the sorry tale of inefficiency, backlogs and injustices, real and perceived, that the Act has led to, but the need for a change is, to say the least, pressing.

Originally it was intended that the CSA would deal with all cases of maintenance for children. People in receipt of benefit had to (and still have to) use the CSA to pursue their spouses for child maintenance;

those not receiving state benefits were given a transitional period in which they could choose whether to use the CSA or the courts. However, the backlog of benefit cases so overwhelmed the CSA that the transitional period was extended indefinitely. Although the power of the courts to hear a contested application for child maintenance has been removed, you can obtain a court order by agreeing the amounts to be paid and having this ratified as an order by the court (see Chapter 12). This is the route that most people who are not obliged to use the CSA have taken.

Powers of the CSA

The CSA calculates the maintenance due to be paid according to the formula laid down in the Act and in subsequent legislation. It will trace the 'absent parent' and pursue him for maintenance. (In this chapter the absent parent is referred to as 'him' and the parent with

---

Terminology and jurisdiction used by the CSA

The absent parent – the non-resident parent (new term)
The absent parent is defined as a parent who no longer lives in the same household as the child for whom the maintenance is applied. (Note that 'parent' could be by either blood or adoption. Step-parents are not responsible for the maintenance of their step-children under the CSA, although they may be in divorce proceedings if the children are 'children of the family'. See Chapter 16.)

The parent/person with care
The parent/person with care is the person whom the child lives with and who has the usual day-to-day care of the child.

The qualifying child
The child must be under 16, or under 19 but still in full-time, non-advanced education.

Habitual residence
The child and both the parents must all be habitually resident in the UK. Habitual residence means usual residence with a settled intention to remain. If the absent parent is abroad, the CSA cannot deal with maintenance, and the court will have to deal with it instead.

---

care as 'her' because in the vast majority of cases this is how things are. However, the Act makes no distinction over gender, so if you are a male parent with care, the formula and rules will be applied in exactly the same way.) It has investigative powers to find out about a parent's income and capital. If the absent parent does not pay, it has powers to compel payment, the most effective of which is by direct deduction from wages.

Who uses the CSA?

Old rules

Parents with care who are in receipt of income support and jobseeker's allowance are obliged to ask the CSA to make an assessment of maintenance against the absent parent. Recipients of family credit (now known as working families' tax credit) and of disability working allowance used to be obliged to as well, but the rules have now changed. If the parent with care is not prepared to cooperate with the CSA, her benefit can be reduced (by 40 per cent of the income support adult personal allowance for up to three years).

Parents with care who are **not** in receipt of benefit can ask the CSA to make an assessment, but are not obliged to. If there is an existing court order that pre-dates 5 April 1993, the CSA cannot make an assessment unless the court discharges the order. Because the CSA has a bad reputation for delay and inaccuracy, most parents with care would prefer not to use it – they would rather keep the threat of an application to the CSA as a fall-back position if negotiations with the absent parent are not successful.

As mentioned earlier, since the 1991 Act came into force, the courts have had no power to deal with a new contested application for child maintenance. If parents can reach an agreement about maintenance for the children, the terms of this can be made into a court order 'by consent'. However, the court does still have power to vary a court order. This means that if an order is made by consent, either party can later apply to the court for it to be varied, either increased or decreased. It has become a reasonably common practice for couples to agree a basic child maintenance order and have it made in the court by consent so that, if they cannot resolve their differences about maintenance during the divorce proceedings, they can invoke the power of the court to order a variation.

It makes sense, when agreeing an order by consent, to do a calculation of maintenance using the CSA formula, to make sure that the figure that you agree is broadly in line with what you might get from the CSA. However, you have to bear in mind that this figure might be altered by other parts of any settlement that you are discussing.

The effect of the CSA has been to create a two-tier system, with one law for those in receipt of benefit, and a more flexible system for those who are not. This is not a happy result, but it seems to be accepted that the task of dealing with all maintenance cases is not one that the CSA can reasonably be expected to take on in the foreseeable future.

New rules

The requirement for parents with care on income support or job-seeker's allowance to use the CSA will remain.

Parents with care who are not on benefit will not be compelled to use the system. If they did, the Agency would be overloaded, so the government wants to encourage people to reach agreements. However, the CSA will offer a collection service to people who have reached their own agreements *but only for collecting maintenance at CSA rates*. The effect of this would be that CSA assessments would replace the court order or agreement if private payment arrangements break down. The plan is that these proposals would not apply to existing court orders and agreements – they will be available only after the reforms come into effect. In addition, CSA collection and assessment services will be available only after a court order has been in place for at least a year, and parents who wish to transfer to a CSA assessment will have to give at least two months' notice. This will allow parents and their lawyers time to renegotiate new voluntary agreements if appropriate. The White Paper on the subject says:

> We believe that these proposals will encourage parents, lawyers and the Courts to come to child maintenance arrangements in the shadow of the CSA. All parties will know that either parent can turn to the CSA in future, and that it would therefore be sensible to determine child maintenance broadly in line with CSA assessment rates. The Courts would still be free, as now, to determine spousal maintenance, property and pension settlements for the couple concerned.

Who can apply, when, and how?

Either parent can apply for maintenance, though normally it is the parent with care. An application can be made as soon as you separate from your spouse; you do not have to wait until you have filed divorce proceedings. You can get an application form from your local DSS office or by writing to or telephoning your CSA branch office. The form is very long and detailed, though it should become considerably shorter and simpler once the new rules are in force.

Once the application has been made, the absent parent will get an equally long form to complete and send back. If he delays for more than 28 days, the CSA can levy an interim assessment, often at punitive rates. This is intended to encourage a quick response.

How long does it take?

It is impossible to give a definitive answer to this because it depends on the speed of the specific office of the CSA you use and also how quickly the absent parent responds. According to the CSA its target time for processing a claim is about 20 weeks, but it appears from its latest report that the target is not always met and that there is a backlog of claims.

How are payments made?

Both parents will be asked whether their preference is for weekly or monthly payments, but the Agency makes the final decision. When the assessment is made, the absent parent can make the payments directly to the parent with care, or to the Agency by direct debit or standing order. The Agency passes on the payments to the parent with care.

What happens if the absent party does not pay?

If the payments are being made directly to the parent with care, she will need to tell the Agency if they are being made late, or not at all. If the payments are being made to the Agency, it will chase them if they are more than two days late. It can also take enforcement proceedings to recover payments. The most straightforward way of doing this is to make deductions from the absent parent's wages. Clearly this will not work if the absent parent is self-employed. The Agency can take court action to enforce payments as well.

Fees

There is no fee payable at present, though there is power in the legislation for a fee to be charged. The fees had to be waived in 1997 because the service offered by the CSA was so poor, and they have not been reinstated. They were originally £34 for assessment and £44 for collection.

The CSA and clean-break orders

One particular matter which received much adverse publicity was the issue of clean-break orders. Previously divorced couples who had opted for a clean break, whereby the absent parent (usually the husband) agreed to settle a lump sum on the wife and children or transfer the home to the wife in return for no maintenance claims being made against him, found that the CSA had the right to re-open the case and ask for future maintenance payments for the children.

A case in 1993 confirmed that while in some cases courts encourage clean breaks to end wives' rights to maintenance, they would never sanction a clean break ending a father's obligation to pay maintenance to his children. The courts confirmed that they would not re-open 'old' clean-break cases decided before the Child Support Act came into effect on 5 April 1993. However, in another change introduced in the package of reforms in 1995, absent parents were given the right to claim an extra compensatory allowance to take into account transfers of the family home as a clean break if the transfer was made subsequent to a court order or written agreement pre-dating 5 April 1993.

In essence, the absent parent is usually given credit for half the net value transferred (i.e. the value of the home at the time of the transfer less the mortgage) and then an extra allowance in his exempt income to reduce the child support assessment. The allowance given is worked out on a band scale, so that if, for example, the value transferred was between £5,000 and £9,999, he will be allowed to keep an extra £20 per week. In some cases this allowance can be given if what was transferred was cash or, say, an endowment policy. This change is actually fairly restrictive: the new departure system may be a better bet for taking into account the financial cost of an old (that is, pre-April 1993) clean-break order. However, note that only old clean-break orders will benefit from the flexibility – for cases since April 1993 there can be no departure from the formula (if it applies) if a clean break is agreed.

The new rules

The Child Support, Pensions and Social Security Act 2000 implements proposals that were mooted in a consultation document 'Children first: a new approach to child support'. The fine detail of the legislation will be added by later regulations, so you will need to check this with a solicitor, your local CAB, the DSS, or the CSA.

The new Act uses the term 'maintenance calculation' in place of 'maintenance assessment' and 'non-resident parent' in place of 'absent parent'. The projected start date for the new rules is April 2002, but pilot schemes may be brought in earlier.

Net income

Net income will mean weekly income after deduction of income tax and National Insurance contributions. The CSA will have power to include overtime payments in the calculation. The old system takes 50 per cent of any contribution to a pension scheme into account when assessing maintenance liability. Under the reformed scheme, it is planned to allow contributions to be deducted in full. However, if a parent with care thinks that the non-resident parent has unreasonably diverted income into a pension scheme to avoid paying maintenance, she will be able to apply to have the child support rates varied to reflect this. The basic rates will take no account of any income that non-resident parents have from savings and investments. However, if non-resident parents get most of their income from this source, the parent with care will be able to apply for a variation of the liability, as with other cases where the non-resident parent's lifestyle is inconsistent with their assessed income.

In calculating income the CSA will also ignore child benefit and non-contributory benefits for disabled people (such as disability living allowance and attendance allowance), housing benefit or council tax benefit. It will also ignore income from boarders (unless it is a significant source of income) and student loans and grants. However, tax credits received in the pay packet like the working families' tax credit will be treated as part of income (unless they are paid to the non-resident parent's new partner in his or her wage packet).

Basic rate

Maintenance will be calculated by taking a proportion of the non-resident parent's net weekly income. This is called the 'basic rate'.

Percentage of non-resident parent's net weekly income	Number of children
15	for one qualifying child
20	for two qualifying children
25	for three or more qualifying children

If the non-resident parent has other children for whom he receives child benefit (these are known as 'relevant children', such as children from a second marriage), the rate of maintenance is calculated by applying the percentages above to the net income after first deducting a similar percentage for the relevant child(ren). So if a father has one child by his first wife and one by his present wife, 15 per cent would be taken away from his net income (as a notional amount for the second child) and then 15 per cent of what is left would be the maintenance for the first child.

Reduced rate

If the non-resident parent's net weekly income is more than £100 but less than £200, he will pay a 'reduced rate'. The detail of this in not in the Bill, but the proposals in the White Paper were that the rate will increase in stages from £5 on earnings of £100 a week to the full percentage rate when earnings reach £200 a week. So, a non-resident parent earning £150 a week with one qualifying child and no second family would pay 12 per cent of his net income, or £18 per week. If his earnings exceed £200 a week, he would pay 15 per cent.

Flat rate

Maintenance would be paid at a 'flat rate' of £5 per week if the non-resident parent's net weekly income is £100 or less, or he or she is in receipt of any of the following:

- income support
- jobseeker's allowance
- retirement pension

- incapacity benefit
- contribution-based jobseeker's allowance
- widows' benefits
- severe disablement allowance
- invalid care allowance
- industrial injuries disablement benefit
- war pension.

Nil rate

A 'nil rate' will be payable for some non-resident parents: those who have an income of less than £5 per week and other people who are not described in detail in the Bill, but who will probably be in the existing categories of non-payers under the present legislation (for example, prisoners, and those in receipt of student grants or loans, or youth training allowances).

Children with different parents with care – apportionment

Where a non-resident parent has children who have different parents with care (for example, if a woman has two children by different fathers), the amount of child support payable will be apportioned between the different parents with care. The amount payable will be divided by the number of children and shared depending how many children each parent with care has.

Shared care – basic and reduced rate

If you share the care of the child(ren) so that from time to time they stay overnight with the non-resident parent, this will decrease the amount of maintenance payable. You have to look at the number of nights that the children have spent with the non-resident parent over the last 12 months, or, if the break-up is new, the projected number of nights in the next year. The reductions are:

Number of nights	Subtract
52 to 103	One-seventh
104 to 155	Two sevenths
156 to 174	Three-sevenths
175 or more	One-half

However, if there is more than one child, you have to decrease the fraction by dividing it by the number of the children. So one-seventh would turn into one-fourteenth if you had two children.

If the fraction is one-half on the table above, you have to make a reduction in the amount paid to the person with care of £7 for each child.

The lowest limit to which the maintenance can be decreased is £5 per week (if there are children with different parents with care, the £5 minimum would be divided as described above).

Shared care – flat rate

If the child(ren) spend(s) at least 52 nights a year with the non-resident parent, who would otherwise be paying at the flat rate, then the maintenance reduces to nil.

Transitional provisions

People who have already got CSA assessments running will be switched on to the new system when it comes into force. The White Paper recognised that if the change were implemented in one go, any change in the amount payable might cause hardship, so transitional provisions are proposed.

Where net earnings are £100 a week or less (or if the non-resident parent is on benefit), the new assessment will be phased in in steps of £2.50 a week. This means that in these cases, where there is no liability under the existing child support scheme, a non-resident parent will have to pay only £2.50 a week – rather than the new liability of £5 – for the first year; where the non-resident parent's net income is between £100 and £400, a week the assessment will be phased in in steps of £5; and for non-resident parents earning £400 per week or more, it will be in steps of £10.

The old rules

The old rules are much more complicated than the new ones. If you feel that you need to read this section of the chapter – because the new rules have not yet come into force or you are already within the CSA system – you will instantly see why there was a need for reform. When the new system comes into force, there will doubtless be press coverage of it, and your solicitor, CAB or DSS office will be able to tell you about it.

The formula

The formula for calculating maintenance under the old rules is much more complicated. Two factors contribute to this: the use of both parents' income and the use of the social security figures to provide a benchmark for the calculation. The calculation has several steps. If you embark upon it, you will find that it is unproductive to ask why something happens as it does. You simply have to go through it steadily and in the end the correct answer should emerge.

A diagram may help you to see the steps in sequence (see over).

At the end of this chapter is a list of the current DSS figures that you would use in the calculation and a set of sheets that you can fill in to do the calculation for yourself if you wish. You should bear in mind the following comments about each of the stages of the calculation.

Maintenance requirement

The term 'maintenance requirement' is deeply misleading, because it does not refer to the maintenance that the absent parent is required to pay at all. It is simply a figure that can be used later in the calculation. The reason that it is based on DSS figures is because of the original intention that lone parents should be 'floated off' benefit. The fact that it uses the adult personal allowance as part of the sum unfortunately led people to assume that the maintenance figure included some maintenance for the mother, even if her claims had been dismissed by the court. This is not the case, as the maintenance requirement is not the amount that is paid in maintenance.

Net income

Both parents' income from all sources has to be included. Tax, National Insurance and only half the pension or superannuation contributions can be deducted. The income of a new partner is not included in this part of the calculation. The application and response form that the parents complete for the CSA does include questions about the income of a new partner, which leads people to believe that this will be added to their own income. In fact, as you can see if you work through the calculation, it is not included in working

Calculating maintenance

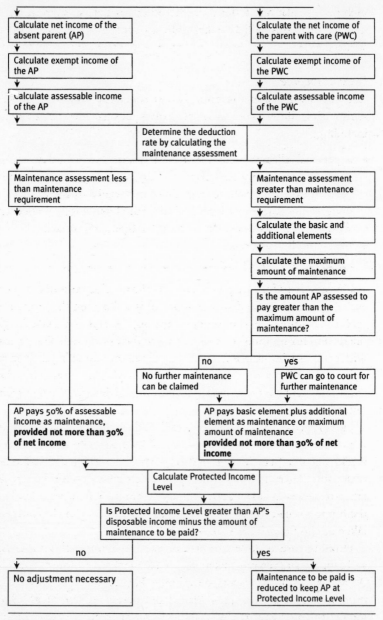

This flowchart is reproduced with grateful thanks to the National Council of One Parent Families.

out how much has to be paid, except at the end where a 'protected income' calculation is done. If the absent parent is supporting a new partner, this will be taken into account and his maintenance reduced.

Exempt income

Exempt income applies to both parents' separate incomes and represents what is allowed for each parent's own personal essential expenses, including:

- a personal allowance to cover both parents' day-to-day living expenses *plus* (if any new partner is not working or otherwise is deemed not to be able to contribute financially to the children's upkeep) the costs of caring for their natural and adopted children who are living with them, assessed on income support rates
- reasonable housing costs
- some travel-to-work costs.

Housing costs for each parent are only the housing costs of that parent's own housing. So if an absent parent is still paying the mortgage on the matrimonial home (as often happens), he cannot include this in the section for housing costs in his part of the calculation. The parent with care in such a situation would include all the cost of the mortgage in her own calculation even if she was not paying it, because it is the cost of the roof over her own head. This can plainly lead to an unfair result.

Housing costs are included only where they are 'reasonable'. Costs which are under the limit of £80 per week, or half a parent's net weekly income (whichever is higher), are automatically assumed to be reasonable. There are some other special cases where housing costs are taken to be reasonable – for example, where the parent who has left the home has had to take on a high mortgage because he has not yet taken out his financial share of the family home.

Housing costs include rent or mortgage repayments (both interest and capital), and repayments made for a loan taken out for some eligible repairs or improvements to the home. Payments of an endowment premium or Personal Equity Plan (PEP) policy are also included as long as the mortgage is £60,000 or under. They do not cover insurance premiums for buildings and contents cover, or payments towards board and lodging if the absent parent has returned home to live with his parents even if the contribution is actually made.

Since April 1995 an allowance towards travel costs has been introduced into exempt income for parents who have to travel long distances to get to work. This is based on the straight-line (that is, as the crow flies) distance between work and home. If the distance is more than 15 miles each way, that is, more than 150 miles each week $(15 \times 2 \times 5)$, 10 pence is included for each mile over 150. The allowance does not apply to the self-employed or if the employer provides certain help towards travel costs.

Exempt income does not include other outgoings like childcare costs or debts; parents who have high payments on any of these may find themselves being treated harshly by the CSA as it will ignore these actual outgoings before assessing what an absent parent can afford to pay. Repayments of debts built up while the family was together could, however, be taken into account now for an application under the new departure system.

Parents on low incomes do get some extra help from the 'protected income' calculation.

Assessable income

Assessable income is the part of a parent's income used for calculating his maintenance obligation. This is worked out by taking his *net income* and then deducting from that the *exempt income*.

There are special rules for the self-employed, childminders and some other cases. While not all sources of income count (for example, social fund payments and attendance allowances are disregarded), the CSA can assume a notional amount of income if a parent deliberately deprives himself of a source of income or, in some circumstances, performs services without pay.

Deduction rate

Assessable income will be shared 50:50 between the children and the absent parent until the *maintenance requirement* is paid. Once that has been paid, if there is any remaining assessable income, further child maintenance at a lower rate of deduction, up to 25 per cent of the excess of income, is payable. The 25 per cent rate is payable only if there are three or more children eligible for maintenance: the deduction rate drops to 20 per cent if there are two children and 15 per cent if there is only one child. There is a cap or ceiling to the maximum amount of maintenance which can be paid.

Protected income

The protected income is designed to prevent the liable parent's income being pushed down to income support levels or below by the amount of child support which he is obliged to pay. For absent parents on low incomes, there is a special formula which gives a margin over and above income support rates and this protected level of income is guaranteed. For all absent parents (since 1995) there is a cap of 30 per cent of net income placed on the level of child support, so that if net weekly income is £300, the maximum child support payable under the formula is £90.

The 'departure system'

In a limited move away from the rigidity of the CSA's formula, since 2 December 1996 for all parts of England and Wales a 'departure system' gives a small amount of discretion to alter child support payments. The system allows for parents to request reductions as well as increases in child support payments; overall the applicant must prove that it is just and equitable to depart from the formula.

Applications for a departure from the formula could be made on any (or a combination) of the following grounds.

Special expenses

- High travel-to-work costs
- high travel costs for maintaining contact with children
- costs arising from the disability of the applicant or a dependant
- debts incurred while the family was together
- pre-April 1993 financial commitments from which it is impossible or unreasonable to withdraw
- costs of supporting stepchildren, where responsibilities were taken on before April 1993.

Property and capital

- Pre-April 1993 'clean-break' property or capital orders
- diversion of income or assets capable of producing income, or higher income (say, if one parent takes out a large amount of

savings from an income-producing account and puts them into a current account where no interest would be earned)
- inconsistent lifestyles (for example, a parent drives an expensive car and goes regularly on foreign holidays but says he has no income from a business).

Additional cases

- Housing costs included in the formula assessment are unreasonably high, or a new partner is capable of contributing to them
- travel-to-work costs in the formula assessment are unreasonably high, or the parent cannot afford them.

Because of the complexities of the formula, any extra expenses sought to be deducted under a departure direction, for example, will not be knocked off pound for pound against the formula but instead will be added to the absent parent's exempt income. So if an absent parent wishes to claim special expenses of £25, this will result in a reduction of only around £10.

When the departure system was piloted, 'inconsistent lifestyle' was the most often cited ground for an application for a departure direction, although it also usually turned out to be unsuccessful – 90 per cent of these applications were dismissed at an early stage as being 'unsubstantiated'. The onus will be on the applicant to provide (probably documentary) evidence, which may not be easy to obtain. An application is made on a special form, available from the CSA, and further information can be requested by the CSA. (Those applications deemed to be 'hopeless' will be weeded out at an early stage.) After the other parent has been invited to make representations, a Child Support Officer will make a decision. There is no fee payable so CLS funding is not available. The CSA predicts that it will take ten weeks to carry out a departure assessment (but it has been overly optimistic in the past about how long it will take to process applications).

So far, the information shows that very few departure system applications have been successful. In a pilot where 6 per cent of those invited to apply did so, only 10 to 15 per cent of applications were likely to be successful, leading to the conclusion either that the departure gateways are far too narrow or that the basic formula may be less harsh than some commentators think.

Challenging a CSA assessment

If you feel that your assessment is wrong, you can seek to challenge it. The first stage in this process is an internal review, which will be carried out by a different Child Support Officer from the one who dealt with your case. If you are still dissatisfied, you can appeal to a Child Support Appeal Tribunal, and thereafter to a Child Support Commissioner; if you feel the decision was still wrong in law, you can appeal further to the Court of Appeal. All this will cost time and probably money – CLS funding is not available until an appeal has been made to the Court of Appeal. If you are on a low income you may, however, be able to ask someone from your local Welfare Rights Advice Agency to come with you to the Appeal tribunal and help you prepare your case.

Child Support Act calculation

DSS rates for CSA formula calculation

The table below lists the rates in 2000–1 for various DSS benefits.

Benefit	£ per week
Child benefit	
Only or eldest child	15.00
Each subsequent child	10.00
Income support	
Personal allowance 25 + [1]	52.20
Child allowances	
Under 16	26.60
16 to 19	31.75
Premiums	
Family premium	14.25

[1]You always use the 25+ personal allowance for child support calculations even if you are younger than 25.

CHILD SUPPORT ACT CALCULATION

Insert values as you work them out for easy reference
MR..........N..........E..........A..........M..........F..........C..........MA..........

1. CALCULATE THE **MAINTENANCE REQUIREMENT (MR)**

use DSS figures in this step

Add together	£ per week
Child personal allowances for each child	
Family premium	
Lone parent premium (if PWC has no partner)	
Adult personal allowance (if one child under 11)[1]	
Subtotal	

Take away:	
Total child benefit for all children[2]	
TOTAL = MAINTENANCE REQUIREMENT	£

2. CALCULATE **THE ASSESSABLE INCOME** OF THE ABSENT PARENT (A)

NOTE:
If the AP is in receipt of income support, A = nil
in which case you do not need to do the calculation but you should check whether he will have to pay the 'minimum contribution'.

A) CALCULATE **NET INCOME (N)**

Add together	£ per week
Gross salary	
Benefits[3]	
Other income[4]	
Any child's income	
Any other income	
Subtotal	

Take away	£ per week
Tax	
National Insurance	
50% of pension contributions[5]	
Subtotal	
TOTAL = NET INCOME	£

[1] Where the youngest child is aged 11 to 13, add 75 per cent of the adult personal allowance; where he or she is 14 to 15, add 50 per cent.
[2] Not one-parent benefit.
[3] Family credit/disability working allowance.
[4] Pension/grant.
[5] Where the mortgage is a pension mortgage, only 37.5% of premiums are allowed as a deduction.

B) CALCULATE **EXEMPT INCOME (E)**

Add together	**£ per week**
Individual personal allowance	
Child allowance for any natural child who lives with him or her[6,7]	
Income support disabled child premium for any natural child who lives with him or her (if appropriate)[6,7]	
Income support family premium (if appropriate)[6,7]	
Lone parent premium[6] (if AP lone parent)	
Income support disability premium/severe disability premium/carer premium (if appropriate)	
Housing costs[8]	
Allowance for transfer of property order[9]	
Travel costs[10]	
TOTAL = EXEMPT INCOME (E)	**£**

C) CALCULATE THE **ASSESSABLE INCOME** OF THE ABSENT PARENT **(A)**

N .... **− E** .... =   £ .... = **A**

If this works out to a negative figure then A is nil

3. CALCULATE THE **ASSESSABLE INCOME** OF THE PARENT WITH CARE (C)

NOTE: If the PWC is not the child's parent, C = nil

If the PWC is in receipt of income support, C = nil

In these cases you can skip this bit of the calculation and go to step 4

A) CALCULATE **NET INCOME (M)**

Add together	**£ per week**
Gross salary	
Benefits[11]	
Other income[12]	
Any child's income	
Any other income	
Subtotal	

Take away	**£ per week**
Tax	
National insurance	
50% of pension contributions	
Subtotal	

---

[6] If the child spends only part of the week with the parent, these allowances should be apportioned.

[7] If the AP's partner has income above a certain level, these allowances may need to be apportioned.

[8] Where the mortgage is a pension mortgage, 25 per cent of the premiums can be added into the housing costs.

[9] Where there has been a qualifying transfer of property before April 1993, an allowance can be made in the calculation of the AP's exempt income. See 1995 amending regulations.

[10] If the average journey to work measured on a straight line is more than 15 miles, 10p for each mile over 150 miles per week (assumes 10 journeys a week).

[11] Family credit/disability working allowance.   [12] Pension/grant.

TOTAL = NET INCOME (M) £

B) CALCULATE **EXEMPT INCOME (F)**

Add together   £ per week
Individual personal allowance
Child allowance for any natural child who lives with him or her[13,14]
Income support disabled child premium for any natural child who
    lives with him or her (if appropriate)[13,14]
Income support family premium (if appropriate)[13,14]
Lone parent premium[14] (if PWC lone parent)
Income support disability premium/severe disability premium/carer
    premium (if appropriate)
Housing costs[15]
Allowance for transfer of property order
Travel costs[16]

TOTAL = EXEMPT INCOME (F) £

C) CALCULATE THE **ASSESSABLE INCOME** OF THE PARENT WITH CARE **(C)**

M .... — F .... =   £............... = C
If this works out to a negative figure then C is nil

4. DETERMINE THE **DEDUCTION RATE**

A .... + C .... = ... × 0.5 = £ .... = MA

5. COMPARE MR AND MA

MR ....   MA ....

If MA is the *smaller* figure take A

A .... × 0.5 = £ .... =

the weekly maintenance which will be paid to the children[17]

BUT!

first calculate: N£................. × 30% = £.....................
If this figure is less than the weekly maintenance that you have just worked out the
maintenance reduces to this figure.

BUT! You will need to check the Protected Income Level FIRST[18]

---

[13] If the child spends only part of the week with the parent, these allowances should be apportioned.

[14] If the AP's partner has income above a certain level, these allowances may need to be apportioned.

[15] Where mortgage is a pension mortgage, 25 per cent of the premiums can be added into the housing costs.

[16] If the average journey to work measured on a straight line is more than 15 miles, 10p for each mile over 150 miles per week (assumes 10 journeys a week).

[17] This is a global figure which is not divided up between them or apportioned individually.

[18] In practice you only need to do this if the AP has a very low salary or the responsibility of a second family.

If MA is the *larger* figure go to step 6.

6. CALCULATE THE **BASIC** (BE) AND THE **ADDITIONAL** (AE) ELEMENTS

A) CALCULATE THE **BASIC ELEMENT**

Where C = nil, MR = BE   £ .... = **BE**

Otherwise:

$$\frac{A\ ....}{A\ ....\ +\ C\ ....} \times MR\ .... = $$ £ .... = **BE**

B) CALCULATE THE **ADDITIONAL ELEMENT**

Where C is nil

A .... − (**2** − **BE** ....) × **0.25**[19] =   £ .... = **AE**

OR

If C has a value:

i) Find G:

$$MR\ .... \div \left\{ \frac{A\ ....\ +\ C\ ....}{2} \right\} = G\ ....$$

ii) Put G in the following sum:

A .... − (**1.0** − **G** ....) × **0.25**[19] =   £ .... = **AE**

Now you have to do a further calculation for AE, and if this second calculation produces a *lower* figure for AE you take the lower figure:

This double check works out for you the *maximum amount* of maintenance which the Agency can order to be paid.

C) CALCULATE THE **MAXIMUM AMOUNT** OF MAINTENANCE
i) Find Q:

	£ per week
Add: The income support family premium multiplied by the number of children in the family	
.... × .... =	
Each child's personal allowance	
....	
....	
TOTAL = Q	**£**

---

[19] 0.25 is the multiplier where there are three or more children; if there is only one child multiply by 0.15, if there are two children, multiply by 0.20.

ii) Put Q in the following sum:

Where C is nil

$1.5 \times Q$ .... = £ .... = **AE**

OR

Where C has a value

1.5................. $\times \left\{ \dfrac{A .... }{A .... + C .... } \right\}$ = £ .... = **AE**

Compare this value for AE with the previous sum and take the lower figure

TOTAL MAINTENANCE PAYABLE IS

AE .... + **BE** .... = £ .... =

the weekly maintenance which will be paid to the children[20]

BUT!
first calculate: N£.................. $\times$ 30% = £.......................
If this figure is less than the weekly maintenance that you have just worked out the maintenance reduces to this figure.

BUT! you will need to check the Protected Income Level FIRST[21]

*A full protected income calculation form has not been supplied with these notes.
The full calculation should be done if the AP is living with someone else or has another child living with him or her. If the AP is living alone, with no new family commitments, the PI calculation may be appropriate if his or her wages are low. The following calculation can be used **only** in these circumstances (it is greatly simplified from the full calculation).*

PROTECTED INCOME CALCULATION
A) CALCULATE **BASIC PROTECTED INCOME**

Add together	£ per week
AP's adult personal allowance	
Housing costs (less any housing benefit)	
Council tax (less any council tax benefit)	
Travel costs[22]	
Margin	30.00
TOTAL = BASIC PROTECTED INCOME (BPI)	£

---

[20] This is a global figure which is not divided up between the children or apportioned individually.

[21] In practice you need to do this only if the AP has a very low salary or the responsibility of a second family.

[22] If the average journey to work measured on a straight line is more than 15 miles, 10p for each mile over 150 miles per week (assumes 10 journeys a week).

B) FIND **DISPOSABLE INCOME**

Net Income (N) as calculated above is the equivalent (in these circumstances) to
Disposable Income = £ ....**(DI)**.

C) DI.................. − **BPI**......................... = ...**(χ)**

D) (χ) .... × **15%** = ... **(γ)**

E) BPI................. + ... **(γ)** = ... = **Protected Income Level**

F) DI................... − **Maintenance Payable**................ = ...*

* is this figure less than the Protected Income Level?

**If it is then the Maintenance Payable is reduced to the difference between the
Disposable Income and the Protected Income Level**

DI .... − **PIL** .... = **Maintenance Payable**

Chapter 7

Protecting your interest in the family home

Lawyers often refer to the family home as the 'matrimonial home'. This term is used in the context of divorce to refer to the home, house or flat acquired by husband, or wife, or both, to be lived in by the family during their time together. However, the term is an awkward one, and by and large the more familiar term of 'family home' is used throughout this book except where legal terminology dictates otherwise.

If you are considering a divorce, you should think about whether you need to protect your interest in the family home, as a precautionary measure.

The spouse who does not legally own the family home – that is, whose name is not on the title deeds – has certain rights of occupation:

- the right not to be evicted without a court order if he or she is in occupation
- the right (if the court thinks fit) to return to the home if he or she has left it
- the right (if the court thinks fit) to exclude the owner spouse from occupying the home for a period (usually only when violence has occurred).

The same occupation rights apply if the home is rented.

These rights were formerly termed 'rights of occupation', but are now called 'matrimonial home rights'. The new terminology has left the old system more or less unchanged. However, one key innovation is that matrimonial home rights are now also available for a property which a married couple intended to use as their home but which they never actually occupied.

Matrimonial home rights are in essence short-term rights which exist while the marriage lasts (until decree absolute is granted). The long-term decisions about the rights to live in the home or to get a share of the proceeds if it is sold will have to be made as part of the divorce financial settlement. If violence has been threatened or used against you, making it unsafe for you to live in the family home, you can apply to the court to protect yourself (as described in Chapter 14) and sometimes gain an occupation order which can exclude your spouse or allow you to re-enter the home. The courts will also be able to make an occupation order overriding one spouse's matrimonial home rights.

Registering matrimonial home rights: owner-occupied homes

If you are a joint owner of the family home, you do not need to register your matrimonial home rights separately. Third parties (for example, a potential buyer or mortgagee) will become aware of your interest when they carry out a search of the property title, so your spouse cannot try to sell or mortgage the property without your consent.

If, however, your spouse, not you, is the sole owner of the family home, you must register your matrimonial home rights to ensure that they are protected against third parties. You can do this without your spouse knowing about it. The Land Registry and the Land Charges Registry do not tell the proprietor that matrimonial home rights have been registered. With registered land (see below), however, any mortgagee will be notified.

How you register your matrimonial home rights depends on whether the title to the family home is 'registered' or 'unregistered'. 'Registered' here means registered at the Land Registry. Most homes will have titles registered at the Land Registry as the whole of England and Wales is now subject to compulsory registration of title, but if your home was, until recently, in an area of voluntary registration, and you bought it some time ago, the title to your home may not yet have been registered.

If you do not know whether the title to your home is registered or not, you may be able to find out from the bank or building society that you have your mortgage with (if the home is mortgaged). If the bank or building society has a 'Charge Certificate' (a Land Registry document), the home is registered. If there is no mortgage and your spouse has a Land Certificate (another Land Registry document), then again the title is registered.

As an alternative, if you do not wish to ask a solicitor to register your rights of occupation, you can carry out an 'Index Map Search' at HM Land Registry★ for your area (usually no fee) to find out whether the title to the home is registered and, if so, what the title number is.

If the title is registered

The district Land Registry for your area will advise you how to register your matrimonial home rights and should provide the various forms and tell you about the procedure. HM Land Registry in London can advise you which is your local Land Registry. There is a helpful leaflet called *Protecting Matrimonial Home Rights under the Family Law Act 1996* (EL4). The Land Registry web site has plenty of useful information and you can download this leaflet and forms you need.

If the title is unregistered

A 'class F' land charge should be registered at the Land Charges Department.★ The form to be used, K2, is available from law stationers' shops and the fee for registration is £1 per name.

The information required includes the full name in which the property-owning spouse bought or acquired the property. If you are unsure of the precise name shown on the conveyance, register the charge against all possible permutations: for example – John Smith, J Smith, John Peter Smith, J P Smith. The charge is ineffective unless it is in exactly the right name. If you are in any doubt, or time is short, apply to register at both the Land Registry and the Land Charges Department until you have sorted out the position. If you find that the title is registered, you should cancel the charge at the Land Charges Department.

The Legal Help scheme allows for a solicitor to deal with registration of a land charge or a notice if you are financially eligible.

All Citizens Advice Bureaux (CABx) can help with filling in the forms to register matrimonial home rights and some have a supply of the necessary forms.

The effect of registering a charge or notice

Anyone buying the property or granting a mortgage on it would, as a matter of routine, check the appropriate registry and discover your notice or charge protecting your rights. (Even if a buyer or mortgagee does not actually search the register or has no knowledge of the registration, the effect of registering a land charge or notice amounts in law to notice of a non-owning spouse's matrimonial home rights.) If the house is then bought or mortgaged, this is done subject to your matrimonial home rights and the buyer or mortgagee cannot turn you out unless you have agreed to give up your rights.

The effect of registration normally ceases once a decree of divorce is made absolute. If the question of the family home has not been settled by then, the non-owning spouse should ask the court, before the decree is made absolute, for the registration of the class F land charge or the notice to be renewed after the decree absolute. Alternatively, if you are making a claim for a share of a property, you should register a 'pending action' claim, which similarly puts third parties on notice of your interest.

Finding out if your spouse owns a second home

Sometimes there may be good reason to suspect that your spouse has bought another home – say if he or she has moved in with a new partner in a newly bought home which he or she says belongs to the new partner. There is now an easy way of checking who legally owns the home, again via the Land Registry. As long as you have the postal address of the new home, you can ask the Land Registry to supply the name and address of the registered proprietor of land. The fee is £4.

If your suspicions are confirmed and your spouse is shown as a legal owner, once you have made financial claims in the divorce proceedings you may also be able to register a 'pending action' claim on the title of the second property if you think that your spouse may try to sell it to avoid paying money.

Moving out

If you hope eventually to have the home to live in permanently, it is tactically best to try to stay there, if possible. Even if you are not planning to remain in the long term but want to persuade your spouse to make other financial provisions for you, staying put may help you in your negotiations. However, the strategy of staying put can some-times be counterproductive: remaining at close quarters with your spouse once the decision to separate has been made can give rise to tensions which may undermine the prospect of successful negotiations. It may be helpful to discuss with your solicitor the pros and cons of moving out, whether on a temporary or permanent basis.

It may be tempting, if the situation between you and your spouse has become very volatile, to lock your spouse out of the home while he or she is away. Remember, however, that your spouse has matrimonial home rights, that is, a right to occupy the home, at least while the marriage is in being, and can apply to the court for an order restoring to him or her the right to occupy the home.

Severing a joint tenancy

If you and your spouse own your home (or any other land or buildings) jointly, you need to check whether the ownership is held under a 'joint tenancy' or a 'tenancy in common'. If you have a mortgage, ask the building society or bank. If you do not, you will need to look at the title deeds or the Land Certificate. You should ask a solicitor to check the point for you.

Under a joint tenancy (the most popular method for spouses to hold the matrimonial home), a spouse's interest in the property is not quantified: both partners own the whole of the house (or flat) jointly. When either partner dies, the whole property automatically passes to the survivor, irrespective of any provision the former may have made in a will. Under a tenancy in common, on the other hand, the interests of each spouse are fixed (usually on a 50:50 basis but it can be in any proportion) and separate, so that each partner can separately dispose of his or her share by will.

Some solicitors advise that you should end the joint tenancy and, pending a financial settlement or a court order, divide your respective interests in the property by becoming tenants in common. Either of you can do this by sending a 'notice of severance' to the other spouse at any time. The notice can simply take the form of a letter to your spouse, stating: 'please accept this letter as notice of my desire to sever as from this day the joint tenancy in our property known as [*insert address of property*] now held by us as joint tenants both at law and in equity so that henceforth the said property shall belong to us as tenants in common in equal shares'. You should sign and date the letter.

A notice of severance will convert your ownership into a tenancy in common. It does not affect your status as co-owners but, when one of you dies, the deceased's share of the property would be part of his or her estate and would be distributed under the terms of his or her will or according to the rules of intestacy. This in effect increases your control over a certain equal share in the property while money matters are being sorted out comprehensively in the divorce proceedings. However, there is also the risk that if your spouse were to die in the meantime, you would lose the chance that you would have had of inheriting his or her share of the home when it was held under a joint tenancy. In summary, you will have to weigh up the risks both for and against – there is no clear-cut right or wrong course of action applicable to all. Whether it would be in your interest to sever the joint tenancy is something you might like to discuss with a solicitor if you decide to go ahead with a divorce. If you sever a tenancy, you must make a will stating where you want your share of the property to go.

Chapter 8

Getting money from your spouse before filing a divorce

Once divorce proceedings have been filed, a whole menu of financial remedies is available to either spouse in the form of orders for both maintenance and capital payments. However, before a divorce is filed, the orders are more limited, but remedies do exist and, in the absence of an agreement between you and your spouse, you can use the Child Support Agency (CSA) or the court to get money on an interim basis.

The alternatives available to you are:

- **agreed arrangements**, which can be informal, or formalised in a separation agreement, *or*
- **in the absence of agreements**, remedies for you (namely, magistrates' court order or county court order) and your children, whether they are with your partner (namely, CSA order) or they are your partner's stepchildren (namely, Children Act order or order linked to your order in the magistrates' or county court).

Agreed arrangements

Informal
Many couples manage to separate successfully and to agree who will pay for what, including the maintenance for any children. If you can do this, you do not need to have a formal agreement or an order (unless you are on benefit, in which case the CSA may insist that you use its services to obtain an order against the 'absent parent' (see Chapter 6), but you will be aware that there is no way of enforcing the payments if the payer is unreliable. Most such arrangements are on a short-term basis only, and it may seem unduly complicated and costly (if lawyers are involved) to formalise the agreement in a written separation agreement.

However, if the separation is going to be long term, for instance, if you propose to separate for two years and then divorce on this basis, it is probably a good idea to draw up a separation agreement. This not only makes the arrangement more certain, but you can enforce the agreement using the courts if your spouse defaults.

Formal separation agreements

Separation agreements are sometimes referred to as 'deeds'. Technically, a legal document is a deed if it is made 'under seal', which means that there will be little round red stickers put on the document next to your signatures, which will be witnessed. The document should generally be drawn up as a deed if 'real' property (houses and land) is being transferred between you, or if it contains a financial obligation that you might later want to enforce.

To ensure that a separation agreement does have effective legal force it should be made only once you are both sure that you know all about each other's financial position: what you earn, you own and you owe. It would be sensible for you each to consult a solicitor and ask the solicitor to draft the agreement.

Separation agreements are usually fairly flexible and are designed to cover the particular things that you want to deal with. A typical deed will probably cover the following issues:

- that you have decided you want to live separately, and the date on which the separation started (this date is useful for tax purposes and also for later evidence to court of the period of your separation)
- agreements about where and with which parent the children will make their main home. You can also deal with contact arrangements if you want them fixed, or simply express a joint intention that contact will be frequent, and state whether or not the children will stay overnight
- who is going to live in the family house, or whether it is going to be sold and how the proceeds are going to be divided
- who is going to pay for what in the future
- maintenance for the children
- maintenance from one spouse to the other
- division of contents of the family home
- ownership of other assets such as the car.

The agreement can also contain an expression of your intention about whether there will eventually be divorce proceedings.

Although part of the reason for making a separation agreement is to avoid being unduly legalistic, you need to make sure that anything you agree to will not have long-term unwanted consequences. Transfers of property or large assets at this stage may have implications for Capital Gains Tax. All the financial arrangements may be considered by the courts (in later divorce proceedings). You need to take legal advice as to whether you are making a commitment that you will later want removed and whether a court would do so.

Most people would like to think that the separation agreement would remove the possibility of any later legal argument in court. But the courts will not let its powers of making orders be removed by private agreement, so you cannot make a binding promise that you will never invoke the power of the court at a later stage. However, the courts will be inclined to uphold an agreement that both parties have made if they both had legal advice at the time that they made it and the financial disclosure on both sides had been full and frank.

If your spouse does not keep to the separation agreement (or, for that matter, if you do not), it is possible to go to the court to enforce the agreement. This does not happen very often, but it can be done. It may be easier, however, if an agreement about maintenance is breached, to make a new application for maintenance as outlined below. This, in itself, is probably enough sanction to encourage most people to keep to the arrangements that they have agreed together.

Maintenance for you

Magistrates' court – Family Proceedings Panel
You can apply to the magistrates' court for maintenance for yourself and a lump sum order up to £1,000. There is no limit on the amount of maintenance that the court can order. You can also apply more than once for a lump sum – there is no limit on the number of applications in the legislation. The court can also order a lump-sum payment, of up to £1,000, for each child.

You can make this application yourself; you do not have to have a solicitor to help you. If you are eligible for Legal Help (see Chapter 1), your solicitor can assist you with this. You can go to the court to get the application form yourself and the court staff will help you to fill it in, but they cannot give you legal advice. No fee is charged for this. There is a fairly straightforward form on which you set out your financial position.

In order to qualify for an order you have to establish that your spouse:

- has failed to provide reasonable maintenance for you or make a proper contribution towards the children of the family (see below), *or*
- has deserted you, or behaved in such a way that you cannot reasonably be expected to live with him (such behaviour could include adultery).

Once you have made your 'complaint', the court will fix a day for the hearing and issue a summons to your spouse, who has to be given at least 21 days' notice of the hearing.

If you manage to agree a maintenance order before, or at the hearing, the court will make an order in those terms, provided it seems to be appropriate. If the order is agreed, a capital sum can be ordered that is more than the £1,000 limit. If you cannot agree, the court will hear evidence from both of you about your financial positions and will then order what it thinks is a reasonable sum.

The court takes into account the following factors in making an order:

- the welfare of any child of the family
- your incomes and earning capacities
- your obligations and responsibilities
- your ages
- any physical and mental disabilities
- the duration of the marriage
- the previous standard of living
- the contribution that each of you has made to the family
- and, if it would be inequitable to disregard it, the conduct of either party.

Normally you will have to wait between one and two months for the hearing to come to court. If you need an order more urgently than this, you should explain this to the court when you make the 'complaint' and the court can be asked to fix an expedited hearing, or to make an interim order to tide you over till a full hearing can be given.

An interim order can last for a maximum of three months, which should give time for a full hearing to take place.

The county court

The alternative to the magistrates' court, which traditionally makes orders which are rather on the low side, is to make an application to the county court under s.27 of the Matrimonial Causes Act. The fee for this is £120. You have to satisfy the court that your spouse has failed to provide reasonable maintenance for you. The application must be accompanied by a sworn statement (an affidavit) setting out your resources and needs.

In theory Community Legal Service (CLS) funding should be available for such an application, but the Legal Services Commission (LSC) will probably want you to use the magistrates' court if at all possible as the costs are lower, so your solicitor will have to justify why the county court would be preferable.

You, or your solicitor, will have to serve your spouse with the application and your statement. He or she, in turn, should file a financial statement in reply within 14 days of receiving yours. The court will fix a hearing, which will be heard in private.

The changes to procedure that are described in Chapter 12 will apply to a s.27 application as well. This means that there will be a First Appointment and a Financial Dispute Resolution Appointment (see Chapter 12 for details) if the case proceeds.

Given the length of time that an s.27 application takes, and its cost, it is probably not a good idea to make it unless you know that you are going to have a long-term separation and that no divorce is contemplated for the time being. Otherwise you are simply going to duplicate the proceedings and run up the costs bill.

Maintenance for the children

CSA

Once you have separated, to the point where your spouse is not living in the same household as the children, the CSA has jurisdiction and you can apply to it for a maintenance order. All the details are set out in Chapter 6.

Children Act application

You can apply under the Children Act 1989 for financial orders for the children of the family at any time. If you think that you are going to be filing divorce proceedings reasonably soon, within a year say, then it is probably not a good idea to start Children Act proceedings as it will simply duplicate the financial proceedings under the divorce and add to the cost.

Financial applications and domestic violence

Since Part IV of the Family Law Act 1996 was introduced on 1 October 1997, it is possible to ask the court to make an order to cover payment of outgoings – like rent or mortgage payments – at the same time as making an occupation order (the new term for an exclusion order: see Chapter 14). This short-circuits the previous necessity of having to make a separate application to the court for financial support to cover basic running costs for the home.

Part 2

During a divorce

Chapter 9

Getting a divorce

Although Part II of the Family Law Act 1996 threatened to change radically the procedure for obtaining a divorce, it has now been shelved. The present divorce procedure dates from 1973, but its origins can be traced clearly to at least the nineteenth century. The concept that one partner in a divorce is at 'fault' still exists, although it hardly carries the stigma it once did. The divorce procedure retains some of the antique language, with terms such as *decree nisi* and *decree absolute* still used today. This may seem off-putting, but in the vast majority of cases the proceedings all take place on paper and nobody has to make an appearance at court.

The present law

There is only one ground for obtaining a divorce in England or Wales, namely that the marriage has irretrievably broken down. You have to show that this has happened by proving one or more of 'five facts', which are set out below.

The five facts to prove irretrievable breakdown are, in essence:

Fact 1: adultery and intolerability
Fact 2: unreasonable behaviour
Fact 3: desertion for a period of two years
Fact 4: separation for a period of two years with consent of the other party
Fact 5: separation for a period of five years.

The full wording of the facts which have to be proved, and explanations, are set out later in this chapter.

You cannot present a petition for divorce until a year after the marriage took place, whatever the circumstances. But you do not have to start off divorce proceedings to apply to the court about problems over the children (for details see Chapter 10). Applications for a residence or contact order, for example, can be made at any time. Similarly, you don't have to start a divorce to ask the Child Support Agency (CSA)★ for maintenance for the children (or the court for maintenance for yourself). So there is no need to begin an application for a divorce until you have finally made up your mind that that is what you want.

Even if you can establish the facts for going for a divorce now, you might want to consider whether to make a separation agreement with your spouse now and then apply for a divorce on the 'no fault' ground (Fact 4) later. Applying for a divorce when you have lived separately from your spouse for at least two years and where you both consent to the divorce going ahead can help to remove some of the bitterness and difficulties often associated with divorce.

Jurisdiction

Where you got married is **not** relevant in determining whether you can get a divorce in England and Wales – that is, whether an English court has jurisdiction to hear your petition. What matters is that either you or your spouse must be 'domiciled' in England or Wales or have been resident there for at least one year before the date of presenting the petition. (Domicile indicates the country of your nationality or the country where you have settled and chosen to live.) Short absences (for example holidays) can be ignored. You should consult a solicitor straight away in connection with any proposed divorce where there is doubt about domicile or where neither of the couple lives in England or Wales.

The law in Scotland and the procedure in Northern Ireland are different and are dealt with in Chapters 18 and 19. Domicile or residence in Scotland, Northern Ireland, the Channel Islands or the Isle of Man is not sufficient to enable you to get divorced in an English or Welsh court.

Where to apply

Divorce proceedings are usually started in a divorce county court or a county court which is classed as a Family Hearing Centre (see *Which court? (England and Wales))*. Not all county courts deal with divorce proceedings, so telephone first to check. Although you do not have to start proceedings in a court that is local to you – choosing a court in another part of England and Wales could be useful in sensitive cases or if you want to avoid publicity – it makes sense to go to the one that is most convenient for you (and your spouse).

Your case may be transferred to the High Court if the divorce proceedings become defended or, in a very small number of cases, where the financial proceedings or the proceedings relating to the children are extremely complex. In London, the Divorce Registry acts as both a county court and High Court.

Legal separation

You do not need to have any formal court order or agreement to be 'legally separated'. If you and your spouse have separated, the simple fact of your separation allows you to describe yourself as separated in any document that you have to complete. A separation which is likely to be permanent, where neither party will wish to be divorced, can be formalised by a 'judicial separation' (see below).

If you think that your separation is going to last for some time before you file divorce proceedings, or indefinitely because neither of you wishes to divorce, then it may be sensible to draw up a separation agreement between you which covers matters such as arrangements for the children, maintenance and property. Mediators and solicitors can help with this. It would be sensible to take some legal advice about the implications of any agreement that you come to (see Chapter 8).

Judicial separation

Judicial separation proceedings can be used where a spouse does not accept that the marriage has irretrievably broken down, or does not want to divorce, for example for religious reasons. The facts that have to be proved are the same as for divorce.

The effect of a decree of judicial separation is that the husband and wife are technically relieved of the obligation to reside with each other. But they remain married, in law, so that neither can marry anyone else, and on the death of one spouse, the other would be his or her widow or widower. This can be particularly important in the case of an elderly couple, where a wife would lose substantial widow's pension benefits if the couple divorced. The decree does, however, affect inheritance rights: if either spouse dies without making a will, they are treated as if they were divorced.

A decree of judicial separation does not preclude a divorce later, and the facts relied on to obtain the judicial separation decree (except for desertion, which formally ends on a decree of judicial separation) may be used in divorce proceedings. The procedure for obtaining a judicial separation is similar to divorce, but there is only one decree, with no interim stage. Applications for judicial separation are made much less frequently than applications for divorce: if ultimately what you want is a divorce, applying for judicial separation in the meantime can double your costs.

Embarking on a divorce

The person who applies for a divorce is called the petitioner. The other spouse is called the respondent. If the basis of the divorce is adultery and the third person is named, he or she is the co-respondent.

In most cases it is fairly obvious who is going to be the petitioner, because generally one party more feels strongly about ending the marriage, and is in a position to say that the other party has been at 'fault', by committing adultery, behaving in an unreasonable manner, or deserting. But it does not have to be as clear-cut as that. Both husband and wife may agree that the marriage is at an end and then they have to decide what is the best way to get a divorce.

Only two of the facts allow you to file a petition immediately: adultery (Fact 1) and unreasonable behaviour (Fact 2). The other three all require a period of separation/desertion of at least two years. If both of you have agreed that the marriage should be ended by a divorce now, rather than after a wait, one of you will have to be the petitioner and the petition (the document that you file at the court) will have to say that the other is at 'fault'. (This does not mean that the respondent will be viewed in a negative light by the court.) The law does not allow the couple to present a petition together.

The petitioner is the one who, to a large extent, has control of the timing of the divorce proceedings. The respondent has less to do. This is reflected in the costs: the petitioner's costs are higher than those of the respondent. A petitioner can ask that the respondent be ordered to pay costs, to redress this imbalance.

In an undefended case you do not actually need a solicitor for the procedure of getting divorced, but the procedure is tricky if you have not encountered it before. It makes sense to take some legal advice before you embark on it. Mistakes could cost you a great deal more in the long run than an hour of legal advice at the beginning. If you have children, or there is property to be sorted out, you must get proper advice at the outset.

Undefended divorce

The vast majority of divorces in this country are undefended and are dealt with by what is called the 'special procedure'. (The term, which is now inappropriate, derives from the fact that the procedure was once applied to very few divorces. It was gradually extended so that all but a very few cases follow this path.) This means that they are dealt with on paper – there are no hearings that the husband and wife have to attend, unless issues about the children or costs arise. The district judge at the county court will read all the papers that are filed in the case and, provided that he or she is satisfied that the case for a divorce has been made out, the divorce will proceed. Everything takes place in private until the pronouncement of decree nisi, which is made, very briefly, in open court. Again, neither party has to attend. There is no public access to the divorce papers.

The proceedings go through a number of stages. The table overleaf shows what they are.

If you decide to act for yourself in the divorce, you can get all the forms that you need for the proceedings by going to your local divorce county court and asking at the counter for them. The court will also give you the helpful information leaflets that the Court Service produces. Alternatively, you could download these from the Court Service web site,* where all the forms and the leaflets are available.

Fees

The fee for filing a petition for divorce is £150. The petitioner will also have to swear an affidavit, the fee for which will between £5 and £9, and pay a further fee of £30 to get the decree absolute.

If you are in receipt of Legal Help, you are exempt from the fees, apart from the affidavit fee.

DIVORCE PROCEDURE

PETITIONER	COURT	RESPONDENT
The petitioner ('s solicitor) prepares the statement of arrangements and sends it to the respondent asking him/her to sign it		If he or she agrees, the respondent signs the statement and sends it back to the petitioner (or solicitor)
The petitioner ('s solicitor) sends the petition and the statement of arrangements to the court for filing		
	The court checks the papers, issues the file with a number, prepares a notice of proceedings and an acknowledgement of service form and sends them to the respondent (and to the co-respondent if there is one).	
		The respondent (and co-respondent) complete the answers to the questions on the acknowledgement of service and send it back to the court
	The court sends the petitioner ('s solicitor) a copy of the completed acknowledgement of service form	

The petitioner ('s solicitor) prepares an affidavit in support of the petition for the petitioner to swear. He/she then files this at court with the request for directions for trial

The district judge reads the file and, if satisfied, gives a certificate of entitlement of decree nisi and a certificate in respect of the children. Both parties are notified of the date fixed for the pronouncement of decree nisi

Decree nisi is pronounced. No attendance is generally necessary. A copy is sent to both parties

Six weeks and one day after decree nisi the petitioner can apply for decree absolute, by sending a form to the court plus fee

If the petitioner does not apply, the respondent can make an application, on notice, three months after the six-week period has elapsed

The court checks the file and issues the decree absolute, sending a copy to both parties

If you are acting for yourself and are on a low income or receiving income support or jobseeker's allowance, you can ask the court to grant you an exemption from fees by completing Form EX 160. You will still have to pay for your affidavit.

There are fees for other applications, such as those concerning property or children. These are dealt with in the relevant sections of this book.

Documents

To start the divorce you need to send, or take, the following documents to the court where you want the proceedings to be. (There are further notes about how you fill them in below.) You should always keep a copy of each of the documents that you have filed.

Petition
- the completed form of the petition for the divorce
- a copy for service on the respondent
- a copy for service on the co-respondent – if there is one.

Statement of arrangements for the children
- the completed form of the statement of arrangements for the children, signed by you, and if possible the respondent
- a copy for service on the respondent.

Marriage certificate
You will need to file your original marriage certificate or an official copy of it. If you do not have the original, the easiest way to obtain a copy is to go back to the Register Office for the area in which you were married, or where you were married. You can apply there by post or in person, and the certificate will cost you £6.50. Alternatively, you can go in person to the Family Records Centre.★ Again, the certificate will cost £6.50, and it will normally take about two weeks. If you need the certificate urgently, you can have it by the next working day for a fee of £22. Yet another option is to make a postal application to the General Register Office.★ The fee is £11, unless you already have their reference for your certificate, in which case it will cost you £8. If you need it sent to you urgently, the charge is £27 to send it within two working days.

If you have a foreign marriage certificate that is not in English, you must have it translated and the translation notarised (which means that a special declaration is sworn by the translator confirming the accuracy of the translation). You should look in *Yellow Pages* for a translator who can perform this service.

Fee – unless you are exempt
- a cheque for £150 payable to HMPG (Her Majesty's Paymaster General).

Certificate with regard to reconciliation
If you have a solicitor acting for you, on a private, not Community Legal Service (CLS)- funded, basis, he or she has to file another form stating whether the possibility of reconciliation has been discussed with you. If you are acting for yourself, this form does not have to be filed.

How the documents should be completed

The petition
There is a helpful leaflet called *D8 Notes for Guidance* which is available from the court and the Court Service web site. This goes through the petition in detail and explains precisely what should go in each part of the petition form. If you are acting for yourself in the divorce proceedings, get hold of a copy of this form and follow its instructions carefully. It is important to get all the parts of the petition form correct because if you make a mistake the district judge may refuse to grant the decree nisi until the error is put right, or further information filed at the court. Court officers may be prepared to help you with the form, but they are not allowed to give you legal advice.

At a later stage in the proceedings you will have to swear an affidavit to say that the contents of your petition are true. If you feel that you have any doubts about or difficulties with the completing the form, you should consult a solicitor.

When it comes to completing the section headed Particulars you should bear the following comments in mind.

Fact 1

That the respondent has committed adultery and the petitioner finds it intolerable to live with the respondent

In the petition, no more need be said than that the respondent has committed adultery with the co-respondent, who need not be named. The petitioner must, in addition, state that he or she finds it intolerable to live with the spouse – what this means in practice is that you must be living apart, even if under the same roof.

If you know the name and address of the co-respondent, you can include these, although you do not have to. Also, if you do not know the co-respondent's identity, you can state, for example, that the respondent 'has committed adultery with [a man or a woman] whose name and identity are unknown to the petitioner'.

You are asked to say when and where adultery has taken place, so far as you know. You can ask the respondent to provide a 'confession statement' admitting adultery at a specific time and place with a person (stating the co-respondent's name and address or stating that the respondent refuses to disclose the identity of the person he or she committed adultery with). Such a statement can be admitted as evidence and you can copy the details given on to the petition. If you do not have details you can be vaguer. You can state, for instance, 'the adultery has taken place from (*insert date* __) until (*insert date* __) at times and places unknown to the petitioner.'

If your spouse refuses to admit to adultery and you have no proof of it, there is a risk that the divorce will become defended (with all the expenditure of money and time that this necessitates). It makes sense, therefore, to agree that a petition is going to be filed alleging adultery rather than 'ambushing' your spouse with an allegation that he or she may be inclined to defend. If he or she will not agree, you may have to consider unreasonable behaviour instead, if it is appropriate.

Fact 2

That the respondent has behaved in such a way that the petitioner cannot reasonably be expected to live with the respondent

There is no simple definition of unreasonable behaviour. Violence or serious threats of violence to the petitioner or to the children, alcoholism, persistent nagging, refusal to have sexual intercourse or refusal to have children knowing that the other spouse wishes to have them, financial irresponsibility such as gambling to excess – these are some serious examples of what can amount to unreasonable behaviour. But many less grave matters are sufficient.

The test is whether the court feels that between a particular husband and wife the behaviour complained of is sufficiently serious to make it unreasonable to expect the petitioner to carry on living with the respondent. Usually, there will have been a number of incidents to evidence the breakdown of the marriage, but one very serious incident (such as severe violence) can be enough. Mere incompatibility is not enough unless it has driven one or both partners to behave unreasonably – for example, by showing no sexual interest or affection, being abusive and derogatory, and so on. If the behaviour of one of the spouses has forced the other to leave home, this would be evidence of the unreasonableness of the behaviour.

In the petition, you should give as precise details as you can. You can allege in general terms the types of behaviour but then you should insert specific incidents, giving details with the approximate dates and places, preferably in date order. But be concise – a few (four or five) short paragraphs giving the bare bones of the allegations will usually be enough.

If it is possible to identify a date when the unreasonable behaviour stopped, you should mention this. If the behaviour is continuing, you should state this as well. It is important that you should not have continued to live as husband and wife for more than six months after the end of the unreasonable behaviour. If you have lived under the same roof, you will have to explain in your affidavit that you have not lived as husband and wife – that you have had, in effect, two separate households.

Fact 3
That the respondent has deserted the petitioner for a continuous period of at least two years immediately preceding the presentation of the petition

Desertion as the basis for divorce means a period of separation of at least two years brought about by a husband or wife leaving his or her spouse against the latter's wishes. You have to state the circumstances, the date on which he or she left and that it was without your consent. This fact is used relatively infrequently these days because two years' separation by consent is more often used. It is useful if the respondent is not prepared to cooperate and give his or her consent after a two-year separation.

Fact 4
Separation with consent: that the parties have lived apart for a continuous period of at least two years immediately preceding the presentation of the petition and that the respondent consents to a decree being granted **or,**

Fact 5
Separation without consent: that the parties have lived apart for a continuous period of at least five years immediately preceding the presentation of the petition (even if the respondent does not consent)

In order to establish separation as proof of the breakdown of a marriage, a couple must have lived apart for at least two years if the respondent consents to a divorce, or for five years if there is no consent. If you are still living under the same roof as your spouse but in separate households, you may be required to give evidence of details of your separation later in the proceedings. In order to be considered to be living apart, you have to be sleeping separately, eating separately and not carrying out any domestic tasks (like cooking or cleaning) for each other.

The date of the separation should be stated accurately in the petition. If the separation has been for more than two but less than five years, the respondent's positive consent to being divorced – not just lack of objection – is necessary. The respondent confirms his or her consent by completing the acknowledgement of service form (see *Service of the petition*, below). If there is a real risk that the respondent may withdraw consent after the divorce papers have been served, it might be worthwhile considering filing for a divorce based on another fact, if appropriate.

After five or more years' separation, the respondent's consent is not required (but there is provision for opposing the divorce on the grounds that it would cause grave financial or other hardship).

In all separation cases, the respondent may request that his or her future financial position be considered by the court before the decree is made final (absolute). This will then be closely scrutinised and, in order to obtain a decree, the petitioner may have to safeguard it.

Time for attempted reconciliation
To allow for attempts at reconciliation, you can have gone on living together for a period of up to six months, or several short periods

which together add up to less than six months, without affecting the facts on which the petition is based.

Six months for attempted reconciliation after adultery: If, after you became aware of your spouse's adultery, you lived together with him or her for a period exceeding six months, you would not be granted a decree. The time begins to run from the date that you knew of the actual adultery which is referred to in the petition. Knowledge does not mean mere suspicion. For example, if you had suspected your spouse for some time but only properly found out about the adultery after you had confronted him or her about it, the six-month period would start to run only from the date of your confrontation. If the adultery is still continuing, you can rely on the latest incident, rather than the date you first knew about it.

Six months for attempted reconciliation after unreasonable behaviour: Where unreasonable behaviour is alleged in the petition, the period of living together is counted from the last act of unreasonable behaviour referred to in the petition and will be taken into account in deciding whether the petitioner can reasonably be expected to live with the respondent. Living together for more than six months would not necessarily prevent a decree being granted, but the court would require a detailed explanation and might well conclude that the respondent's behaviour was not unreasonable.

Six months for attempted reconciliation after separation: Although periods of living together (up to a total of six months since separation or desertion) will not invalidate the divorce petition, you cannot include such a period of time in the two- or five-year period. For instance, if you lived together for three months in an attempt at reconciliation and then parted again, the petition cannot be filed until two years, three months and one day have elapsed since the original separation.

The prayer

The last page of the petition asks the court for various things:

- a prayer (request) for the marriage to be dissolved (ended)
- an order for costs to be made against the respondent and/or co-respondent; in the case of a petition for adultery, unreasonable behaviour or desertion, it is usual to ask the court to make an order for costs against the respondent

- under the heading of 'ancillary relief', orders for maintenance (called periodical payments), lump-sum payments, property adjustment and pensions; such applications are made in general terms at this stage, so you do not need to specify any actual amounts.

Do not cross off the claim for financial relief because it may be complicated or even impossible to apply for it later: you would have to make a special application to the court for leave (permission) to apply later for any required order. Such an application may not be granted if it is made after a long time lapse or if, for example, the respondent says that he or she decided not to defend the petition only because of the absence of any request for ancillary relief. So, even if you have agreed with your spouse that no financial claims will be made, you should nevertheless include them in the petition so that they can be formally dismissed by the court (only if claims have been made can they be dismissed and a full and final settlement order be made). But to avoid misunderstanding when your spouse receives the petition, explain to him or her that the claims are being included only so that they can be dismissed by the court later.

Similarly, you can include a prayer for costs even though you may agree or decide not to follow this request through. What you are claiming here is costs only in respect of the divorce itself (not ancillary issues such as finance or claims about the children). These will be comparatively low, as they are worked out on a standard, limited basis, and are unlikely to cover the full costs of your solicitor.

In the case of a divorce based on periods of separation, the petitioner and respondent often agree that costs will be divided between them, so the petitioner would seek an order for only half the costs to be paid by the respondent. It is possible to seek costs against a co-respondent, but it would be wise to discuss this with a solicitor.

The last page of the petition should be signed by you if acting in person or receiving Legal Help or by your solicitor if one is acting for you. You should also include the names and addresses of the respondent (and co-respondent) for service of the petition, and your address. Home addresses can be used, but if solicitors are acting for either or both of you, their address(es) should be inserted instead here.

Statement of arrangements for children

All 'children of the family', whatever their ages, have to be named in the petition. Children of the family are, in broad terms, those who are:

- children of both husband and wife
- children adopted by them both
- stepchildren
- other children who have been treated by both at any time during the marriage as part of the family, but not foster children.

'Relevant' children are those under the age of 16, or under the age of 18 and still in full-time education or undergoing training for a trade, profession or vocation (even if the child is also earning). If your child is over 16 and under 18 but is in full-time employment or is unemployed (that is, no longer in the education system), it is important to say so because he or she is no longer a 'relevant' child.

A statement about the present and proposed arrangements for relevant children (Form D8A) must be prepared by the petitioner. A blank printed form of statement is available from the court office (or can be downloaded from the Court Service web site★): you should try to agree its contents with the respondent in advance of starting the divorce, and get his or her counter-signature if possible. If the respondent refuses to cooperate, you can file your own statement of arrangements and the respondent will have the opportunity to produce his or her own statement later. If the respondent has not signed the statement of arrangements, some courts will want the petitioner to confirm that he or she has tried to obtain the former's signature.

The statement of arrangements form is eight pages long and requires detailed information about the children of the family. Despite its length, however, it is fairly jargon-free. You will need to set out details about the home where the children currently live, their education or training, any child-care arrangements, amounts of support payable for the children and whether a claim has been made to the Child Support Agency (CSA), contact (access), their health and whether there are any other court proceedings about them. If you do not agree with the current arrangements, any proposed changes should be set out. At the end of the form you are asked whether you would agree to attend conciliation (mediation) with your spouse if arrangements are not agreed. You must sign the form.

The aim of making the form so detailed is to get parents to look in

Agreed arrangements for children: a quick guide

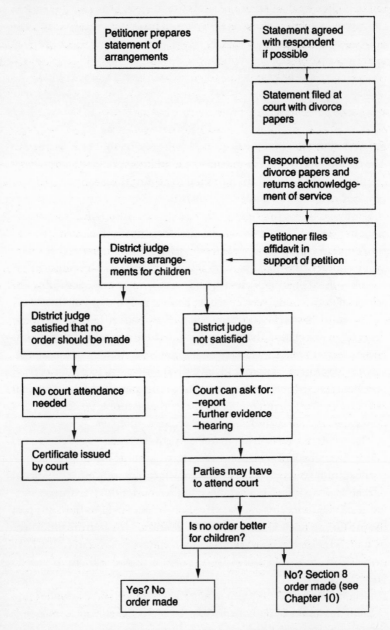

depth at the realities of how their children's lifestyles will change as a result of separation and or divorce. As the courts will not be able to ask the parents in person about the children (most divorces now proceed on the basis of paperwork alone), they want to have as complete a picture as possible of the arrangements for the children. If your future is uncertain, it may be difficult to complete the form fully; if so, just include as much information as you can, indicating where necessary what arrangements have yet to be decided upon.

Service of the petition

The court posts to the respondent, at the address given in the petition, one copy of the petition and of the statement of the arrangements for any children.

The court also sends with the petition an acknowledgement of service form, which the respondent has to complete and return to the court within eight days (although this time limit is, in practice, not always adhered to). If adultery is alleged and a co-respondent is named, a copy of the petition is also sent to him or her, again with an acknowledgement of service form to be returned to the court.

The court has to be satisfied that the respondent (and co-respondent) has received the divorce papers or that all reasonable steps have been taken to serve the documents on him or her. The return of the acknowledgement of service form to the court is normally taken as proof of service. If, however, the acknowledgement of service form is not returned, the petitioner can apply to the court for a fresh set of documents and arrange for 'personal service'.

The petitioner cannot personally serve the petition, but any other person over the age of 16 can effect service by delivering the set of papers to the respondent personally and then completing an affidavit of service and taking or sending it to the court. If the petitioner has had difficulty in serving the papers, he or she can apply to the court for the petition to be served by the bailiff of the county court for the area in which the respondent lives, or can employ an enquiry agent (a private detective) to act as process server. This can prove expensive, however.

If the respondent (or co-respondent) fails to return the acknowledgement of service form but has acted in a way which makes it clear that he or she has received the petition, an application can be made by the petitioner for service of the petition to be deemed to have been effected.

If service turns out, in practice, not to be possible, the petitioner may be able to get an order dispensing with service.

Being the respondent

It may seem very hard to be the person who is, on paper, being blamed for the marriage coming to an end, but in practice this will rarely have any effect on the way in which the court treats the respondent. In issues concerning money the court will consider the question of conduct only in cases where it is so very bad that it would be wrong to disregard it. A typical example would be where the husband attacked his wife so violently that she was unlikely to be able to work again as a result of her injuries. Adultery will generally not influence the court one way or the other.

In cases about children, too, the court will consider only evidence that relates to the mother or father's fitness as a parent. If you receive a petition based on unreasonable behaviour and there are allegations about your behaviour as a parent which you feel are untrue and could be brought up against you if there were any disagreements over the children, you should consult a solicitor before returning the form to the court.

Documents the respondent should complete

With the documents sent to the respondent are explanatory notes called 'notice of proceedings' telling the respondent about the implications of the answers he or she may give on the acknowledgement of service form.

The acknowledgement of service form does not serve merely as an acknowledgement that the petition has been received; it also includes questions about the respondent's intentions, namely:

- **whether he or she consents to the divorce proceedings**

In an adultery case, the respondent is asked to indicate if he or she admits adultery, and must sign the acknowledgement of service even if a solicitor is also signing. In most other cases, if the respondent has instructed a solicitor, only the solicitor will sign the form.

In a separation case, the respondent has to reply to the question on the acknowledgement of service form as to whether he or she intends to apply to the court to consider the financial position as it will be after the divorce.

Where the divorce petition is based on separation with consent, the respondent has to confirm that consent by writing 'yes' and also putting his or her signature on the form.

- **whether he or she objects to a claim for costs; if so, why**

If a prayer for costs has been made in the petition, the respondent is asked whether he or she objects to paying the petitioner's costs and, if so, why. The respondent may, for example, have agreed with the petitioner that no order for costs will be pursued against him or her, and a comment to this effect on the acknowledgement of service form should remind the petitioner to delete that request in the affidavit following the petition.

- **whether he or she wishes to make his or her own application for an order about the children**

If the respondent does not agree with the proposed arrangements, he or she should first make sure that what he or she is objecting to are actual proposals and not mere intentions, and should try to discuss them with the spouse. If there is underlying disagreement, the respondent should send counter-proposals to the court by filing his or her own statement of arrangements.

All financial matters and any disputes about the children are dealt with as separate issues, irrespective of whether the divorce itself is defended or undefended.

The respondent has to sign the acknowledgement personally where there are children and a statement of arrangements has been filed.

Defending the divorce – cross-petitioning

Defending a divorce is extremely difficult largely because the sole ground for divorce is that the marriage has broken down irretrievably. If one party is so certain that the marriage has broken down that he or she has filed a divorce petition, it is virtually impossible for the other to say that the marriage is still in existence.

Defending a divorce is also extremely expensive, and it is almost impossible to obtain CLS funding for it. Moreover, if the divorce gets to a full hearing, it is done in public, which could be humiliating.

However, there are some cases in which the spouse who is made the respondent feels very strongly, and can prove, that the breakdown of the marriage has been largely caused by the other spouse's action, whether as a result of adultery or unreasonable behaviour. In such cases, it is possible for the respondent to file a cross-petition. This can be coupled with an 'answer', or denial of some or all of the allegations in the particulars of the petition. A cross-petition must be filed within 29 days of the petition being served.

In most cases, even when the respondent feels that the petition is very unfair, the advice of most solicitors would be to allow the petition to proceed undefended, because to do so would be cheaper and, in the long run, the respondent will not be placed at any disadvantage in the rest of the proceedings. The acknowledgement of service form where an unreasonable behaviour petition has been filed asks the respondent: 'Do you intend to defend the proceedings?'. One way of reserving the respondent's position is for him or her to answer: 'No. But I do not admit the truth of the petitioner's allegations of behaviour made against me in the petition'. This does not amount to a defence, but the respondent can then feel that he or she has not admitted that the allegations are true.

If a cross-petition is filed, the divorce can go ahead, on the basis of either the cross-petition (if the petitioner does not dispute it), or cross-decrees (where each party gets a decree on the basis of the 'fact' that he or she has alleged).

If the petitioner does dispute the allegations made in the cross-petition, he or she can file a 'reply' at the court. The case cannot then proceed under the 'special procedure' – instead, either party can apply to the court for 'directions for trial'. Normally, this will mean a hearing in private at which the district judge will try to see whether any agreement can be reached so that the case can proceed undefended.

Only if these efforts fail will the district judge allow the case to go forward to a hearing of the divorce. In practice only a tiny number of defended divorces proceed to a full hearing.

The full divorce hearing will be in open court before a judge. Each party should instruct his or her own solicitor who may in turn instruct a barrister for representation in court.

Getting back together

Some couples find that there is a chance of saving the marriage when the divorce procedure is well under way but feel that they are bound to continue with the court action until the end. This is not necessary.

The proceedings are not a rollercoaster – you can pause them or stop them altogether. If you feel at any stage that you and your spouse might like to give the marriage another try, you are quite free to do so; it is best to tell the solicitor and the court what is happening if your spouse wants to give the marriage another try too. You can apply to the court to dismiss the petition when you feel the reconciliation is working. It is particularly important to tell the court if you have obtained an order to get or keep your spouse out of the house and/or not to molest you. Such an order will automatically lapse once you start living together again.

Recent studies of divorced couples suggest that not only did some of them regret the decision to get divorced, but also that many started to feel uneasy about the process long before getting the decree but felt unable to halt it once it had gained momentum. Remember that it is you who must make decisions, not your solicitor. If you are not sure about wanting to go ahead with a divorce you can always call a halt (if you are the petitioner) as long as you do so before decree nisi (even a decree nisi can be rescinded by an application to the court).

You may want to consider whether some or all of the differences with your spouse can be resolved with outside, non-legal, help. A fresh viewpoint can often be useful. Such help can, for example, be obtained from a marriage guidance counsellor (such as RELATE);★ see also Chapter 5.

Continuing proceedings

The next stage in getting an undefended divorce is to apply to the court for a date for the decree nisi to be pronounced, by completing the 'request for directions for trial (special procedure)' form.

The petitioner can make this application only if he or she can prove that the respondent and any co-respondent have been served with the petition and have had the opportunity to defend it. Usually, proof of service is provided by the respondent's filing the acknowledgement of service. The court then sends a copy of this to the petitioner, usually together with a blank form of 'request for directions for trial' and a blank form of affidavit. The court also normally sends a helpful leaflet (D186, *The respondent has replied to my petition – what must I do now?*), which can also be downloaded from the Court Service web site.

The petitioner must complete the 'request' and affidavit and lodge them with the court. In the 'request' form, the petitioner should fill in only the top part by inserting the name of the court, the number assigned to the petition, the names of the petitioner and respondent, and then date and sign it. The rest of the form is completed by the district judge and court staff.

Affidavits

The 'special procedure' affidavit is a fairly straightforward document, mostly in the form of a questionnaire. The questions refer to the petition, asking for confirmation that its contents are true and for any alterations or additions. (Knowingly giving false information is perjury, which is a criminal offence.) The petitioner also has to state whether he or she is going to pursue any requests for costs made in the prayer of the petition.

There is a slightly different form of affidavit for each of the five facts on which a divorce can be based.

If the respondent has signed the acknowledgement personally, a copy of it must be 'exhibited' to the affidavit (attached and sworn with it). Similarly, if the respondent has signed the statement of arrangements for the children, the signature must be identified. The fee for swearing an affidavit is £5 plus £2 for each document exhibited.

Affidavit where the 'fact' is adultery

The petitioner must refer to the numbered paragraphs on the petition that refer to the adultery and state that the allegations are true to the best of his or her knowledge and belief. If the respondent has admitted the adultery on the acknowledgement of service form or by making a written confession statement, the petitioner should identify the respondent's signature on the document. A co-respondent does not need to have admitted the adultery for the divorce to go through, provided that the respondent has made the admission or that the petitioner can prove the adultery.

If the adultery has not been admitted by the respondent (and provided that the petitioner can prove service of the petition on the respondent and co-respondent), the petitioner should give all the first-hand information available, such as the date of confession of adultery or details of circumstances to show that the respondent has committed adultery.

'Hearsay' evidence, that is, indirect information from somebody else, is not usually acceptable: the petitioner may need to supply further affidavits by people who can give first-hand information to back up the allegation. In the past, an enquiry agent's report often provided additional evidence, but this form of investigation is used less often now.

The petitioner also has to confirm in the affidavit that he or she finds it intolerable to live with the respondent.

Affidavit where the 'fact' is unreasonable behaviour
The form also asks the petitioner about the effect that the respondent's behaviour has had on his or her health. This needs only a short response that will fit in the box provided. Normally the information given in the petition will be enough to satisfy the district judge that a decree should be granted. If not, he or she can call for further evidence to be supplied.

In order to clarify whether, and for how long, the petitioner has gone on living with the respondent, he or she is specifically asked whether the behaviour described in the petition is continuing and, if not, when the last incident took place. The petitioner then has to say whether he or she has lived at the same address for more than six months since then; if so, he or she has to describe what arrangements the couple has for sharing the accommodation. This involves giving details of sleeping, cooking and cleaning arrangements and so on.

Affidavit where the 'fact' is desertion
The date on which desertion began has to be given, and the petitioner must state that he or she did not agree to the separation and that the respondent did not offer to return.

Affidavit where the 'fact' is separation
Where you and your spouse have been living in separate households for the whole of the period apart, the relevant dates and separate addresses should be given and details of when and why you decided that the marriage was at an end. Merely living apart is not always sufficient; separation starts from the time you considered the marriage had actually broken down.

You are asked to say when you came to the conclusion that the marriage was at an end – not when you decided to get divorced, which could well have been at a later date.

You may have had to continue living at the same address because it was impossible or impracticable to live completely apart, even though the marriage was at an end. You may not consider that you have been 'living together' if you have merely been under the same roof and, for example, sleeping separately, not having sexual intercourse, and barely communicating; but a court could hold that you have in fact been living together in one unhappy household and would need to be convinced that there were, to all intents and purposes, two households. You will therefore have to give the fullest possible information about the separateness of the households. (If the space provided in the standard affidavit form is inadequate, attach an extra sheet dealing with this point.)

If the district judge is still in doubt about the circumstances, he or she may remove the case from the special procedure list, to be heard in open court so that fuller evidence can be given. If this happens, you should consult a solicitor; if your financial position makes you eligible, you can apply for CLS funding to be represented at the hearing.

Completing the affidavit

An affidavit can be sworn in front of a solicitor (other than the one acting for you), a commissioner for oaths or the court office. Most solicitors' firms are very willing to offer this service and you can go to a firm convenient for you. As mentioned earlier, the fee is £5 plus £2 per exhibit, that is, any document attached.

The completed affidavit, signed and sworn, has to be sent or taken to the court with the application form requesting directions for trial.

You do not need to serve the respondent, or notify him or her that you are doing this, but normally it would be courteous to do so.

District judge giving directions

About the divorce

Provided that the district judge is satisfied about the service of the petition on everybody concerned, that an opportunity for defending has been given and, in a consent case, that the respondent's consent has been confirmed, and that all the paperwork is correct, he or she will give directions for the case to be entered in the special procedure list.

If the district judge is not satisfied with the information in the petition or affidavit, the petitioner (or a witness) may be asked to lodge a further affidavit or give additional information on the points of concern.

If the district judge still does not accept that there is sufficient evidence for a divorce, he or she may direct that the petition be removed from the special procedure list. A fresh application then has to be made for directions and for a date to be fixed for a hearing in open court before a judge.

When the district judge is satisfied that there is sufficient evidence to support the petition, he or she will certify that the petitioner is entitled to a decree nisi of divorce (or decree of judicial separation). The court will then fix a date for the judge to pronounce the decree nisi.

About the children

At the same time that the district judge looks at the divorce papers, he or she must also consider the arrangements for the children and decide whether *no* order is better for the children. (Since the Children Act 1989, the court will incline to making *no* order, unless it is plainly better for the children that an order is made. See Chapters 4 and 10.) If the judge decides that, a certificate of satisfaction will be issued to this effect and the decree nisi pronouncement will go ahead.

If, however, the district judge has doubts or concerns about proposals for the children, or if there is a clear dispute between the parents, then further evidence will usually be called for. The judge can ask for the parents to attend a special appointment at court, or for affidavits or a welfare report to be filed. In that case the decree nisi will usually be postponed until the district judge is again satisfied that no court order needs to be made, or that a residence and/or contact order will be made where appropriate.

Decree nisi and decree absolute (final decree)

The decree nisi is a provisional decree and does not end the marriage. It entitles the petitioner to apply to the court for the decree to be made absolute after a period of six weeks and one day have elapsed. Until this is done, you are still legally married.

In an emergency a decree can be made absolute earlier than the six weeks if the petitioner applies for this when the decree nisi is pronounced and attends to explain to the judge in person the reason for the application. The respondent must be given notice of the application by the petitioner. An application will be granted only in urgent circumstances, for example to enable one of the couple to marry again before a child is born.

The procedure for applying for a decree absolute is simple. The form 'application for decree absolute' (obtainable from the court office) is completed by the petitioner by inserting the date of the decree nisi, the date of the application and his or her signature and lodging this form, together with a fee of £30, at the court office. A certificate of decree absolute will then be issued by the court and sent to the petitioner and respondent (and co-respondent). It is normally sent out in a day or two. If there are very urgent reasons for getting the decree absolute immediately, you can ask the court office if they will do this for you, explaining your reasons.

If you want your decree absolute for use abroad, for a remarriage, say, you will need to get the document specially signed by the district judge, so that the document can be legalised at the Legislation Office at the Foreign and Commonwealth Office, London.

If the petitioner does not apply for the decree nisi to be made absolute when the time comes, after a further three months have elapsed (that is, six weeks and one day plus three calendar months after decree nisi), the respondent may apply to the district judge for the decree to be made absolute, with an affidavit setting out the reasons why it is he or she rather than the petitioner who is applying. This will result in a hearing at which the district judge will decide whether the decree should be made.

If decree absolute has not been applied for within 12 months of the decree nisi, the delay must be explained when the application for decree absolute is lodged, giving the reason for the delay and stating whether the couple have cohabited since decree nisi and whether the wife has borne any more children. A district judge may require further explanation or even affidavit evidence before the decree is made absolute.

It is important to keep your certificate of decree absolute in a safe place. You would, for example, need to produce it for the registrar or priest if you wanted to marry again.

Chapter 10

Disputes about children

In any case involving disputes over children, it is wise to consult a solicitor and obtain legal advice. Court disputes are costly, both financially and in emotional terms. There is rarely any winner in battles over who will have primary care of the children on a day-to-day basis.

Wherever possible, you should try to negotiate with your spouse either directly, or through a mediator or solicitors, to avoid a full-blown battle over the children. In such battles, you are forced to lay bare your private family life and will accuse your spouse of not being fit to be awarded the day-to-day upbringing of the child or even to have contact with the child. A bitterly fought court case can make it harder to establish a decent parenting relationship with the other parent later. In all cases, consider carefully whether, from the child's viewpoint, it is best for you to go ahead with an application to the court.

If repeated and, in the courts' eyes, vexatious applications are made to the court by an adult, the court can make a special order under section 91(14) of the Children Act 1989, preventing a named parent from making further applications without the court's prior permission. The aim of such an order is to prevent further unhappiness for the children. This order is, however, used only sparingly. The criteria for using it are fairly tight. It will not be enough that there is deep bitterness between the parties, for example: the parent on whom the order is served must be shown to have gone beyond what is reasonable.

Orders the court can make

All the following orders are made under section 8 of the Children Act 1989 so they are called 'section 8 orders'. They all restrict in some way the exercising of parental responsibility (see Chapter 4).

Residence order

This settles the arrangements about whom a child will live with, and where. In most cases it will be with one parent (usually the mother), but a residence order can allow for shared parenting, so the children divide their time between their parents' homes. It could also be applied for by two people together, for example a parent and a step-parent.

Contact order

This requires the person with whom the child lives to allow contact with the applicant (the person looking after the child is responsible for making the order work). It can be by way of visits or stop-overs, telephone calls or letters, or all or any of these.

Specific issue order

This decides a specific question connected with parental responsibility, for example, which school the child should go to.

Prohibited steps order

This has the effect of restraining in some way the actions of a person in relation to the child. No step stated in the order can be taken without the consent of the court. This could be used, for example, to stop one parent from changing a child's surname or from taking the child out of the country without the other parent's or the court's consent.

Both specific issue and prohibited steps orders have their origins in wardship proceedings, which are now much less likely to be used. Both types of order can be applied for in an emergency 'ex parte', in other words without the other party having to be notified of the hearing in advance.

The court may attach conditions in certain circumstances to the new orders. For example, it could state that contact should take place only in the home of the parent who looks after the children or that another adult should be present during the visit.

Who can apply for section 8 orders?

Either parent can apply for an order, if necessary even before the divorce itself has started. The new court orders can be used much more flexibly than before, and indeed other people, such as relatives or even the child him- or herself, may also be able to apply where appropriate (see *Applications by a child*, below, and Chapter 16).

The court itself can make a section 8 order in any family proceedings, thus widening its own powers. But the court is supposed *not* to use such orders without proper consideration: court orders, as mentioned earlier, should be made only if it is better for the children that they are. If the parents can decide between themselves about who should look after the children and when the other parent should see them, then it is likely that no formal court order will be made, and the situation will continue fluidly with both parents having parental responsibility and thus both deciding together how the children will be brought up. In the vast majority of divorce cases, the end result is precisely that – both parents with parental responsibility and no court order.

The procedure

An application for a residence or contact order (or other section 8 order) is triggered off when you apply for one to the court, stating clearly what order you are seeking. The fee for an application is £80. (If you get income support, working families' tax credit, disabled person's tax credit or Community Legal Service, CLS, funding, you will not have to pay the fee.)

You make the application by filling in the appropriate application form available from the court office. If you have not already started divorce proceedings you have to fill in form C1; if proceedings are already in the court, you use form C2, which is shorter because the court already have much of the information in the divorce papers. However, some courts still prefer you to use form C1: check with the court before you start. Three helpful leaflets (*Children and the Family Courts, Filling in the forms* and *Serving the forms* are available from the court and the Court Service web site.* You will need to have three copies of the form, one for the court, one for service on the other parent and one for your records.

The form asks for all the details of the child or children and asks you to say what sort of order you want made. There is a very small section for you to say why you want the order made. This is deliberate; at this stage the court does not want long detailed evidence filed. If the case cannot be resolved at an early stage, you will have the opportunity to set out your reasons in greater detail.

The proceedings have been designed to be accessible to people who are not used to the law. You should fill the form in carefully to make sure that all the facts are correct, but if you ask for the wrong order the court has power to correct an application, or even make an order that it has not been asked for.

The first stage will be that the court will fix a 'directions appointment' or a 'conciliation appointment'. You and your spouse, and your solicitors (if you have them) will be asked to attend an appointment before the district judge. This is in the judge's room, in private, as all hearings under the Children Act are. There will also be a court welfare officer, who is someone who is trained and experienced in dealing with children's legal issues.

In most courts you will be asked to go with your spouse to talk to the court welfare officer privately. Legal advisers are generally left out of this meeting. The court welfare officer will try to explore with you what the issues and difficulties are. He or she will try to see whether an agreement can be reached. This is really a compressed form of mediation and there will be quite a lot of pressure on you both to try to reach an agreement. For this reason alone, it would be sensible to try to use mediation first, before you get to the stage of filing an application.

If you can reach an agreement, then the district judge will be told what you have agreed. You may feel at this stage that you want to agree only to a short-term arrangement, to try it out. Most judges will understand this and think that this is sensible. You could, for instance, agree to a pattern of contact visits for the next three months. The judge can then fix another appointment for the end of that period that you can make use of if you want to. You may well find during the trial period that you can start to look ahead and agree plans for the future. The judge, together with you and your legal advisers, has to decide whether it would be better to make no order (simply recording what has been agreed in a note on the file) or whether you need an order. The bias is always towards making no order, but if you have had a very difficult time in the past, and one or other of you has not been reliable at keeping to agreements, the judge may feel that an order would help you both to know where you stand.

If the conciliation process has not been successful, the judge will decide whether any short-term orders or arrangements should be made pending a final decision of the court. He or she will make an order about who is to file evidence and by when. The judge will also order that a court welfare officer (a different one to the one you saw earlier) should prepare a report about the children. Time limits will be set which must be strictly complied with (the Children Act specifically recognises that delay may be harmfully prejudicial in a children application). In practice, however, you may find that owing to the workload of the court welfare service, the welfare report may take several weeks to be filed. You should also be told the 'return date' – in other words, when the case will next come to court.

In your evidence, try to confine yourself to setting out the facts, rather than inserting emotional arguments. 'The facts' can extend in children cases to hearsay evidence (information you learned second-hand), but the courts are far more influenced by clear, concise, factual and accurate information than they are by gossip.

The welfare officer will usually interview both of you and the children. The older the children are, the more weight their views will carry. The welfare officer may also make enquiries of the children's schools, and other relevant parties – for example, a child's grandmother, if it is proposed that she will be looking after the child while her son or daughter (the child's parent) is at work. The welfare officer will prepare a report which sets out the facts and circumstances and his or her impressions, and occasionally a recommendation to which the court will pay great attention (but not necessarily follow).

A copy of the welfare officer's report will be sent to you directly or through your solicitors, if appointed. **It must not be shown to any third parties without prior permission of the court**. Before a final hearing the court may set a date for an interim hearing to try to resolve which issues are in dispute. Again at this stage the date for a final hearing will be fixed.

The court's considerations

The overriding principle of the Children Act is that 'the child's welfare shall be the court's paramount consideration'. In applying this welfare principle, the court has a checklist of matters it must look at in particular:

- the ascertainable wishes and feelings of the child (in the light of the child's age and understanding)
- the child's physical, emotional and educational needs
- the likely effect on the child of any change in circumstances
- the child's age, sex and background, and any characteristics the court considers relevant
- any harm the child has suffered or is at risk of suffering
- the ability of each of the child's parents, and of any other person in relation to whom the court considers the question to be relevant, to meet the child's needs
- the range of powers available to the court.

The checklist is neither exhaustive nor exclusive, but one which lays out simply what the court *must* consider. The court *may* of course consider that other factors are important in an individual case. For example, the parents' wishes and feelings, although not listed, may often have an important bearing on the eventual outcome of a case.

The wishes and feelings of the child

The fact that the child's wishes and feelings have been placed at the top of the checklist highlights the child-centred approach of the Children Act: children should, wherever possible, be put first. At a hearing, the judge may occasionally ask to see the children in private in chambers, without parents or legal advisers present, to talk to them and ask them what they want. If so, the court will ask the parents to bring the children along to court (usually this applies only to children of about ten or over). Far more often children's wishes and feelings will be explored by the court welfare officer when preparing the report.

As mentioned above, the older the child, the more persuasive will be his or her views. Teenage children in any event often 'vote with their feet' over where they want to live, whereas younger children may find it very difficult to put what they want into words. In practice, the child's wishes are extremely influential. The views of mature, articulate children from around ten upwards, who have sound reasons for choosing a particular outcome, will often be the decisive factor. But if the court suspects that children have been coached by one or other parent, 'their' opinions will carry little weight. Although children's views will be respected, they should not be forced to choose unwillingly between two people both of whom they love. Ultimately, especially for younger children, it is up to adults to make decisions.

The child's physical, emotional and educational needs

If the child is very young or sickly or otherwise especially needs a mother's care, a residence order is more likely to be made in favour of the mother. In the past the courts have usually decided that a child's welfare is best protected by being with the mother rather than with the father. One case decided since the implementation of the Children Act confirmed the presumption that a baby would stay with his or her mother. There is thus an in-built bias in favour of mothers, although that bias becomes less strong as the child gets older. It is not unusual, for example, for a court order to provide for older boys to live with their fathers. The courts will always look at each individual family: whichever parent has primarily looked after the children and with whom the children have the closer bond is likely to have a residence order made in his or her favour.

The effect of change

The courts have long recognised that changing the status quo can compound the difficulties of a child adjusting to the parents' separation. So a parent who is already looking after the children usually has a much stronger claim. This, however, does not apply if the children have been snatched from their usual home environment: the courts can act quickly to return children to the parent best able to care for them.

Likewise, splitting the family is almost always regarded as undesirable, so that wherever possible siblings (sometimes even half-brothers and -sisters) should be kept together.

The child's age, sex and background

The inclusion of this factor in the Children Act is an attempt to get away from a stereotypical view of the family which does not 'fit' an individual family unit. So if, for example, it is the cultural norm that the parents go off to work while the grandmother cares for their children, the court might well feel it is best for the children to continue to be cared for by the grandmother. Each case will be decided on its own merits.

Harm or risk of harm

Alcoholism, drug abuse or violence (whether towards a partner or the children) will prejudice a parent's case. Also, if there is a real risk of sexual abuse by a parent, that parent would definitely not get a residence order. A contact order might be given, but only if it would be in the child's best interests (for example, if there were a strong bond between parent and child, if the parent were seeking treatment and if the contact were supervised properly).

Homosexual parents (of both genders) used to find the courts prejudiced against them. But recent cases have made it clear that sexuality is immaterial. The most important considerations are whether the parent's relationship with the child is loving, caring and considerate.

It is still sensible for a homosexual parent to obtain professional advice from a solicitor experienced in this area. There are several organisations concerned with lesbian and gay parenting; for most of them the first point of contact would be the London Lesbian and Gay Switchboard,★ where someone can make a referral if necessary.

If there is a real and significant risk of harm to the children – like sexual abuse for example – the local authority's social services department may become involved and may apply for an order that the children be taken into care. Such a case would then become a 'public law' case (that is, where the state, here the local authority, gets involved) instead of just a 'private law' case (that is, just between individual people) and is likely to be heard in a different court. It will be important to have a solicitor acting for you who is experienced in public law cases and is (ideally) on the Law Society's Children Panel (whose members have been specially trained in dealing with children cases).

Since Part IV of the Family Law Act came into force in October 1997, the courts also have new powers to make court orders excluding suspected abusers from a child's home – where the local authority wants to take emergency protective action to protect the children. Interim care orders and emergency protection orders are also now available, and if domestic violence occurs, children as well as adults can be protected by court orders.

Capability of the parents

This can range from practicalities, such as whether a parent works outside the home, to an ability to respond to the child's needs. Overall it is a matter of trying to assess which parent will be better able to look after the children during the week (contact orders may be made for the children to see the other parent during the week, at weekends and/or holidays); sometimes the claims of both will be equal. Note that this factor does not refer to the parents' conduct as individuals, and a distinction must be drawn between a person's behaviour as a parent (which will be looked at) and as a partner (which will often be ignored unless it has directly affected the children).

A parent who can offer a stable home life (perhaps particularly if remarrying) will usually have a stronger claim than an unreliable and unpredictable parent. A parent who abandons the children and puts the interests of a lover first is likely to be at a disadvantage when applying for a residence order.

Where relatives or other people (like childminders or full-time nannies) are involved in bringing up the children, their capabilities too may be explored.

A child's right to contact

The chief principle is that it is the right of every child to have contact with both parents. The advantages of regular contact with both parents are undeniable – if the parent who is looking after the children wants to deny the other having contact then he or she will have an uphill battle in doing so.

In very rare cases, where the parent looking after the children can show an 'exceptional and cogent reason' why the other parent should be denied contact, the courts may accept that for the time being contact should not be ordered. The courts have described the process in making such a Solomon's judgment as follows:

The court must ask whether the fundamental emotional need of every child to have an enduring emotional relationship with both parents is outweighed by the depth of harm which the child would be at risk of suffering by virtue of a contact order.

Factors such as actual or potential abuse of a child obviously counteract the in-built presumption towards contact. But where a father has, say, a history of criminal conduct and lacks control over his aggression he may be denied contact in any form. In very exceptional cases a mother's (or even sometimes a stepfather's) implacable hostility to a father having contact has been enough to stop him from having contact, but the court has often insisted that he should have indirect contact via letters or telephone calls. In an unusual case in 1996, a father who wanted to apply to re-establish contact with his child after some time was ordered by the court to make videos for the children, which were pre-viewed by the mother, to help prepare them for meeting him face to face. However, if a father is extremely violent, abusive, abuses drugs and/or alcohol or in other ways will have a profoundly negative effect on the children, the negative effects are likely to outweigh the in-built balance towards contact.

If an order for contact is made and the parent looking after the children disobeys it, the ultimate sanction is imprisonment – although the courts are very reluctant to resort to such extreme action.

Contact centres

In many towns now there are contact centres, which offer a safe space in which parents can have contact with their children in a supervised environment. These are sometimes run by the local Court Welfare Service (which will shortly be replaced by the Children and Family Court Advisory and Support Service, CAFCASS), and sometimes by local volunteers. Couples can choose to use them, or a court may stipulate that contact takes place there. The centres can be used in cases where there is genuine concern about the way in which one parent behaves during contact – this may arise where there has been violence or abuse in the past – or where a parent has threatened to take a child away from the parent that he or she lives with and there are worries that the threat might be carried out. Sometimes they can be used in less upsetting cases, where contact has lapsed and the absent parent needs to rebuild a relationship with the child.

Using such centres is seldom seen as a permanent arrangement. The hope is that a relationship can be rebuilt and that both parents can come to trust each other again and the children can feel comfortable with seeing the parent whom they do not live with. In any case, some centres, owing to a shortage of space, can offer the service only on a short-term basis.

Appeals

Successful appeals against decisions made by the trial judge (the one who originally heard the case) are extremely rare. The judge has a wide discretion, and appeals will be allowed only if the first decision can be shown to be 'plainly wrong'. This is so even if the appeal court feels it would have come to another decision itself. But if further important evidence comes to light, then an appeal might work. If you do go to the Court of Appeal, you may be offered a mediation session to see whether the problem can be resolved out of court.

An appeal against a decision of either the county court (for family cases this is called a Family Hearing Centre) or the Family Proceedings Panel within a magistrates' court will go straight to the High Court. From the High Court an appeal will go to the Court of Appeal.

Challenging an old order

If a parent wishes to vary or change an old court order made before the Children Act 1989 came into force (14 October 1991), the application will usually be made under the Children Act 1989. Although an application to reopen an old decision has a better chance of success than an appeal, the situation would have to have changed fundamentally before it would be worthwhile going to court again.

Prior to the implementation of the Children Act, there were three different legal concepts applicable to children: custody, care and control, and access. The legal usage of some of the words was (and is) different from ordinary English usage. Because these terms are still popularly used even though they no longer apply, it is useful to be aware of what they mean. (You may also have an old court order which uses these concepts.)

Custody

This meant the bundle of responsibilities that parents have towards their children, for example, the right and duty to make major decisions concerning their upbringing, their religion and education.

There were two different court orders for custody: sole custody (for one parent) or joint custody (for both). Joint custody was the court order that resembled most closely the pre-divorce role towards the children. In a sense, the effect of a joint custody order was primarily psychological, because it confirmed for the parent who did not look after the children the fact that he or she had a recognised role to play towards his or her children. ('Parental responsibility' now fulfils this function.)

Care and control

This meant the actual physical 'possession' of the child. Orders were made only for sole care and control: an order for care and control could not be split (unlike the new residence orders). Care and control was what most people meant when they talked about custody.

An order for care and control was granted to the parent with whom the children were living on a regular basis. Even in the unusual cases where children divided their time equally between their parents, only one parent used to have to have an order for care and control.

Access

This meant the visiting periods for the parent who did not have care and control. This could have been 'staying access' (when the child stayed with the non-custodial parent) or 'visiting access' (when the non-custodial parent simply visited or took the child out for the day).

Where parents were able to agree, the courts usually made an order for 'reasonable access' which left the terms of the access visits, or periods of staying access, up to the parents to agree between themselves. Where the parents could not agree, the court may have made an order for defined access, determining when the child would visit the non-custodial parent, sometimes specifying the time when the child should be collected and brought home again.

Other issues

Changing a child's surname

If a child is to be brought up in a new family, a parent (usually the mother) may want to change the child's surname to that of her new partner when or after she remarries. Whether there is anything in the law preventing her from doing so depends on whether there is a residence order (or an old custody/care and control order) in force.

If such an order is in force, there will automatically be a provision stating that the child's surname cannot be changed without the consent of the other parent or the court. But if no such order exists, the mother can in theory change the child's surname, as she has parental responsibility which she can exercise independently. (If you wish to change a child's surname by making a deed poll, which is then enrolled at the court, every person with parental responsibility must give his or her consent. However, a name can be changed legally simply by usage, without going to the lengths of using a deed poll.) However, in practice, where two parents both have parental responsibility, the parent who wants a name change should first try to obtain the other parent's consent. He or she can then apply to the court for permission if the other parent objects. A parent who objects can in any event apply to the court for a specific issue order. The court application will be decided by the principles that the child's welfare is of paramount consideration and that no court order will be made unless this is better for the child.

It is likely that the courts will be influenced by the old case law which broadly disapproved of changes of surname. The courts usually took the line that the link between a child and his or her natural parent, as symbolised by the surname, should not be broken, so changes of surname were usually refused.

However, a mature child him- or herself may apply for a change of surname by way of a specific issue order. If the child has strong feelings about wanting to be included in the new family and sound reasons for making the application, the court may be persuaded to make an order for a change, given that the child's wishes and feelings rank number one on the welfare checklist.

Taking a child abroad for a holiday

If there is a residence order, the usual rule is that a parent who wants to take a child abroad (this includes going from England or Wales to Scotland) should obtain the other parent's written consent first. This is because it is a criminal offence to remove a child from the country without the written consent of both parents or the consent of the court.

Where a parent simply wants to take the child on holiday and has a residence order in his or her favour, he or she can take the child abroad for a period of up to a month. If the other parent objects, an application can be made to the court for its permission by way of a section 8 order. (See also Chapter 15 on child abduction.)

If there is no residence order, the civil law says nothing either to permit or prevent a parent from taking a child abroad. Again, if the parents are in dispute, one or other should apply for a section 8 order. But whether or not a residence order exists, the criminal law still applies.

Applications by grandparents and others

When a marriage ends, sometimes the contact between the children and one set of the grandparents ends too, as families divide into opposing camps. This is rarely good for the children: often they can be helped to cope with their distress by grandparents (or other close relatives or friends, say, perhaps a godparent), who can give a helping hand to guide the children through their trauma.

Grandparents (or for that matter any other interested relative or family friend) can apply to the court for a contact order or other section 8 order. They do not have to wait until divorce or other proceedings have been started (as under the old law). Children Act applications are not limited to new cases either: if an old order is already in existence, an application can still be made for a section 8 order under the new law.

Before such an application can proceed, the court's permission may first have to be sought. The Children Act gives some categories of people the automatic right to make an application. So, if the potential applicant has had the child living with him or her for three years or more *or* has the consent of the person with a residence order in his or her favour, *or* has the consent of everyone with parental responsibility (or that of the local authority if the child is in care), he or she can apply as of right to the court for a contact order or other section 8 order. Otherwise, the court's permission must be obtained before the application will be given the go-ahead. The court will then take into consideration:

- the nature of the proposed application
- the applicant's connection with the child
- the risk of harmful disruption to the child's life.

(The local authority's care plan for the child would also be a factor if the child is being looked after by the local authority.)

If applicants, for example grandparents, have lost contact with the children over many years and formerly had a bad influence on them, it is possible that their application for permission to apply to the court will fail. The legal test is whether a grandparent can show that he or she has a 'good arguable case' and that there is a serious issue to try. Usually the court will grant permission to apply and leave a full investigation of the facts to a proper court hearing involving all sides.

Applications for contact by grandparents will more likely than not be granted unless there is deep bitterness between the families which would be exacerbated by making a contact order. Contact orders can be in the form of letters, cards and telephone calls, so the court may make an order for contact in stages, building up contact from letters and telephone calls before a face-to-face meeting, especially if the grandparents have not met their grandchildren for a long time.

Applications for residence orders by grandparents may be unlikely to succeed unless the natural parents (or the local authority if the child is in care) are fully in support and the child has established a pattern of living with a grandparent.

Legal representation for children

In cases where parents present opposing views of what their children think, the court could order the child to have separate representation – in other words, to have his or her own advocate at court.

In public law cases (where the local authority is concerned), children are usually represented by a 'guardian *ad litem*', a person skilled and experienced in dealing with children, who will put the arguments for what is in the child's best interests. Occasionally the courts have taken the step of appointing a guardian *ad litem* in private law proceedings (that is, those involving disputes between private individuals). In other cases the courts have asked the Official Solicitor (a public official who is a lawyer and acts for children and others who do not have full legal capacity) to intervene and present the case from the child's viewpoint. Appointing the Official Solicitor is still a relatively unusual step and costs can be a problem: the courts will need to be sure that the costs are met from some source (which may be a costs order against one of the parents). Solicitors have also been instructed to act for a child directly.

Applications by a child

The Children Act also allows children themselves to make an application for an order under section 8: the extra hurdle that the child has to overcome is to show that he or she is of 'sufficient understanding' before an application will be allowed to proceed.

The first stage in seeking independent legal representation for a child is for the child him- or herself to approach a family law solicitor to give instructions. The solicitor will have to decide whether the child is mature enough to make an application to court – whether he or she sufficiently understands the consequences. The legal test is often termed 'Gillick competency', after a case involving a Mrs Gillick and one of her daughters, namely 'the attainment by a child of an age of sufficient discretion to enable him or her to exercise a wise choice in his or her own interests'. A solicitor must first assess whether a child passes this test, and then the Legal Services Commission (LSC) has to be convinced too. CLS funding will be available on the grounds of financial eligibility (assessed on the basis of the child's own resources, if any) and merits.

Although applications by children in their own right are still relatively rare, a lot of publicity has been given to the handful of cases where, according to the media, children have applied to 'divorce' their parents. In law, to use the term 'divorce' in this context is incorrect. Children cannot actually divorce their parents: parents will still continue to have parental responsibility and thus be legally connected to their children. The courts have endeavoured (not always with success) to protect the privacy of children who have made their own court applications, on the basis that conducting family battles in the full glare of the media is not conducive to resolving family problems calmly and reasonably. More often than not the cases brought by children have been sorted out without a full court battle: the much-publicised case in the early 1990s of a teenage girl who wanted to live with her boyfriend and his parents eventually ended amicably, with the teenager agreeing to go back home to her mother.

It is still relatively early days since the Children Act was implemented, and so far the new right of children to make their own court applications has not yet been fully tested. Cases have been brought by children to ask the court for a residence order that they live somewhere else or for a contact order that the parent who has left the home be made to see them (sometimes against that parent's will). In many cases, the disputes have been resolved by the family themselves eventually.

In general, remember that court applications by children must cross three hurdles. First, a child will have to convince a solicitor to act for him or her (and the solicitor must usually get CLS funding). Second, the courts must be asked permission for a child's application to go ahead; the child will have to show that he or she has got sufficient understanding. Only if that stage is passed will the courts go on to the third stage, which is to look at the merits of the case. The courts need to be convinced that the child making the application is mature and has sound reasons for asking the court for help, and is not just making the application on impulse because of a row with a parent.

Once the second hurdle is crossed, the courts may sometimes appoint the Official Solicitor to act for the child in place of an ordinary solicitor. If a child wants to ask the courts for help, care should be taken to get the advice of a solicitor experienced in dealing with children cases. Contact the Solicitors Family Law Association* or the Children's Legal Centre.* The law may not be the best remedy for sorting out children's problems – also consider mediation or a form of therapeutic help.

Financial applications for children

As well as reforming the legal framework of the relationships between parents and children, the Children Act 1989 codified the law about financial applications for children. It also enables children over 18 to apply for periodical payments or a lump sum. Since the Child Support Act 1991 came into force on 5 April 1993, most claims for child maintenance have been made through the Child Support

Agency (CSA), although the courts retain their powers for stepchildren and any other children for whom the CSA cannot act. This would include children whose absent parent is working – and is thus habitually resident – abroad. Even if the CSA has jurisdiction over maintenance, however, capital sums or even property orders can be sought for the children.

To make an application under the Children Act 1989, a parent, guardian or anyone with a residence order for a child can apply to court for an order that either parent (or both) pays:

- periodical payments (maintenance) – this applies only if the CSA has no jurisdiction. Periodical payments can be secured
- a lump sum
- a settlement of property
- a transfer of property to the applicant for the benefit of the child or directly to the child (a transfer of property could cover a transfer of a tenancy too).

Applications can be made to either a magistrates' court (Family Proceedings Panel), the county court (Family Hearing Centre) or the High Court, although the magistrates' court has power to order only periodical payments or a lump sum.

The court must look at all the circumstances, including the income, earning capacity of the parties (and the financial position of the child), their needs and obligations, any physical or mental disability of the child and the way in which the child was (or expects to be) educated or trained (this approach is often summed up as 'needs and resources').

See also Chapter 6 about applying for child support under the Child Support Act 1991.

Applications by sons or daughters over 18

A son or daughter over 18 can apply for periodical payments (like weekly or monthly payments) or a lump sum if he or she is in full-time education or training (although this would also cover situations where the son or daughter was working in the evenings to supplement his or her income while in continuing education). The courts will take the approach as outlined above.

There are, however, some restrictions on applications: they can be made only if the parents (whether married or not) are no longer living together in the same household and there was no previous maintenance order in existence before the child's sixteenth birthday. In other words, this provision is intended primarily for sons or daughters who plan to go on to further education and whose parents have comparatively recently split up and where the parental part of the grant (for example) is not being paid. Instead of the parent being forced to go to court to chase up maintenance payments, the son or daughter can make his or her own application. Such children can also apply if they are not covered by the CSA, that is, they are 19 or over.

Chapter 11

The family home in divorce

The family home is generally the biggest single asset that a family owns. Chapter 7 advises you on how to protect your interest in it when a divorce is pending. This chapter tells you how the courts tend to treat the house when looking at the division of assets between spouses. The kinds of order that a divorce court can make about the family home are for:

- a sale, with division of the proceeds
- outright transfer of one spouse's interest to the other
- a transfer of one spouse's interest to the other with a lump-sum adjustment
- a postponed sale – usually until the children complete their education but sometimes beyond that, the house then to be sold and the proceeds divided in specified proportions.

There are no special rules about when and what order a court should make: the courts have a fairly wide discretion. A sale and 50:50 division of the proceeds is appropriate in some cases (especially where the marriage has been short and there are no children); in many others, this would operate unfairly against one or other of the parties. A court's decision in a particular case depends on whether or not there are children, the ages of husband, wife (and any children), the length of the marriage and whether the spouse who will move out has potentially secure accommodation.

Rented property

The courts have power to make a transfer order on divorce with regard to 'property', which includes some but not all rented property, under section 24 of the Matrimonial Causes Act 1973.

The Matrimonial Homes Act 1983 gave the courts power to transfer certain tenancies from one spouse to another on granting a decree of divorce or at any time after that. The power was contained in section 7 and schedule 1 to the 1983 Act, and covered:

- protected and statutory tenancies under the Rent Act 1977
- statutory tenancies under the Rent (Agriculture) Act 1976
- secure tenancies under the Housing Act 1985
- assured tenancies under the Housing Act 1988.

If a non-tenant spouse has been deserted by the tenant spouse it is important that he or she should ask the court for a transfer of tenancy order *before* the divorce decree is made absolute. This is because the occupation of the accommodation by the non-tenant spouse is keeping alive the protected, statutory, secure or assured tenancy arising from the 'deemed occupation' rules contained in section 1 of the 1983 Act.

Once the marriage is ended on divorce (decree absolute), these rules no longer apply, and the tenancy will lose its protected, secure or assured status, or in the case of a statutory tenancy will simply cease to exist. If there is no longer a protected, statutory, secure or assured tenancy in existence, there is nothing for the court to transfer under the 1983 Act.

The general rule is that a transferee spouse cannot get better tenancy rights than the tenant spouse, so if the home is rented on a short-term basis the court will not be able to extend the term of the tenancy, and if rent payment debts have been built up then these would be passed on to the transferee. Some doubts have been raised about whether a statutory tenancy created, for example, under the Rent Act 1977 counts as property which can be transferred under the Housing Act 1983 – this point has not specifically been tested by the courts. However, a case decided in 1997 – *Newlon Housing Trust v Al-Sulaimen and Another* – confirmed that a contractual periodic tenancy is classified as a matrimonial asset and can thus be transferred by the courts as part of the financial arrangements on divorce. Similarly, an earlier case held that a council tenancy counts as 'property' and is thus transferable too.

Rented property: changes under the Family Law Act 1996

Under a part of the Family Law Act 1996 which is already in force, the courts specifically have the power to transfer tenancies between spouses on divorce (or on a decree of judicial separation) and can also, in rare cases, compensate the transferring spouse by an order for compensation against the transferee. The types of tenancy covered are those specified above but also categorically include protected or statutory tenancies under the Rent Act 1977 (although it excludes shorthold tenancies or long leases). The new power extends to cohabitants and former cohabitants as well as former spouses.

Owner-occupied property

If the property is in joint names and expressed on the title deeds to be for the benefit of both parties equally, each technically has a half-share in the 'net equity' (or value after deducting any mortgage debts) of the home. Occasionally, the deeds may express a different division of the property, say 60:40, but this is more common where two cohabitants buy a property. Where spouses buy a property together this is usually done on an equal basis.

However, whatever the title deeds may say, the courts can act on their own discretion about how to divide up the equity of a home.

The courts need to assess what the financial interest of husband and wife is in the home, but in most cases this is only the first stage of the process by which the courts decide what is to happen. The courts have a fairly wide discretion and each individual case is decided on its own merits.

Whose name the house is actually in (husband's, wife's or both), who put up the deposit and who paid the mortgage are obviously important, but are by no means the only factors when decisions are made. The longer the marriage, the less important who contributed what becomes.

Where the home has dropped in value

During the recession of the 1980s it was not uncommon for the value of the home to be less than the amount of the mortgage (that is, to have 'negative equity'), especially if the original mortgage was for

100 per cent of the purchase price. Even now that house prices have been rising again, it may take a little time for the value of a property to rise to more than the amount of the mortgage. Remember also that for properties where the value is slightly higher than the unpaid mortgage, the added costs of selling the home, including legal and estate agents' fees, may mean that the home is worth nothing or even less than the mortgage.

Where your home in effect has negative equity, you will need to weigh up carefully what your best course of action might be. The reasons for retaining the home and carrying on meeting the mortgage repayments would be that a spouse and any children would keep a roof over their heads and that property prices may rise later to make the investment worthwhile. Sometimes estate agents may suggest a very low price for the home just to ensure a sale, but keeping the property until the market has improved can raise the price that the home would eventually fetch.

On the other hand, continuing the mortgage repayments if the home is unlikely to increase sufficiently in value to cover your indebtedness may only be throwing good money after bad, so it could be tempting to consider handing the keys in to the mortgagee (the bank or building society) and leaving it to them to sell. The drawback of this option is that the mortgagee may sell the property at a considerable loss and will look to you for the balance of what is owing under the mortgage at a later stage, plus interest which will still continue to run against you. This may make it difficult for you to get another mortgage later.

None of the options that you face may look attractive, and you may be forced into choosing the least unattractive, namely the one that costs you least. Ask several estate agents for a free valuation of the home and for their views on the property market. Although some of what you are told may be speculative rather than factual, you should get a clearer picture on which to base your decision. Talk to your bank or building society to see whether they offer any schemes to help out homeowners in your situation. Make sure that you also talk to your solicitor or Citizens Advice Bureau to discuss your options before finally making up your mind.

Where there are no children

Where there is a divorce after a short marriage, the courts may look mainly at what financial contributions relating to the house or flat had been made and decide that the person who put in the most should have the most out. As mentioned earlier, the longer the marriage has gone on, the less the courts are interested in who put in what, in money terms, and the more they are prepared to recognise the other party's non-financial contribution. For instance, the wife's contribution in keeping the home going may count as much as the husband's financial contributions.

The main consideration is likely to be whether the net proceeds of sale of the house are sufficient to enable each spouse (with the aid of such mortgage loan as each might be able to obtain) to buy an adequate new home. If so, the courts may well order a sale of the house without delay. Even if one spouse wants to stay on, it may not be practicable or fair to the other because the latter would need his or her share of the value of the house in order to buy a new home. The house may have to be sold where the combined resources of husband and wife are insufficient to keep up the mortgage repayments on the existing home and to provide accommodation for the other spouse.

Where the home has been bought from the local authority under the 'right to buy' with a discount and is sold within three years of buying, the couple have to pay back to the local authority part of the discount they were allowed. This could be grounds for asking the court to defer a sale until the three-year period is up.

Division of proceeds

When determining how best to share out the money from the sale of the house (or flat), the courts will take into account direct financial contributions by the non-owning spouse towards the purchase (payment of part of the deposit or part of the mortgage repayments) or for the improvement of the house. They will also consider indirect financial contributions – for example, where the wife has worked for all or part of the marriage and has used her earnings to pay some of the household bills, food, or clothing or has paid her earnings into the couple's joint bank account.

If the wife's share would be insufficient to enable her to buy a new home, particularly if her earning capacity puts her into a less favourable position for getting a mortgage, the courts could order that the wife should get a greater share of the proceeds of sale. They may compensate the husband by ordering him to pay relatively low maintenance to the wife – or none at all.

Not selling

A sale of the family home may, however, not be the right solution. The expenses of selling, and of buying two other houses, will have to be met, and the net proceeds of sale may not be sufficient to enable either spouse to buy another home. A court can order that the wife remain in the house:

- until she wants to move out, or marries again, or cohabits permanently (this is normally taken to be the case after, say, six months of living together, but preferably should be defined in the order) or she dies; *or*
- for a period of time specified by the court.

After that, the house would be sold, and the net proceeds divided in the proportions decided by the court at the time of making the order (these cannot be varied later).

The wife might have to compensate the husband in the meantime by a (notional) payment of rent. In practice, this might be achieved by an appropriate reduction of his maintenance obligations to her.

An arrangement which leaves the wife with uncertainty as to her future home, and the husband having to wait a number of years before he receives his capital while he has to continue paying maintenance, can cause bitterness. The courts try to avoid some of these difficulties by arranging a 'clean break'. For example, it might be fair for the house to be transferred outright to the wife, and for the husband to be compensated by dismissal of the wife's claims for maintenance for the present and the future. No clean break can, however, be made in respect of maintenance for the children – parents continue to be financially responsible after divorce. So the cost of child support will need to be weighed up to see if this option is affordable (see also Chapter 6).

If an order is made for the transfer of the whole of the home into one of the spouses' sole name or from one into the joint names, a transfer or conveyance will have to be drawn up. On the transfer of property by court order following the break-up of a marriage, no stamp duty is payable irrespective of the value of the property.

One spouse 'buying out' the other

An alternative clean-break arrangement is for the spouse who is going to remain in the house to buy out the departing spouse, by paying him or her a lump sum for his or her share in the house.

Beware, however, the danger of a delay in the lump-sum payment if the house market is volatile. In a case in 1989 (*Hope-Smith v Hope-Smith*) the husband had been ordered to pay his wife a lump sum of £32,000 within 28 days; if he failed to do so, the matrimonial home was to be sold forthwith and £32,000 of the proceeds given to the wife. The husband unsuccessfully appealed against this order, but three years later the house was still unsold. His former wife then successfully appealed against the original order and the court substituted a larger payment to her because of the increase in house prices over the three years.

Wherever there is likely to be a delay in payment, it may be better to express the payment in percentage terms of the equity of the house, rather than as a fixed lump sum.

Where there are children

The courts' priority is that an adequate home should be provided for the children. Recent cases continue to stress that, while the courts have a number of matters to take into account, the interests of the children have priority over others.

The Child Support Acts have made a significant impact on the way the courts and lawyers deal with the home following a divorce where there are children. The full extent of the changes has not yet been fully tested in the courts. One thing, however, is clear – the fact that in general child support payments have increased substantially.

Because the spouse who has left the home is likely to end up having greater outgoings in the form of child support payments, one knock-on effect is that he (or, more rarely, she) may no longer be able to afford to transfer his share in the home to the parent remaining to look after the children. So the advice which follows here must be tempered by the consideration that there may not be enough money both to achieve proper child support payments and changes in ownership of the family home. As payments of child support are usually fixed, the absent parent may have to retain a share in the family home unless there are sufficient funds to meet both child support payments and the costs of his re-housing (see also Chapter 6 for more information).

However, a case in 1997 (*B v B*) highlighted that where there are sufficient funds to stretch to two homes, each party needs a home, particularly when children are involved. The case is more important for families who are financially slightly above the position of being able to afford only one owner-occupied house – but where there is not a lot of extra capital. The judge in the case made it clear that the courts will expect families to try to make the financial effort to buy two homes.

Selling

It is unlikely that the courts would order a sale unless selling the home would bring in enough money to buy other adequate accommodation for the parent (usually the wife) who is going to have the children to live there with her.

The house would, however, have to be sold if the wife could not keep up the mortgage repayments with whatever assistance by way of maintenance the husband could finance. More economical accommodation would then have to be provided for her and the children out of the proceeds of selling the house.

Not selling immediately

In order to secure the house as a home for the children, the courts may order the husband to transfer it into joint names if it was in his sole name. When a house is in joint names, it cannot normally be sold without the agreement of the joint owners, but either party can apply to the High Court for an order to enforce a sale. To prevent this, the divorce court normally directs that the house shall not be sold for a specific period while the wife and the children live there – usually until the youngest child reaches a particular age, usually tied to the time when he or she is expected to leave school (or until the wife remarries, or cohabits on a settled basis).

A more usual alternative is to transfer the house into the wife's sole name, subject to a charge securing to the husband whatever sum or proportion of the net proceeds of (eventual) sale the courts think proper. A 'charge' over the property means that when it is sold, the charge (which is like a mortgage) comes into effect and the other spouse will get his or her money out of the proceeds. The husband's position becomes just like that of a bank or building society to whom money is secured on the property. He does not have rights to enter the house, for instance, or interfere in its management. The husband may have to pay Capital Gains Tax (CGT) on the money he eventually receives. Normally, the provisions for inflation and his personal exemptions cover this but it may be worth bearing in mind if there is an anticipated gain, or if the husband is likely to use up his exemptions in some other ways.

In either case, the court specifies at what point the husband can realise his interest in the house. This is likely to be when the youngest child of the family comes of age or when any child undergoing full-time education ceases to remain normally resident in the home. The husband can then enforce the sale.

Selling later – pros and cons

A difficult consideration is whether the house should be kept as a home for the ex-wife even after the children have left home. The courts will take into account whether the wife's share of the proceeds, if the house were sold then, would enable her to buy another house, and also the husband's need for the capital. The courts can only gauge what the situation is likely to be at a time possibly 12 or 15 years ahead – how much the ex-wife would receive from the sale of the house, her likelihood of employment, and her earnings and mortgage capacity. Her share would need to be sufficient for her to buy a flat or a smaller house at an age when she might be unable to raise much by way of mortgage. Meanwhile, the husband will have been able to start afresh with another mortgage because of his lower age and possibly higher earnings at the time of the divorce.

Another disadvantage of delaying a final resolution of a division of the parties' capital assets is that, when the time eventually does come for a sale, the ex-wife may well be reluctant to move out, particularly if she sees her former husband doing comfortably in another property. In a sense, this type of order can prolong the agony of a divorce. But sometimes there is no alternative.

If it seems likely that the ex-wife will have insufficient funds to enable her to buy another house when the children are no longer dependent, a court may either award her a larger share of the value or defer the sale (or enforcement of the ex-husband's charge) for the remainder of her life (or until she remarries or cohabits). However, if such an order would cause even greater hardship to the ex-husband than to the ex-wife, the court would be reluctant to make such an order.

Where either party has Community Legal Service (CLS) funding, the Legal Services Commission's statutory charge (if applicable) will not be levied until the house is sold. By then, the rise in house prices may have reduced the practical effect of the charge (but remember there will be accrued interest on the charge to be paid in addition).

When the house is eventually sold, liability for CGT may arise for an ex-spouse who is still a joint owner but who had moved out of the house.

If there is no mortgage to be paid off, the ex-wife will, in effect, be living in the house at the ex-husband's expense. The court therefore may make an order requiring her to pay the ex-husband an occupation rent from the time that the children cease to need the house as a home. If she is paying off the mortgage on the house, the ex-wife will be contributing to the value of the ex-husband's eventual share of the proceeds of sale. This would generally be taken into account in the proportions in which the sale proceeds are divided.

If the house or flat is mortgaged

Mortgages cannot simply be transferred, and the court has no power to order the transfer of a mortgage, only the transfer of a property subject to a mortgage. The consent of the building society or other mortgagees is necessary, otherwise the mortgagor (usually the husband) remains liable for the mortgage even if the property is transferred. The mortgagees must be served with notice of an application to the court for a transfer of ownership and have the right to object.

It may well be the ex-wife who is going to be responsible for meeting the mortgage repayments in future, possibly out of an income (from maintenance payments) on the basis of which the building society or bank would not have agreed to make a mortgage loan. It is advisable for her to contact the mortgagees as soon as possible to discuss ways of making repayments if and when the house is transferred.

The building society or other mortgagee must agree before the transfer can take effect. If it does not, it may be necessary to try to pay off the mortgage and find a new mortgagee – if necessary through a mortgage broker (although remember that mortgage brokers usually charge fees at around 1 per cent of the amount borrowed).

It is not uncommon for building societies to ask a former husband to guarantee a mortgage that is being taken out by a woman whose income comes from his maintenance payments either in whole or in part. The ex-husband would have to meet the mortgage repayments only if his former wife defaulted. (He can ask her for an indemnity so that she is liable to compensate him if this does happen.) In practice, her default is likely to happen only if he defaults on the maintenance.

Where there is an endowment mortgage

A mortgage on an endowment basis is linked to an insurance policy that aims to pay out enough to repay the loan at the end of the mortgage term or on the policyholder's death. In the meantime, only the interest has to be paid on the loan, plus the premiums on the insurance policy. Doubts have recently been raised about whether in reality endowment policies sold in the 1980s and early 1990s will realise sufficient funds to cover the mortgage, especially if the policies were affected by the stock-market crash in 1987. It may be worthwhile checking with your mortgagee or insurance company how financially healthy your particular endowment is.

The application for a property adjustment order where there is an endowment mortgage should include an application to transfer the husband's beneficial interest in the insurance policy to the wife (or vice versa). If this is not transferred, the ex-wife would be in a position of getting nothing under the policy and would have to pay off the whole mortgage loan out of the proceeds of sale of the house. When the mortgage term comes to an end, a decision has to be made regarding any bonuses on the policy over and above the amount required to repay the loan. This surplus could be ordered to go to the ex-husband to compensate for the loss of use of capital, or to the ex-wife, particularly if she has been paying the premiums for many years, or to be shared between them.

Capital Gains Tax

Capital Gains Tax is payable on gains arising on the 'disposal of assets'. (A helpful leaflet to do with CGT, IR281, called *Husband and Wife*,

Divorce and Separation, is available from the Inland Revenue. It can also be downloaded from the Inland Revenue's web site).⋆ Before the Finance Act 1988, capital gains were treated differently from income for tax purposes. For disposals made after 6 April 1988, the amount of a person's chargeable capital gains is added to his or her income. He or she is charged the appropriate income tax rate (in 2000–1 at 10, 22 or 40 per cent) calculated by treating the capital gain as the top slice of income.

A specified amount of gains in any one tax year is exempt. Husband and wife each have their own £7,200 annual exemption (2000–1 figures).

So long as a husband and wife are living together, and for the rest of the tax year after the separation, no chargeable gain results where one transfers his or her share of the house to the other. But when the asset is eventually transferred or is sold to someone else, the gain (or loss) is calculated over the whole period of ownership, not just since the date of transfer to the ex-spouse.

For the calculation of gain on disposals of property owned before 1982, the base cost is the market value of the asset on 31 March 1982 (subject to certain special rules mostly dealing with business). To calculate the inflation since that date, reference is made to the increases in the Retail Prices Index (RPI) based on the figure at March 1982.

On divorce or separation, the major areas where disposals are likely to arise are:

- household contents – antiques, for example
- other assets such as a car, a second home, stocks and shares, savings ('assets' means practically everything capable of being owned and sold or transferred)
- the home.

Most consumer goods decrease in value, so the question of 'gain' does not arise. Most chattels with a life span of less than 50 years are exempt from CGT, anyway.

Cash and cars are specifically exempt from CGT, and so are any sums received on the surrender of life insurance policies. So if, for one reason or another, you cash in an endowment policy which is linked to a mortgage, there is no question of liability to CGT. A sale of other assets, such as stocks and shares, can give rise to CGT.

The home and CGT

Any gain made on the sale of a person's principal private residence (PPR) is normally exempt from CGT. But CGT liability arises when the home is sold if you had stopped living there more than three years earlier.

On divorce, it is likely that you will do one or other of three things with the home:

- sell it and split the proceeds
- transfer it to your spouse outright
- put it into joint names (or leave it in joint names) and postpone sale and division of the proceeds until a future date.

Sale and division of proceeds

If you sell the house and split the proceeds within three years of one or other of you ceasing to reside there, you will be entitled to claim PPR exemption provided the home was your only, or main, residence throughout the period that you owned it.

If at any time you have two or more homes, either of them is potentially eligible for the PPR exemption. If, therefore, you have bought another home and the old home has not been sold, you may make a choice, usually within two years of divorce or separation, as to which one you wish to have treated as your PPR. (If you do not, your tax inspector will.) It may make sense to claim the exemption in respect of the house that is being sold, if this is at a gain.

Where the sale takes place more than three years after one of you has left, the person who ceased to reside there may not be fully exempt. Only a portion of the gain will be exempt: namely, the period of his or her actual occupation plus the last three years of ownership. (The last three years of ownership are always exempt.) Thus, the longer you wait beyond three years after separation before selling your old home, the greater the possibility of CGT having to be paid by the person who left. (The person who remains will not be liable for CGT provided he or she has remained permanently in residence.) However, do remember that indexation relief will be available as well as an annual personal exemption. On top of these exemptions, Extra Statutory Concession Form D6 may be applicable, and is available from the tax office. This is designed to cover the situation where a home (occupied by one spouse) is sold as part of a settlement and the other spouse has not elected to treat another property as his main residence. Although these rules are complex, the net effect is that CGT can very often be avoided.

Transfer of the home to your spouse outright

Although no money changes hands, the transfer would in theory be a 'disposal', based on the market value at the date of disposal. Quite apart from the fact that there may well not be a capital gain anyway (after taking inflation into account and the current year's exemption), the transaction would qualify for PPR exemption if made within three years of the transfer or of the spouse leaving the home.

House in joint names sold much later

Transferring the house into joint names will not attract CGT liability.

When the house is sold many years later and the proceeds divided, the spouse who has remained in the home will not have to pay tax on his or her share because that will be fully covered by the PPR exemption. But the one who moved out might be liable to some CGT. The same applies if the house is not in joint names but the one who moves out has a charge on the property. On realisation of the charge, that spouse will be liable for CGT on the rise in the value of the charge after taking into account the increase in the RPI and his annual exemption. The extra statutory concession mentioned above may, however, cover this.

Second home

Selling a second home to raise money may render you liable to CGT if there is a sufficient gain. (By 'second home' in this context is meant a property for which PPR did not apply while you were living together.)

It could make more sense to transfer it to the spouse who is moving out of the matrimonial home for him or her to live in it as his or her PPR. When it is eventually sold, it will be possible for him or her to claim PPR exemption on the whole of any gains from the date when the property had first been acquired – provided that the transfer between the spouses took place before the end of the tax year in which they separated.

Seeking advice

You may feel that you need specialist advice about CGT, perhaps from an accountant. For someone in receipt of Community Legal Services funding, it might be better for the solicitor to instruct the accountant since he or she can then pay the accountant's fee if it will be recoverable from the Legal Services Commission (LSC) as an expense reasonably incurred; prior authority of the LSC to incur the accountant's fees would be needed. If the accountant were instructed directly, the client would have to find the money more or less straight away (whereas the statutory charge may not be payable until considerably later).

Chapter 12

Money in divorce

Sorting out your finances in divorce is a separate matter from the divorce proceedings themselves. However, the timings have to coincide at some points. You cannot actually file a financial application until the divorce petition has been filed (though this does not stop you starting to negotiate about finances). A final financial order cannot be made by the court until decree nisi, but often the terms of such an order are agreed before decree nisi and submitted to the court for approval at the same time as the decree. The final financial order cannot actually take effect until decree absolute, the final decree of divorce. The order may well come some time after the decree absolute, so that you can be divorced and free to remarry but not have your financial situation sorted out.

The rules about when final orders can be made do not stop interim orders for maintenance or maintenance pending suit orders being made, if necessary, pending decree absolute.

It is open to the husband and wife to settle the financial issues between them at any stage. Sometimes these are sorted out with relative ease and no financial applications are filed: a consent order is simply submitted for the court's approval (see below). More often, a financial application will be filed and proceed to a greater or lesser extent before both parties feel comfortable enough with the information that they have obtained about each other's finances to be able to settle. Sometimes such settlement is not reached until the very day of the final hearing, 'at the court door'. Perhaps surprisingly, given the way that these things are reported in the press, only a very small percentage of cases actually end up before a district judge who has to decide how the assets are to be divided.

When you start to consider how your assets should be divided you need to be aware that there is no fixed formula for the division. The only formula in family law is the Child Support Agency's (CSA's) formula for the maintenance of the children. Each case is decided on its own particular set of circumstances; what suits one family may not be best for another, even though superficially they seem to be alike. This may seem to make the whole thing a lottery, but there are clear criteria laid down by law (see below) and an experienced lawyer will be able to give you a good idea of the sort of order that a court might be expected to make in your case.

As a court order is the 'bottom line' when you are negotiating – what you will end up with if you cannot reach a settlement – it makes sense to consult a solicitor about money, even if you feel that you can deal with the basic divorce proceedings yourself. Otherwise, you are negotiating in ignorance and may well sell yourself short, or think that your spouse is being unreasonable, when in fact he or she is simply asking for the sort of order that the court might make.

This chapter first sets out the statutory criteria, with explanations of the weight that is to be given to them. It then looks at the orders that the court can make and the general approach that the court takes in balancing these issues. The procedure that you have to follow in making a financial application is then set out. This is a new scheme that came into force in June 2000, having previously been piloted in various areas of England and Wales.

Factors that the court has to take into account

When you look at the way in which the court will approach a final financial order it is important to understand that the judge is not concerned to reward or penalise one party or the other for behaviour during the marriage. This would be an impossible task and the law does not require it. Instead, the judge will be looking forward, and trying to make sure that the children of the family are properly looked after and that both parties are provided for in the future. When you are thinking about your financial settlement, you too need to look to the future, however bitter you are about what has happened in the past.

The courts no longer have a wholly free rein in deciding how the family income can be divided, as the CSA usually has jurisdiction over child support (where there are children covered by its jurisdiction). After that has been worked out, the lawyers (and ultimately the courts, if the case proceeds to a full hearing) will examine how much is left for division and will apply the court-based guidelines given below.

The other important question to be decided is with whom (in cases involving children) the children should live and whether the family home needs to be kept on. From these decisions, all other matters will flow.

In deciding whether to make financial orders on a divorce and if so what orders, statutory guidelines require a court to take account of:

- the income, earning capacity, property and other financial resources of both spouses, both now and in the foreseeable future, including any increased earning capacity which the court could reasonably expect either person to try to acquire
- the financial needs, obligations and responsibilities of both spouses, both now and in the foreseeable future
- the standard of living before the breakdown of the marriage
- the ages of both spouses
- the length of the marriage
- any physical or mental disabilities
- the contributions of each spouse to the welfare of the family including any contribution in caring for the family or looking after the home, both in the past and in the foreseeable future
- in some circumstances, the conduct of either spouse
- the value of any benefit, such as a pension, which either spouse would lose the chance of acquiring as a result of the divorce.

These guidelines are set out in section 25 of the Matrimonial Causes Act 1973, as amended by the Matrimonial and Family Proceedings Act 1984. The 1984 Act altered the previous guidelines in various ways and specifically directed that the court must give first consideration to the welfare of any child of the family under 18 when considering all the circumstances of a case. In practice, the needs of dependent children have long determined what course the court could reasonably follow in making appropriate orders, but the specific endorsement of this principle gives recognition to the role of the parent with whom the children make their main base, while also discouraging any assumption that that parent is automatically entitled to life-long support without further question, purely as a result of having looked after the children.

The 1984 Act abolished an old and quite unrealistic objective, namely that the court should try to place both spouses in the financial position they would have been in if the marriage had not broken down, insofar as was practical and just. The thrust of the guidelines is now more clearly forward-looking – but only after careful note is taken of the circumstances relating to the marriage and the family. The court must still consider the standard of living enjoyed before the breakdown when considering appropriate provision for the future.

Part of the emphasis of the 1984 Act was that the guidelines specifically mention contributions that will be made to the family's welfare in the foreseeable future (as well as those made in the past).

Before deciding on the amount of maintenance to order, the district judge will look first at the shortfall between the child support and the needs of the parent looking after the children. Factors particularly relevant to maintenance are:

- the gross income of the husband and any necessary expenses of his work that can properly be set against his gross income together with any future earning capacity
- the gross income of the wife and any necessary expenses of her work that can properly be set against her gross income, together with any future earning capacity
- the needs of the children, now and in the foreseeable future
- the needs and outgoings of husband and of wife
- the possibility of each being financially self-sufficient (a 'clean break')
- the effect of tax on any proposed order
- the effect of any order on welfare benefits entitlements.

When dealing with a request for a property-adjustment or a lump-sum order the district judge will consider:

- the full extent of each party's capital and details of any other assets
- the value of the family home and of any other properties owned by either the husband or the wife or by both
- the amount owing on any mortgages
- the needs of each for accommodation
- whom the children live with

- the financial contributions or other contributions made by each towards the purchase or improvement of the family home and any previous homes
- if husband or wife is CLS funded, the effect of the Legal Services Commission's (LSC's) statutory charge on a property-adjustment or lump-sum order.

In all cases, the overall question of costs must be considered.

Earning capacity

The court is specifically directed to consider whether either spouse could reasonably increase his or her earning capacity. The 1984 Act reflected the desirability of a husband and wife aiming at financial independence from each other after divorce, to the extent that this may be realistic. Courts recognise, however, that women who have long been out of the job market may not be able to return straight away and, even if a job is found, it may well turn out to be with low earnings, little job security and few career prospects. A case in 1997 (*Flavell v Flavell*) held that it would not usually be appropriate for the courts to order an end to maintenance for a wife in her mid-fifties or so who has not worked for a long time.

Generally speaking, if there are very young children at home, a court would not expect a mother to go out to work unless she had been working before the breakdown of the marriage, in which case she would be expected to go on earning if practicable. This is also true of a father if the children live with him, except that it may be more realistic for him to go out to work, particularly if his level of earnings would mean that he could afford a housekeeper or childminder.

As the children grow older, the courts expect mothers to be able to return to work, at first perhaps part-time, or after a period of retraining (which the husband might need to finance).

A woman who has not worked outside the house throughout the marriage, who has grown-up children and is herself only a few years from retirement age, is recognised as having a very limited earning capacity, perhaps none. The extent to which it might be reasonable to expect her to find paid employment would depend very much on how realistic an option this is, set against the background of the marriage, the husband's earnings, her health, her tangible job prospects and all the other circumstances. Her need for a form of pension, to cover her maintenance needs after retirement age, will also very much need to be taken on board.

The court cannot order anyone to get a job but it can 'deem' a level of income which it considers either spouse could reasonably get. This can work both ways. If a wife is felt to be unreasonably refusing to work when there are job opportunities available, her maintenance order might be reduced. If a husband gives up his job simply to avoid paying maintenance, a bullish court might still make a maintenance order against him based on the amount that he should realistically be earning, in the hope that this will spur him back to work. The court will, however, take account of economic realities.

Conduct

The courts are directed to have regard to conduct if it is such that in the opinion of the court it would be inequitable to disregard it. 'Run of the mill' conduct as a partner, for example having an affair, will usually be ignored. Only in exceptional cases will conduct be brought into account and then only where one party's conduct has been 'gross and obvious' while the other party's conduct has been comparatively blameless. (Conduct which has had an obvious impact on the financial position of the couple, such as the husband who injured his wife so badly that it impaired her earning capacity, is more likely to be taken into account.) Where both parties have behaved extremely badly, the court is likely to disregard conduct. Even where conduct is relevant, it is only one of the factors that the court must look at.

New relationship

If either or both parties in a divorce have formed a new relationship and are moving out to live with the new partner, the break-up of the marriage may be less damaging financially. Such an eventuality may be the best thing that could happen as far as accommodation costs are concerned: it reduces the biggest financial strain of all – the cost of funding two homes from one income. Where an ex-spouse's living expenses and accommodation costs are substantially reduced because of a new partner's contribution, there is more of the ex-spouse's money to go around and be shared out. (See also Chapter 16 on Step-families.)

Length of marriage

The question of whether the court should take into account any time of pre-marital cohabitation when making an order has caused some legal controversy. It is likely to if children were born during that period, or if one party had made a substantial financial contribution to the shared home before marriage. It is likely to be considered under the provision dealing with 'all the circumstances of the case' rather than the factor relating to length of the marriage.

After a short marriage in which there are no children, the court may be inclined not to order maintenance, or perhaps only for a limited period. The question as to what constitutes a short marriage is not clear: a marriage of three years has been held by the court not to have been a short marriage, whereas a marriage of five years was considered 'of short duration'. A short marriage between a young couple who are both working or able to do so is likely to be treated very differently from a short marriage between two people in, say, their mid-fifties where the woman had given up secure accommodation and/or a career and/or maintenance from a former spouse when she married, or if she is or was suffering from some kind of disability.

No strict definition exists of what a long-lasting marriage is.

The orders that the court can make

The court can make the following orders:

- an order for maintenance 'pending suit' – which means before the decree absolute is granted
- an order for periodical payments – often referred to as maintenance
- an order for secured periodical payments
- a lump-sum order
- a property-adjustment order
- an order directing pension fund trustees to pay part or all of pension rights as they fall due.

These are the only orders that the court can make, and the effect of each is described in more detail below. If you can manage to agree a consent order with your spouse, you can add to the orders made by the court by binding promises – undertakings – which extend the range of matters that can be covered by the order. This makes a consent order much more flexible (and therefore generally desirable).

Maintenance pending suit

This refers to maintenance that one spouse can be ordered to pay the other before decree absolute is made. In most cases temporary maintenance can generally be agreed between the couple prior to a final financial settlement being reached. This can be formalised by a consent order, but in many cases couples simply rely on the agreement and do not bother with the extra expense of making a court order. However, in some cases, where one spouse (it will generally be the wife) is not being maintained by the other and has no other adequate source of income, she can apply to the court for maintenance pending suit.

Because of the costs involved and the time taken up in the procedure, it is not likely to be cost effective unless the maintenance is going to be significantly higher than state benefit. For this reason, maintenance pending suit applications are comparatively infrequent. But the power to make the application, and the threat that it will be made, often produces an offer to pay on an interim basis.

Periodical payments (maintenance)
For the children

Maintenance for children where the court has jurisdiction to make such an order (see below), is generally expressed as an annual sum, to be paid weekly or monthly. If the order does not state that it is to be paid in advance it is paid in arrears. The sum for each child should be stated. Maintenance will normally run until each child's seventeenth birthday, but the order can be worded to go on to the child's eighteenth birthday if he or she is expected to still be at school, or even continue until the child has ceased full-time education or training.

Children covered by the CSA: The implementation of the Child Support Act 1991 in April 1993 has made the issue of how much maintenance should be paid paradoxically both more and less certain for parents with children. As long as the children come within the jurisdiction of the CSA (see Chapter 6), the amount of child support that should be paid can be worked out in most cases relatively precisely. If the necessary information is available to make the calculation, a 'right' answer can be arrived at, which leaves only the question of how much spousal maintenance should be paid.

The figures to be included in the calculation may not be easily available – say if one spouse plans eventually to leave the home but has not yet moved out, his (or her) future housing costs will not yet be known, so a vital element of the calculation will be missing (but this will not be significant when the new formula – see Chapter 6 – is implemented). Even so, it should be possible to guess how much rent will be paid approximately and thus make a good stab at the eventual figure. This will provide a starting point for working out how much maintenance should be paid for the wife (or, where the wife is comparatively wealthy and the husband has no income, for the husband). See Chapter 6 for further information.

Children not covered by the CSA: Some children are not covered by the CSA's powers, and so an application must be made to court for their maintenance. Those *not* covered by the Agency include:

- stepchildren
- children who are, or whose parent(s) are habitually resident abroad
- children whose parents made a pre-existing agreement for maintenance.

If an application is made to the court for children's maintenance, the court may look at how much child support would be if the CSA formula were used, in addition to the factors it would have taken into consideration in the past. It may also look at other yardsticks – a report published by the Joseph Rowntree Foundation in autumn 1997, for example, noted that the 'average' yearly cost of bringing up a child was nearly £3,000. However, the courts take pride in being flexible in family cases and will be able to take other outgoings – like travel, child-care costs and debts – into account before deciding how much should be paid.

Having worked out child support, the court will then address the question of spousal maintenance.

For the spouse

Maintenance for a spouse, as for children, is generally expressed as an annual sum, to be paid weekly or monthly. Occasionally, the court can specify that it is for life, in which case it will end on the death of either party; it will also end on the remarriage of the recipient (but not her cohabitation) or if a court order terminates it. A later court order can also vary the amount paid. (See *Changes in circumstances: variations*, at the end of this chapter).

It is becoming more common for spousal maintenance to be ordered for a fixed period. The typical situation where this would happen would be where a wife has had a period away from work to care for a young family but intends to return to work in a few years, or after a period of re-training. If maintenance is for a fixed period, the order can dismiss the wife's claims at the end of that period so that no further order can be made at all, or leave them open, which would give the opportunity for the order to be extended if unforeseen circumstances prevented the anticipated return to work.

There are no set guidelines on how much should be paid for spouses. The old rule was that a wife might expect to receive something like one-third of the overall gross income. Now that way of dividing up incomes is out of date: families often have two incomes, and most of the tax advantages that used to exist in paying maintenance have been abolished. The court has instead adopted a more realistic approach, often dubbed the 'needs and resources' approach. It looks at how much each partner needs and then what the overall resources are to meet those needs. Producing a budget of how much each spouse needs to live on will be helpful.

As mentioned above, the courts first work out child support before looking at spousal maintenance. Their primary concern is to see that the needs of the children and those of the parent looking after the children are met. Where these are not met by the income of the parent looking after the children, the courts will where possible set a level of spousal maintenance to top up that income. If not enough money is available to do this, the courts will merely order the absent parent to pay what he (or she) can reasonably afford (if anything). Welfare benefits may be available to top up maintenance levels. Remember, however, that maintenance will be deducted pound for pound from income support, but is not taken into account for the working families' tax credit.

A court's overall task is to evaluate all the various factors, balance them one against the other, give what weight is considered appropriate to each factor and then try to arrive at an order which is fair and reasonable. Capital and income are looked at together. It may be appropriate for a wife to receive more capital and less maintenance even if there is not to be a clean break.

The Finance Act 1988 changed the tax treatment of maintenance orders on divorce. Before then, parties had been able to maximise the tax effectiveness of maintenance orders by utilising each child's single person's tax-free allowance through orders for maintenance payments to the children, to reduce the burden of tax upon the payer.

The changes in tax law mean that it is now easier to calculate the tax burden on the family; no skilful manipulation of maintenance figures can result in a decrease of the tax burden on the family after divorce. Divorcing families thus have to translate into reality a problematic equation: the division of (often) one income to support two households.

Capital orders

When the court looks at capital orders – lump sum, transfer of property and pension adjustment – it first has to consider what the available resources are and how they can be sensibly divided up. It is unlikely, for example, that a court would order the sale of a small family company simply in order to divide the proceeds, because it might make better economic sense to keep it as a going concern. In addition to the needs and resources of both parties, what the individuals have contributed to the marriage is also taken into account.

In most cases, the needs of the wife used to be the major consideration, but in 2000 a case called *White v White* in the House of Lords changed the assumptions on which cases had been fought and settled for many years. Briefly, the case established that rather than concentrating on the needs of the wife and adjusting shares in the family capital accordingly, the court should start with equality as the basis, and then consider whether there are any good reasons for departing from it.

White v White was a case which involved a lot of money, and a half-share would have, it was deemed, given the wife more than her 'needs' required. In cases where there is less to go around, a half-share may not be adequate for the wife's needs if she is to house the children with her, and so there could be good reasons for giving one party a larger share of the capital.

Lump sum

A lump-sum order is a capital order. One spouse can be ordered to pay the other a lump sum either all at once, or by specified instalments. The date by which the payment(s) should be made should be in the order. The order can provide for interest to be paid if the payment is late.

Before the Family Law Act 1996, the court had power to make only one lump-sum order – this was a final order which could take effect only on or after decree absolute. However, the 1996 Act has modified this to some extent. In addition to any final order that the court might make, the court can now make a lump-sum order at a later stage if a periodical payments order is ended by a court order. This can be a useful way of creating a clean break between husband and wife where this was not possible at the time of the divorce. A typical situation is where a husband has been paying maintenance and wishes to end the obligation by paying his former wife a large lump sum which she can invest and live off instead. Before the 1996 Act this could be achieved only if the spouses both consented, but now the court can order this.

Transfer of property order

A transfer of property order generally involves the transfer of the matrimonial home between the spouses, but property is defined widely and can include a council tenancy, or shares, and not just what lawyers call 'real' property (houses or land).

The court can order one spouse to transfer property to the other, or adjust the proportion of the property each spouse owns. It can order the sale of a property and the shares in which the proceeds are to be divided. It cannot order a third party to make a transfer, nor can it order a mortgagee – the building society or the bank – to cooperate in the transfer. For this reason, the consent of the mortgagee must be obtained in advance, or an order will not be effectual.

The court can make a transfer of property order only on or after decree nisi, to take effect on or after decree absolute.

Pension rights

There has been increasing concern about women being potential losers over pensions when their marriage breaks up. This is particularly the case if:

- the wife has spent her time largely looking after the children and home and has either no, or relatively low, earnings from which to make her own savings for retirement, *or*
- a more mature wife, who fully expected to share in the benefits of her husband's pension, and again has devoted herself to children

and the home, finds she is divorced and will have insufficient time to build up a reasonable pension, even if she were able to get a job of her own.

Pensions present complex legal and mathematical problems and you need good legal advice on these issues. From 1 December 2000, for divorces filed on or after that date, there are various ways in which the courts might take account of any pension rights outlined below – (for clarity, we have assumed the wife is being compensated for loss of the husband's pension rights, but the options are equally valid where a husband requires compensation from the wife):

- giving the wife a bigger share of other assets to offset the loss of her interest in the husband's pension
- giving the wife a lump sum to compensate her for the loss of specific benefits, such as the right to receive a widow's pension
- earmarking part or all of a future lump sum payable on death of the husband for payment to the ex-wife
- requiring the husband to swap part of his pension for a lump sum at retirement (called 'commutation') and earmarking part or all of that lump sum to the ex-wife
- earmarking part of the husband's pension (either a future pension or one currently being received) to be paid to the wife, or
- 'pension-sharing' – in other words, transferring part of the husband's pension rights to the wife.

For divorce proceedings started before 1 December 2000, only the first five options are available to the courts.

Compensating

In general, compensating (also known as offsetting), that is, giving one spouse a greater share of the family home or a larger lump-sum payment in recognition of the loss of his or her pension rights, is to be preferred by the courts to earmarking (see below), which will be used only if no assets are available to compensate. Two considerations are likely to reduce any payment made. The first is the fact that the receiving spouse will be getting a certain amount right away and will therefore not be subject to uncertainties about the performance of the funds invested or whether the pension member might die before retirement or soon after. Second, the lump sum or assets transferred (often the family home) is likely to be tax free (whereas earmarked pension payments will bear income tax on current rates of between 0 and 40 per cent).

Earmarking

Under the Pensions Act 1995, which covers petitions filed since 1 July 1996, courts must now take pension rights into account. They have the power to redistribute other assets as compensation for loss of pension rights or to order pension trustees or managers to 'earmark' part of the pension to be paid at retirement to the ex-wife, in other words to allocate a share of the husband's pension (and any tax-free cash he takes at retirement) to the wife for the future. (The courts can also order part of a lump sum payable on death to be paid to a non-pension member.) The first option – to compensate – is what courts will do by preference, but if other assets are not available, the courts do have the earmarking powers and are given teeth to use them.

The husband can also make parallel applications for his wife's pension to be, for example, earmarked in his favour, but as this situation is less common, in the rest of this section we assume that it is the husband who has the pension rights and the wife who wants to claim.

The part which is earmarked can either be a percentage of the whole pension or a fixed sum. Once it starts to be paid – namely, when the husband retires – the earmarked pension will be paid directly from the pension scheme itself to the ex-wife. The court has been able to make full earmarking orders both for a lump-sum and annual payments payable from April 1997, and can specifically make the pension trustees pay up, overriding their discretion.

The earmarking approach is an improvement on the previous system, but it still suffers from a number of drawbacks.

- Valuing the pension is still problematic, and the designated cash equivalent transfer value (CETV, see *Pension valuations*, below) which the courts must now use in working out pension values undervalues occupational schemes, according to pensions experts.
- The earmarked pension will be payable only as long as the ex-wife does not remarry – on remarriage she would lose the maintenance-style pension previously and provisionally assigned to her (although probably not a lump sum). An earmarked pension will also cease on the death of the husband or ex-wife.

- The health (and remarriageability prospects) of each of the spouses will also have to be examined for a realistic appraisal of how earmarking might work in practice.
- There are also tax considerations. The Inland Revenue treats earmarked periodical payments orders as being taxable in the hands of the payee at the payer's marginal rates. So while other forms of maintenance are not taxable in the hands of the payee, earmarked periodical payments will be.
- The wife cannot begin to draw her earmarked pension until the pension benefits are payable – usually when the husband retires. This would be a particular problem where the wife is older than the husband or if the husband decided to defer his pension beyond normal retirement age.
- If the husband has already retired or is close to retirement, the system could work fairly equitably. But if the husband is many years from retirement, he could stop the pension plan or leave the pension scheme in which the rights are earmarked – if he changes job, for example. The wife would then have the right only to a share of an early leaver pension, which will be substantially lower than the retirement pension would have been if contributions or membership had continued. A new pension arrangement started by the husband after the divorce settlement would not be affected by the earmarking order.
- If the husband dies before his planned retirement, the wife may receive nothing at all. Moreover, if he remarries and divorces, perhaps more than once, before retirement, what share the first ex-wife would be entitled to is not clear. If, for instance, she had been awarded 30 per cent of the pension payable to him, it is not yet known whether she would get 30 per cent of the whole pension or 30 per cent of what is left of the pension after his second ex-wife (if he remarries and re-divorces) claims an earmarked portion too. The law may become clearer once some test cases give enlightenment about the courts' approach.
- Earmarking flies in the face of the clean-break approach favoured by the courts; an earmarking order in effect keeps a couple tied together financially after their divorce even if they have no other ongoing maintenance or other financial obligations.
- The ingenuity of pension trustees (or that of their lawyers) should not be underestimated. Considerable legal fees are already being

spent to see whether there are any loopholes in the new law that will allow trustees to hold on to their discretionary powers and pension scheme holders to keep their hands on their full pensions. As cases come up before the courts to test the limits of their powers, expect to see strong legal arguments testing any potential weaknesses.

It is not just the future retirement pension that an ex-wife or ex-husband may lose on divorce. Most pension schemes pay lump sums or pensions (called 'death-in-service benefits') to widows and widowers if the pension holder dies before retirement. The tax rules still allow these payments to be made to the ex-spouse after a divorce, but the trustees or plan-providers generally have the power to decide who receives them and will tend to follow the wishes of the scheme-holder or plan-holder. If the ex-spouse can show that he or she was financially dependent on the deceased pension-scheme holder – say receiving maintenance payments from the latter – he or she may qualify for some or all of the dependants' benefits, but that will also depend on who else is making a claim.

However, it is possible under the Pensions Act to apply for a lump sum order in respect of a lump sum payable on death. The courts can also require the spouse with pension rights to nominate the person to whom a lump sum payable on death is paid, if he or she has the power to do so.

Pension-sharing

For divorce proceedings started on or after 1 December 2000, the courts have a further option: pension-sharing (formerly termed pension-splitting). Unlike earmarking, pension-sharing is expected to a fairly popular option. The government estimates there could be 35,000 to 65,000 pension-sharing orders a year.

Following the style above, in this section we look at the new rules in terms of a husband's pension rights being shared with his ex-wife. But the same rules apply where, less commonly, a wife's pension rights are shared with her ex-husband.

Under pension-sharing, the value of the husband's pension rights is calculated using the CETV method (see *Pension valuations*, below). Part of that value is then transferred to the wife to fund her own pension. The value of the husband's rights is reduced by the sum transferred.

In England and Wales, the amount transferred is a given percentage of the CETV. In Scotland, the amount transferred may be a percentage or alternatively a specified cash sum.

There are two types of transfer:

- **internal transfer** The money stays in the same pension scheme to which the husband belongs and the wife becomes a member of that scheme. She gets pension rights according to the rules of the scheme
- **external transfer** The money is moved to another pension scheme, generally chosen by the wife. This might, for example, be a stakeholder scheme or another employer's scheme to which the wife already belongs. She will then get a pension in accordance with the rules of the new plan or scheme.

If the husband works in the public sector, usually only an internal transfer will be allowed. This is because many public-sector pension schemes – for example, for the police, civil servants and teachers – are unfunded, which means that any payments out of them are met using taxpayers' money. The government was reluctant to risk an immediate tax burden caused by transfer payments from these schemes, so it drew up the rules to prohibit external transfers in the case of unfunded public-sector schemes. Where (less commonly) a public-sector scheme is funded – for example, the local authority superannuation scheme – external transfers must be offered.

Where the husband is a member of a private-sector scheme which is funded (as is normally the case), external transfers must be offered and internal transfers may be available. An unfunded private-sector scheme does not have to offer external transfers.

The government has estimated that three-quarters of transfers will be external ones.

It is important to note that a court cannot make an order to 'earmark' and 'share' the same pension. You cannot, for instance, have an order for a share in the lump-sum death-in-service benefit **and** share the other rights. Key features of the new scheme are:

- the court can direct that a very wide range of pension rights be shared, including any SERPS pension, additional voluntary contributions and contracted-out pension rights. However, pension-sharing cannot apply to the state basic pension (which is already subject to special rules on divorce), state graduated pension, widow's and widower's pensions or lump-sum death benefit

- there will be no automatic 50:50 split – each case will be determined (or settled) on its merits – there are likely to be no minimum requirements, so in theory the court could order, say, a 10:90 split
- the valuation method will still be the CETV method – even though many pensions experts argue that it undershoots the true value especially of occupational schemes
- the husband's pension and other benefits are normally treated as if they have not been reduced when it comes to working out how much extra he can pay into the scheme to top up his benefits. However, by concession, the reduction due to the pension-sharing is recognised if he earns less than a given amount (£22,950 in 2000–1) and he is not a 'controlling director' of the company which runs the scheme
- the pension and other benefits received by the wife are ignored when it comes to working out how much she can pay into a pension scheme
- the pension scheme managers or trustees can make reasonable charges for the costs involved in administering a pension sharing order. These are expected to be around £750 to £1,000 per case
- the ex-wife's rights to a pension are not dependent on uncontrollable factors, such as her ex-husband's retirement plans or premature death
- pension-sharing makes a clean break between the husband and wife.

Pension valuations

Pensions can often be the most valuable matrimonial asset, especially if the family home has minimal equity. (For information on the different types of pensions see Chapter 13.) However, there can be problems in working out exactly how valuable a pension is. One of the main ones is to do with the period of time that should be taken into account when valuing a pension. Although the Pensions Act 1995 updated the law on pensions in divorce generally, it is silent about what period of the pension should be valued. In Scotland the law is clear – a husband or wife is entitled to a share of the contributions made by a spouse only during marriage. In England and Wales a younger spouse will potentially be able to claim a share of the entire pension pot accumulated during a partner's whole career. It is possible that later on the courts may limit claims to pensions built up during marriage, but at present this is one of the uncertainties faced under the current legislation.

The next problem is how best to value a pension. Personal pension plans, in which regular amounts are paid in to the pension, are in some ways similar to a savings account and thus can be more easily valued. The same is true of those occupational schemes which work on the same basis (called 'money purchase' because you build up a fund of money and then use it to buy a pension). However, working out the CETV for the pension from an occupational salary-related scheme is more complicated because in such scheme, you do not have your own pot of pension money. Instead you are promised a pension which is worked out according to a formula and is usually based on your pay at or near retirement, the number of years you have been in the scheme and a fraction (called the 'accrual rate', often one-sixtieth) which you get for each year. In general, the CETV ignores the future. It is normally based on your pay when you have the pension valued rather than at retirement, which may be many years away, and it looks only at the years you have clocked up to date, not any future years you might build up in the scheme. Once your pension is estimated, assumptions are made about how investments might grow between then and your retirement. This allows the pension to be expressed as a cash lump sum – the CETV. This is the lump sum which, if invested now, might be expected to provide enough cash by retirement to buy the pension.

Regulations issued in 1996 to implement the Pensions Act 1995, (which, among other things, allows for a share of a pension to be 'earmarked'), laid down that the value of a pension would be the CETV. The Welfare Reform and Pensions Act 1999 applies the same approach to pension-sharing. Pensions experts advise that this valuation method can undershoot the real value because it crystallises the value of the pension rights now, ignoring how they would have changed in the remaining time until retirement. So, as pointed out above, with a salary-related pension, the CETV ignores future increases in earnings and, with a money purchase pension, hefty transfer charges might be deducted. This means that CETV tends to favour the person giving up the pension rights and short-change the person (usually the ex-wife) being compensated or given a share of the rights.

Most computerised pension schemes can produce a CETV fairly simply. A fee for preparing the valuation by the pension trustees or managers will have to be paid by the pension scheme holder (or some-times the spouse); the amount is likely to be set by each individual plan.

Once the basic information about the pension is available, if the pension is potentially valuable, solicitors will often advise their client to instruct an actuary to prepare a valuation. Pension valuations can be prepared from instructions given jointly by the husband's and wife's solicitors. The Divorce Corporation,★ for example, charges £250 plus VAT for a combined actuarial calculation of pension rights for compensating and suggested earmarking, which it prepares on an even-handed basis. It states that the same valuation will be provided whether instructions are given by the husband or the wife. The advan-tage of joint instructions are that later arguments over pension value will be minimised.

The Divorce Corporation will accept instructions only from other professionals such as solicitors. Other firms which offer pensions valuations could be contacted, for example via the Society of Pension Consultants★ or the Association of Consulting Actuaries.★ Again fees will be charged – check how much before asking a pensions specialist to prepare a report.

Secured payments

The courts have the power to order that periodical payments be 'secured' by a capital asset that the paying party possesses. A secured order is rare and is relevant only where there is a lot of available capital. It should not be contemplated without legal advice. A secured order can last for the life of the recipient because it survives the death of the payer; no other maintenance order does so.

The clean break

The courts have the explicit obligation, when making an order for financial relief, to consider whether it would be appropriate to make an order which would lead to each spouse becoming financially inde-pendent of the other 'as soon after the grant of the decree as the court considers just and reasonable'. They can (although this is rare) make a clean break even in the face of adamant opposition from a wife (or, very rarely, a husband).

The ability of the husband to finance a clean break may, however, have been adversely affected by his having to pay higher levels of child support under the CSA formula. Child support levels will usually have to be worked out first, and only then can the husband's ability to make a clean break be assessed. Clean breaks apply only in respect of spousal maintenance, never for maintenance for the children.

Where an order for periodical payments is to be made to a spouse and a clean break might be appropriate, the court should consider whether the payments should be for a specific period only and then cease. The specified period should be what, in the opinion of the court, would be sufficient to enable the recipient to adjust without undue hardship to the ending of his or her financial dependence on the other spouse. In practice, courts are reluctant to look more than two or three years into the future, and only if the future is pretty clearly foreseeable will a limited term order be appropriate. Time-limited periodical payments are much less likely to be appropriate where there are dependent children than, say, where there has been a short, childless marriage and the wife requires just one or two years of financial assistance while she re-establishes herself.

A clean-break settlement is sometimes fair and reasonable especially if one spouse buys out the other's maintenance claims with an additional capital payment. The availability (or more usually the non-availability) of funds is critical. The court will look at all the circumstances, including the wife's prospect of remarriage and any future earning capacity.

In cases involving wealthier couples, the amount of the lump sum which could buy out the wife's maintenance is worked out according to a 'Duxbury' calculation. In essence the idea is that a lump sum will be calculated which will be sufficient to meet the wife's needs for the rest of her life on the basis that she draws capital as well as income. The calculations are complex – they try to take account of foreseeable changes such as reductions in expenses when the children leave home (when a wife may move to a smaller house). In general Duxbury calculations tend to work only where there is a large amount of free capital available and where the wife is not too far off retirement age – the cost of buying out a young wife's claims with a Duxbury calculation is usually prohibitive. A wife of 42, for example, with a further life expectancy of 43 years would need to be paid £178,000 to give her an annual income of £10,000, whereas if she were ten years older, at 52, with a life expectancy of another 33 years, the lump sum Duxbury calculation would fall to £144,000. Of course, a wealthy wife may be ordered to pay a lump sum to her husband, perhaps to enable him to buy a house, just as a wealthy husband can be ordered to pay a lump sum to his wife.

Since July 1996, with the new law on pensions earmarking in place, even if a clean break is ordered, the court can still award a wife a share of her husband's pension, payable on retirement, thus eroding the 'pure' clean-break principle.

A clean-break order should include a provision to prevent one spouse from having a claim on the estate of the other spouse after death under the Inheritance (Provision for Family and Dependants) Act 1975, as amended by the Law Reform (Succession) Act 1995.

The courts have a duty to investigate whether it is realistic to expect a husband and wife to be moving towards financial independence, but where there are dependent children, this may very well not be in their interests, and the courts have a specific duty to give first consideration to the welfare of children. It cannot be over-emphasised that the clean-break approach can extend only to the parties in the marriage, not to provision for children.

Advantages and disadvantages

The main advantage of a clean-break order is certainty, in terms of both the husband knowing that his maintenance obligations to his ex-wife will end and the wife knowing that she will receive a specific sum of money. It can also encourage both parties to create independent lives after the divorce. However, following the implementation of the Child Support Act 1991, even if a clean break and lower levels of child maintenance are agreed now, the CSA is likely to have the right to review child support in the future and can raise the levels in line with the formula.

Another disadvantage for the recipient is that the capital awarded is unlikely to produce as high an annual income if invested at standard rates as the maintenance provision that there might otherwise have been. Moreover, the lump sum cannot later be increased to keep pace with inflation or a husband's financial fortune. If something un-expected happens, such as the wife falling ill and being unable to work, she will not be able to look to her ex-husband for support. Similarly, the spouse making the payment must remember that it is possible that the recipient could get remarried a short while later. If he or she were receiving maintenance, this would end on the remarriage.

Even if there is no capital other than the net equity of the family home, a couple may prefer the wife to receive all or a disproportionate part of the net equity and to have her maintenance claims dismissed. But this is not always a realistic solution and must be considered very carefully. The court will be unwilling to provide for a clean break in circumstances where the wife's only means of support is income support. Where the marriage has been long-standing and the wife is in, say, her mid-fifties without ever having worked outside the home during the marriage and without reasonable prospects of working in the future, it is highly unlikely that the court will willingly grant a clean-break order.

Applying to the court for an order

In 1999 the civil justice system underwent a complete overhaul. Many new developments were introduced under what are referred to as the Woolf reforms. Matrimonial law largely fell outside the scope of these reforms but the new ethos has affected the approach of the courts, and the changes to financial relief (ancillary relief) proceedings that were introduced in June 2000 reflect these changes.

The effect of the changes is to give the courts more control over the progress of litigation. Strict timetables for the progress of cases have been introduced. The courts want to keep a close eye on the level of costs so that they do not escalate unreasonably. Parties are encouraged, even obliged, to be frank about their negotiating positions, rather than play cat and mouse. For the same reason, simultaneous exchange of information is prescribed; this takes the place of the old system of one party filing an affidavit, then the other replying with his or her side of the story, then a reply to that and so on. The content and format of the initial exchange of information is also laid down.

As pointed out, the purpose of all of this is to try to reduce the length of time spent on litigation, and the costs. The judge in a case will try to mediate a solution, or may refer the couple to mediation. Moreover, the parties themselves can decide at any point to settle the matter.

Making the application

If you want to apply to the court for an order, you start by filling in a Form A (which is available from the court or the Court Service web site★) and filing it (and two copies of it) at the court where the divorce proceedings are taking place. The fee is £80 (the usual exceptions apply). The form simply notifies the court and your spouse that you intend to proceed with the financial application. You tick boxes to show which of the orders you intend to apply for:

- an order for maintenance pending suit
- a periodical-payments order
- a secured provision order
- a lump-sum order
- a property-adjustment order
- a pension-sharing/attachment order.

If you intend to make an application for periodical payments for the children, you have to tick boxes to show why the court has jurisdiction and the CSA does not.

By contrast with the old procedure you do not have to file evidence of your financial position at the time that you make the application. This comes later (see below).

It is important to bear in mind that once you have filed Form A you are on a tight time scale with which you must comply. It would be prudent to make sure that you are going to be able to get together all the financial evidence that you need in time before you start.

The 'First Appointment'

Once the court receives Form A it will fix what is officially known as a First Appointment. This must take place between 12 and 16 weeks from the date on which you filed Form A. The court will not change the date for any trivial reason, and it can be changed only with the court's permission or with the consent of your spouse.

Before the First Appointment

At least seven weeks (35 days) before the First Appointment you must exchange with your spouse full details of your financial position on Form E. This form is extremely detailed, and it must be completed thoroughly. (See below, on disclosure.) You, or your solicitor, will need to contact your spouse, or his or her solicitor to agree the date on which the forms are to be exchanged. Depending on the date on which the court fixes the First Appointment, you will have between five and nine weeks to complete Form E. This may seem a long time, but the detail that the form requires means that it is going to be quite a task unless your financial position is very straightforward. If you are the applicant, it makes sense to start compiling the information as soon as possible. If you think that your spouse is going to be an applicant, you should also be putting the information together as soon as you can. It will save you solicitors' time and costs if you can do much of this yourself.

Form E has to be sworn (like an affidavit) and filed at court, as well as being served on the other party.

At least two weeks (14 days) before the First Appointment, you must file at court, and serve on the other party:

- a statement of the apparent issues between you
- a chronology (which will set out the dates of the principal significant events in your marriage such as births, job changes, separations and so on)
- a questionnaire or a statement saying that you do not intend to use one
- a notice on Form G saying whether you are in a position to proceed to a Financial Dispute Resolution (FDR) meeting, giving your reasons for saying so.

What happens at the First Appointment

You and your spouse have to attend the court. If you have solicitors, they will be there too. If you do not attend, you can be penalised in costs. (The costs sanction applies to any non-compliance with the new procedures.)

At the First Appointment the judge may take the view that there is a need for further information to be provided by one or both parties and will make orders ('directions') about what needs to be filed and when the next hearing will be. If enough information has been filed and you and your spouse are in a position to agree a settlement, a final order can be made. If financial issues cannot be sorted out in this way, the judge can either adjourn the case so that you can go to mediation, or refer the case to an FDR appointment.

Financial Dispute Resolution appointment

This type of appointment is new to family proceedings (except in areas where the scheme was piloted). Again, both you and your spouse should attend (unless the judge orders otherwise). The hearing is described as 'informal', which means that the judge can run it as he or she thinks best. Each judge will have a slightly different style of dealing with the matter, so it is impossible to describe exactly what will happen. It is intended that the appointment will give an opportunity for negotiation and discussion. The judge will attempt to find a settlement that both parties feel that they can agree to.

One of the new aspects of the FDR is that at least seven days before the hearing the applicant must file at the court a bundle of all offers and proposals that have been made or received by either party; this applies whether the offers were made 'without prejudice' or not. If the case does not resolve at the FDR, this bundle will not be shown to the judge at the final hearing, who will in any case be a different judge to the one who conducted the FDR. This means that the 'privileged' aspect of 'without prejudice' correspondence is preserved.

The expectation is that most cases will be settled at (or before) the FDR. But if you still cannot resolve matters, the judge will set the case down for a final hearing, at which the judge will hear all the evidence and make an order in the usual way.

Costs disclosure

The new rules require both parties to come to each hearing with a statement of the costs that they have incurred so far. This has to be filled in on Form H. The court will expect the costs to be 'proportionate' to the issues in the case. You and your solicitor will be criticised if you have run up costs out of all proportion to the money that you hope to recover.

Disclosure

It is a fundamental principle in dealing with financial matters that both parties should give 'full and frank disclosure' of their individual financial positions, supplying documentary proof where appropriate. Before the new rules this was done by means of affidavits filed first by the applicant, then by the respondent. Further affidavits could be filed as well. If either party thought that information supplied by the other was defective, he or she could ask for further questions to be answered, or documents supplied by sending a 'questionnaire'. This was largely unregulated; parties could draw up affidavits in a form they chose and ask as many questions as they liked. Inevitably in some cases, the paperwork and costs grew out of all proportion to the assets involved as parties and their solicitors lost sight of the total picture in the hunt for some elusive fact or detail.

Form E

Under the new rules disclosure of financial matters is very much more controlled. Form E lays down what information should be filed. The form should have the following documents supplied with it:

- a valuation of the family home (if obtained in the last 12 months)
- a copy of your most recent mortgage statement
- bank statements for all your accounts for the last 12 months
- surrender-value quotations for any life policies
- if you have a business, accounts for the last two years and any other document that supports a valuation
- last three payslips and most recent P60
- if you are in a partnership, accounts for the last two accounting years.

You can attach any other documents that explain or clarify any information given on the form.

Because the form is exchanged simultaneously with your spouse, you may well find that the two of you have duplicated some of this information.

Questionnaires

Once you have read your spouse's Form E you may feel that he or she should provide more information about his or her assets. You can still send a questionnaire to elicit this information. However, instead of sending it simply to your spouse, it has to be filed at the court, and you have to notify the court that you want to do this, at least two weeks before the First Appointment (as described above). If you do not feel the need for a questionnaire, you have to state that you are not going to use one.

Because of the tight time scale you may only have five weeks to draw up a questionnaire or decide that you do not want one, if you have exchanged Form E at the last possible date. At the First Appointment the judge will be able to rule on any aspect of the questionnaire and say whether the questions are reasonable and should be answered.

Further disclosure

No further evidence of finances can be filed or sought without the leave of the court. The implication of the new rules is that it will be hard to get leave unless you can make out a convincing case that information has been withheld **and** that it will make a material difference to the outcome of the case.

Expert evidence

Occasionally you may need the evidence of a third party before the court. If this is an expert, such as a valuer, the court will give directions on this and if possible both you and your spouse should instruct the expert. This is to prevent each party producing partisan witnesses whose fees will increase the overall costs. The expert is expected to address the report to the court and the evidence can be submitted only with the permission of the court.

Third parties

You may feel that it is important to get evidence from a third party – the most likely situation is where you want to find out about the finances of your spouse's new partner. Your spouse cannot be compelled to produce evidence about him or her, and in any case may claim not to know any details. The other person cannot be compelled by the court to file a Form E because he or she is not a party to the proceedings. But the court does have power to require a third party to attend the court with documents, which can then be inspected. To obtain such an 'inspection appointment' you have to file an affidavit explaining what documents you want to see and why they are relevant to the case. It is then for the judge to decide whether it would be appropriate to order the attendance of the third party. Mere curiosity on your part would not be sufficient.

The final hearing

If you are unable to resolve the case at the First Appointment, the FDR appointment, or by negotiation as the case goes on, then the matter will come to a final hearing. This will be, like the other appointments, in private, 'in chambers' as lawyers sometimes say.

You both have to go into the final hearing having 'shown your hand' about the orders that you want the court to make. You have to file at court and serve on your spouse a statement that sets out, with the details of the amounts involved, the orders that you want the court to make for you. If it was your application in the first place, you have to file and serve this statement at least 14 days before the hearing. The respondent has to file his or her statement within seven days of receiving yours.

At the hearing both you and your spouse will have an opportunity to state your case, either in person or through your solicitor or barrister. Either of you may be asked to give evidence on oath, if only to bring the financial disclosure up to date. The convention is that the applicant gives evidence first and can then be cross-examined. Then the other party gives evidence and can be cross-examined, if appropriate.

If you have to give oral evidence, here are some tips:

- always listen carefully to any questions put to you
- answer the questions clearly and simply, and do not ramble or mumble
- try to answer the question, and not what you think is the motive behind it
- remember that the person whom you need to convince is the district judge (or judge), not the lawyers. It can be helpful to turn slightly towards the judge and answer him or her directly after a question has been put to you by a lawyer
- take a deep breath before answering any questions and try to speak slowly: often the other party's solicitor and the district judge (as well as your solicitor, if instructed) will be taking notes of what you are saying
- avoid becoming heated or emotional in response to the other party's questions; the district judge will want to confine his or her enquiry to the facts.

If any witnesses are called, they will not be able to come into the district judge's room until they give evidence – sometimes this may entail a long wait. Witnesses should give evidence only about matters that have been raised before the court hearing. You should not spring something on the other side (although where a new piece of evidence has only just come to light and is relevant in the proceedings, the district judge will usually use his or her discretion to hear it).

When oral evidence is not asked for, neither side is subject to cross-examination, but both sides can make submissions or comments after the affidavits are read.

Negotiating a financial settlement

You may be relieved to know that only a small percentage – about 10 per cent – of divorce cases end up in a full-blown battle over money. The rest are settled by agreement at some stage along the line: at the very beginning of the separation (or before), or even on the steps outside the court doors just before the final financial hearing is to be held. The fact that mediation is now more widely available and can be used by families who want to save on legal costs also offers another option to resolve family disputes speedily, efficiently and effectively.

Whenever an agreement is made, the family as a whole is likely to save significantly on legal costs. There are rare cases where a spouse pretends to make an agreement while in reality he or she is determined to drag out the process of resolution, but as a general rule making agreements will save you money, and the earlier you can do so the more money will be saved on legal fees.

Although you have the option of keeping your agreements oral and relying on your spouse's sense of honour, the problem is that such agreements have a habit of unravelling over time as one or other spouse claims no longer to be able to 'remember' the terms. So, to protect yourself properly, an agreement should be drawn up in the form of a separation agreement or deed, or, better still, a consent order made by the court. If you have reached a settlement through media-tion, this will usually be drawn up in the form of a 'Summary' or 'Memorandum of Understanding'. This again should be translated, usually by solicitors, into a court order which you seek from the court to make the settlement financially watertight.

In your negotiations, your objective must be to achieve a workable financial settlement with your spouse. If you have carefully prepared an overall summary of your financial circumstances (as described in Chapter 2) and calculated how a division of your income and assets might work out in practice, you will have a good idea as to whether the proposals that you intend to make are realistic or not.

Proposals

Once you are satisfied that you have a clear view of the overall financial picture and that both sides have fully disclosed their financial positions to each other, you can put forward proposals for settlement on a 'without prejudice' basis. This means that if the proposals do not result in settlement and litigation does follow, they cannot be referred to in a final hearing before a court (as described earlier, they must be disclosed to the FDR appointment judge). Any 'open' negotiation (as opposed to one that is 'without prejudice') you (or your solicitor) have with your spouse would place you in a vulnerable position in that he or she could later use in court any admissions you have made. Accordingly, if your solicitor is conducting negotiations for you, he or she will automatically head proposals with the words 'without prejudice'; if you are conducting negotiations yourself, you should do the same.

Usually it is the spouse who will be paying maintenance and/or a lump sum who puts forward the first proposals; frequently (but not always) these result in counter-proposals from the other spouse. Generally, the eventual agreement will fall somewhere between these two sets of proposals.

You may, therefore, be tempted to pitch your first proposals very low (or very high as the case may be). This is, on the whole, not a good idea. Although whatever proposals you make may be interpreted as just an opening bid, unrealistic proposals will sour the atmosphere and prolong the agony, with inevitable consequences in terms of both acrimony and legal costs. They are also likely to prompt your spouse into being equally unrealistic when it comes to counter-proposals, and you will be faced with what appears to be an unbridgeable gulf.

Calderbank offers

Calderbank offers, which are named after the case in which they were originally approved, are offers that are made 'without prejudice', but where the writer reserves the right to reveal the contents of the offer to the court at the final hearing, when the question of costs comes to be decided. If at the end of the case the applicant is awarded less by the court than was in the offer, he or she will be made liable for the costs from 28 days after the date that the letter was written. The justification for this is the argument that the applicant should have settled for that offer and not run up the subsequent costs.

When you are in the process of negotiating a settlement, you may get to the point where it is appropriate to write a Calderbank letter, or you may receive one. It should be a realistic offer, intended to be taken seriously. You need to think about what the court is likely to order and pitch the level of the proposals accordingly. A Calderbank letter should not be written until the process of financial disclosure is completed. The offer should cover all the aspects of the settlement. If disclosure is not complete or the settlement proposed does not cover some essential points, it is open to the recipient to argue that it could not be accepted for these reasons alone, and so the protection against an order for costs that it is designed to achieve would be ineffective.

If you receive a Calderbank letter, you have to consider whether you are really going to get more if you pursue the case all the way to a final hearing, and whether the costs of doing so will outweigh any increase that you might hope to get. You need to consider this carefully with your solicitor. If you have been acting for yourself up to this point, it would be sensible to take some expert legal advice at this stage.

Recent changes in the rules about costs that have been brought into matrimonial proceedings have added an unwelcome complication to the strategy of sending Calderbank letters. It applies where the respondent (who will generally be the husband) makes a Calderbank offer to settle and the applicant replies with a counter-proposal, also written in the form of a Calderbank letter. If the matter does not settle and goes to court and the applicant does not do better than the original offer and the counter-proposal, not only will she be liable for the costs, but the court can also order her to pay interest (at a rate not exceeding 10 per cent above bank base rate) on those costs as well. This rule has been adopted wholesale from the rules that apply to general claims in the civil court, and does not really suit the family law situation, where the parties are husband and wife: indeed, it may put unwelcome pressure on wives to settle. It certainly reinforces the need for careful legal advice at this point. The best tactic for the wife may be not to make a counter-proposal in a Calderbank form.

Financial agreements and divorce

If couples agree a financial order, rather than have one decided by the court, it is known as a 'consent order'. An application for a consent order involves the drawing up of a draft court order which the parties would like the court to make: this is usually called by lawyers 'minutes of agreement and consent order' or 'minutes of order'. This too can be tailor-made to fit your own requirements (and so can often suit an individual family far better than can a court order made by the court after a battle).

One of the main reasons why lawyers emphasise that a court order should be drawn up instead of leaving an oral or written agreement as it stands is the issue of a clean break. The husband and wife may have amicably agreed to a clean break: that they will divide their assets to give the wife a greater share to compensate her for giving up her claims against the husband for maintenance. But so long as no court has formally ordered a dismissal of the wife's maintenance claims, they can still be activated at a later stage. If she were to fall on hard times or were to see her husband's financial standing improve, she would still be able to make a further claim for maintenance from him (unless she had remarried). Indeed, as long as she had included capital claims, say, in the petition, these would continue, even after remarriage, unless dismissed by the court.

To ensure that the form of a proposed consent order is as watertight, tax-efficient and comprehensive as possible, a solicitor should be instructed to draw up the documents. Note that making a clean-break order by consent will not preclude a future application for child support via the CSA. A 1993 case confirmed the long-standing principle that clean breaks can end only a wife's (or, more rarely, a husband's) right to maintenance and never a parent's responsibility to maintain the children. Some parents who had previously agreed clean-break orders are now finding that the amount of child maintenance, if the CSA becomes involved, dramatically increases beyond their initial expectations. Since 1996 parents can apply for a departure direction in the departure system if the result appears unfair – see Chapter 6.

Drawing up a consent order

An order made by consent, as has already been mentioned, can be much more comprehensive than an order made after a contested hearing. This is because you and your spouse can include undertakings (formal promises) in respect of matters over which the court could make no order: for example, an undertaking by a husband to retain sufficient funds in his own bank account to meet his obligations, to arrange the transfer to his wife of a car owned by a company of which he has control, and so on. Undertakings are enforceable, so make sure that you do not undertake to do anything which might turn out to be impossible.

You can also include 'recitals' setting out the background to the order: for example, that you intend it to be in full and final settlement of any claims. If you have agreed the form of a clean break, it is also wise to include a recital that neither you nor your spouse will be entitled on the death of the other to make a claim against the estate of the deceased spouse under the Inheritance (Provision for Family and Dependants) Act 1975 as amended by the Law Reform (Succession) Act 1995. You can also note 'for the record', for example, that the family home has been sold and the proceeds divided (and, by implication, taken into account in the overall settlement).

Do not forget to include reference to costs, whether for payment by one party of the other's costs or 'no order for costs', and deal, too, with orders for costs 'reserved' on any interim applications where there has been some litigation between the husband and wife before reaching the stage of applying for a consent order.

The words 'liberty to apply' are sometimes written into the wording of consent orders. This confirms that either spouse can go back to the court for implementation of the order. It does not allow either party to seek in any way to vary the terms of an order for a lump-sum or of a property-adjustment order.

An application can be made by a couple at any time within the divorce proceedings for an order to be made by consent for maintenance pending suit (temporary maintenance payments made to a spouse until the decree absolute) and for interim periodical payments for children. For a final order (lump-sum, property-adjustment or periodical payments) the application cannot be made before you apply for 'directions for trial' under the special procedure. The order will not be made until the decree nisi has been pronounced and will not become effective until decree absolute.

To apply for an order, you will need to lodge with the court:

- agreed 'minutes of agreement and consent orders', signed by both parties and their solicitors if instructed, in duplicate; only one copy need be signed

- a short synopsis of the family's financial circumstances (known as form M1)
- the court fee – £30 for the consent order.

Form M1. Financial information form on the lodging of a consent order

This form is obtainable from the divorce court office. The information it seeks includes details of:

- the length of the marriage, the age of each party and of any minor or dependent child of the family
- an estimate in summary form of the approximate amount or value of the capital resources and net income and the value of any benefits under a pension scheme (the value should be taken from the most recent valuation provided, if there is one) of each party and of any minor child of the family
- what arrangements are intended for the accommodation of each of the parties and any minor children, and what child support payments are being made
- whether either party has remarried or has any present intention to marry or to cohabit with another person
- where the terms of the order provide for the transfer of property, a statement confirming that any mortgagee of that property has been served with notice of application and that no objection to such transfer has been made by the mortgagee within 14 days from such service
- where the terms of the order provide for payment to be made by the trustees of the pension fund, a statement confirming that the trustees or manager of the pension fund have been served with the application and no objection to such an order has been made by them within 14 days of such service
- any other especially significant matters.

There is a very serious obligation on each party to give full financial disclosure. Just how serious that is was shown by a decision by the House of Lords, the highest appeal court in the country. In the particular case, decree absolute was pronounced in April, terms of agreement were reached in August and about one week later the ex-wife became engaged to be married without telling the court or her ex-husband. On 2 September an order was made by consent; on 22 September, in accordance with the order, the husband transferred his half-share in the home to the wife who, two days later, remarried. In these circumstances, the court order was held to be invalid for lack of proper disclosure and the ex-husband was entitled to have it set aside.

These circumstances were somewhat exceptional. You would not be able to have an order set aside on the grounds of failure to disclose some minor matter which would not have made any difference to the order the court would have made.

Making of the consent order

Once the consent order minutes, financial statement and applications have been lodged at the court, the district judge will review them. Provided the district judge has sufficient information to be satisfied that the proposed terms are reasonable and both parties are in agreement, he or she is likely to accept the agreement and issue a formal consent order as requested.

If the agreement is put forward by solicitors on each side, the district judge may approve it without either spouse having to attend in person, but if you are acting for yourself, the district judge will probably make an appointment to discuss the proposed order with you and your spouse, and may require further evidence, especially if no affidavit has been filed. Approval by a district judge is not a rubber-stamping procedure: in certain cases, where the district judge feels that the order is unfair to either party, he or she may refuse to make it (although, again, this is unlikely if you have negotiated terms through a solicitor).

Effect of a consent order

Consent orders, once made, are as effective as orders made by the court after a full hearing. You can apply to have a consent order set aside only on grounds of:

- fresh evidence that could not have been known at the time
- fundamental mistakes, such as wholly erroneous information, on which all parties, including the court, relied
- fraud (which may include evidence that the other party had no intention of ever abiding by the terms of the order)
- lack of full and frank disclosure if such disclosure would have

resulted in an order substantially different from that which was made

- in certain rare circumstances, where the fundamental basis on which the order was made has been destroyed.

What to do with your court order

If you are acting for yourself, the court will send the court order to you. If you have a solicitor, he or she will be sent the copy and will send it on to you.

Check it

The first thing to do is check it through carefully. Sometimes errors creep in even if the order was made by consent. If there is anything that is the result of a typing or transcribing error, the court can put it right under what is called the 'slip rule'. If there is anything that you do not understand in the order (and with a consent order this is unlikely to happen because you should have seen it before it went to the court), you should discuss it with your solicitor straight away – or go back to the court if you are acting for yourself.

Make sure the order is carried out

You need to make sure that you keep to any promises that you have made or things that you have been ordered to do. There may be time limits that you need to keep to. You do not want to find yourself in breach of the order simply because you have overlooked part of it. Also, you need to check that your spouse keeps to his or her part of the order. It is important to realise that no one else polices the order for you; the court does not have any supervisory role, and your solicitor will not get involved in the implementation of the order unless there is something legal to be done like the transfer of the home.

Arrears of maintenance can quickly build up after an order is made unless the payer makes immediate arrangements and the payee makes sure that payments are made on the correct dates. The longer maintenance remains unpaid, the harder it is to recover, so it is important to be alert at this stage.

Keep the order safe

You must keep the order safe. It would be a good idea to take a photo-copy and put the court copy away securely. Some orders have a long-term effect – such as orders where the sale of the home is postponed until the children grow up. By the time the order takes effect your solicitor may have put away or even destroyed your file (generally, solicitors do not keep matrimonial files for more than six years, though if there is a continuing obligation in the order they should). Courts have been known to lose old files as well, so rely on yourself in this.

After you have obtained a court order

Once you have a court order, it may feel as though there is nothing else to do. However, sometimes one or other party will not be satisfied and will wish to appeal. Alternatively, you may find that your spouse does not do what the order says, so you may consider enforcement. You may also need to sort out your tax position.

Appeals

An appeal against an order or decision of the district judge can be made to a judge by filing a notice of appeal within 14 days. The fee for this is £80. The notice setting out the grounds for an appeal is best prepared by a solicitor. From a judge's decision, an appeal proceeds to the Court of Appeal and thereafter to the House of Lords, although it is very rare (and expensive) for a case to get this far.

Tax, separation and divorce

When spouses separate and where the separation is likely to be permanent, the married couple's allowance is available (in full) for the year of separation (up to the next 5 April) but not in later years. This allowance will go to the husband, unless a claim has been made to transfer half or all of it to the wife. (This date of separation is a question of fact.) Note that the wife can claim half the married couple's allowance as of right – she can get more than half only if she has her husband's agreement.

However, after 5 April 2000, the married couple's allowance was abolished for couples unless one or other spouse was 65 or over on that date.

Additional personal allowances may be claimed by both the husband and the wife in the year of separation if they each have a qualifying child resident with him or her for all or part of the remainder of the year. The definition of a qualifying child means under 16 years (or older, if in full-time education), at the beginning of the year of assessment. 'Resident' is taken to mean that the child is resident with you for all or part of the year – the Inland Revenue's view is that 'resident for part of the year' means more than just the occasional short visit. If the child has his or her own bedroom and belongings at the home and spends significant time there, that would qualify.

If the husband and the wife both claim in respect of the same child, the allowance is apportioned between them, but two allowances are available if each has a qualifying child resident with him or her for at least part of the year. But the available allowance is reduced by any married couple's allowance to which the husband or wife is entitled. The additional personal allowance will continue in later years as long as the conditions are satisfied. If, however, either of them lives with someone else as man and wife, note that only one additional personal allowance is available per household – so if each of the new partners has a qualifying child from a former marriage, only one additional personal allowance is available and it will be given for the youngest qualifying child. This allowance is to be replaced by a new children's tax credit for the tax year 2001–2. Full details have not yet been made public.

Tax and maintenance payments

Tax relief used to be available (to a limited extent) on maintenance payments but this has now been wholly abolished except where one party to the marriage was born before April 1935. In such cases, up to £2,000 (2000–1 figures) will qualify for tax relief. No tax is paid on maintenance payments; they do not form part of your income for tax purposes.

Advising the Inland Revenue of the date of separation

You and your spouse should endeavour to agree the date on which you separated, for tax purposes. You may be able to choose a date between the date of your separation and decree absolute for the date of final separation. Although, given the Finance Act 1988, this is unlikely to have much effect on your maintenance position, it may affect your position with regard to Capital Gains Tax.

Enforcement of payments

Whether you actually receive maintenance following a court order or CSA assessment often depends on the continuing ability of the ex-spouse to make the payments.

Should the payer (usually the ex-husband) fall into arrears with maintenance payments, there are several channels for enforcement, none entirely satisfactory. The sooner steps are taken to enforce the arrears, the better. If arrears are allowed to accumulate, they may prove impossible to recover: courts will not enforce arrears that are more than a year old.

If child support is paid through the CSA, you can ask it to use its collection and enforcement service. The main advantage of this service is that it is likely to be a lot cheaper than going to court. The CSA also has extra powers to trace a disappearing ex-husband, through access to Inland Revenue and Department of Social Security (DSS) records, for example. The CSA can make a deduction of earnings order, like an attachment of earnings order, which takes the maintenance due (plus a small administration fee) directly from the payer's salary. It can also apply for all of the enforcement procedures set out below: the ultimate sanction is committal to prison (although this is likely to be used only rarely). Since April 1996 the CSA has also been able to collect and enforce spousal maintenance.

A defaulting spouse getting away with not paying has traditionally been part of the wider problem of trying to enforce civil debts in general: your chances of success in enforcing a debt may not be particularly high.

An application for enforcement has to be made to the divorce court that made the order (unless the order has been registered at a magistrates' court). The divorce court will not automatically chase arrears and will make an order for enforcement only if asked to. But you can apply to the Family Proceedings Panel (FPP) to register an order in the magistrates' court. The burden is then on the court to chase the arrears.

Enforcement in the county court

The main methods of enforcement are:

- a warrant of execution
- an attachment of earnings order
- a judgement summons for committal to prison.

Warrant of execution

A warrant of execution is an order issued by the county court for the district where the defaulting payer lives for the court bailiff to seize sufficient of the person's goods as will, on sale by auction, discharge the debt shown on the warrant.

Second-hand goods seized and sold at auction rarely produce much money. It is worthwhile getting a warrant of execution only if the goods are in good condition, but, on the other hand, merely the threat of seizure and sale may produce payment.

To get a warrant issued, you must swear an affidavit showing the amount of the arrears, provide a copy of the order, complete the appropriate county court forms and pay the appropriate fee (ranging from £20 to £45).

Attachment of earnings order

Provided that the ex-husband is in regular employment, an attachment of earnings order may be a more effective way of collecting arrears. (Since the Maintenance Enforcement Act 1991, it can be applied for even before arrears build up, at the time the maintenance order is made.) It requires the employers to deduct regular weekly or monthly amounts from his wages and to send the money to the court which will then pay it to the former wife. The amount of deductions can include not only a regular sum off the arrears until they are discharged, but also the ongoing maintenance. (The employers can deduct £1 in addition each time for their pains.) The procedure is no use where the man is unemployed or self-employed.

The application for such an order usually has to be to the divorce county court which made the maintenance order. The appropriate application form (in duplicate), with a copy of the maintenance order, must be supported by an affidavit giving details of the arrears and, if possible, the name of the employers. The court fee for this is now £50.

A notice of the application is served on the ex-husband, together with a form asking for details of his income and financial commitments. The court can ask the employers to supply information about the man's earnings over the past few weeks. The applicant should attend the hearing to give up-to-date evidence about the arrears.

Any order the district judge makes will be on the basis that it must not reduce the man's net income below the protected earnings rate. This is the amount which would be allowed for him and his dependants for income support together with the amount of his rent (or mortgage payments) and rates, and other essential and reasonably long-term commitments, such as other court orders or a hire purchase agreement.

When making an attachment order, therefore, the court may well take the opportunity – after an adjournment, if needed, for a formal application to be made – to adjust the maintenance order to take account of the realities of the situation as disclosed at the time of enforcement proceedings.

Committal to prison

A judgment summons can be issued for maintenance arrears if it can be shown that the ex-husband has the means to pay maintenance and has failed to do so; in theory, he can be sent to prison. A judgment summons is a potentially effective means of enforcing payment of arrears where a man has capital or is self-employed and cannot be touched by an attachment of earnings order.

A request for a judgment summons can be made to any county court convenient to the applicant. CLS funding is not available for a judgment summons in the county court but it is in the High Court. (If the applicant would be financially eligible, the solicitor should consider whether it might be possible to have the case transferred to the High Court.) The county court fee is £80.

The former wife, or her solicitor, should attend the hearing of the judgment summons in order to question the ex-husband in an attempt to prove that he could have paid the maintenance but neglected to do so. If it is proved that he had the means, an order committing him to prison can be made. If an ex-wife is applying for the ex-husband's committal to prison, it is essential that the application is drafted accurately. This is because the courts view committal as a remedy to be used only in extreme circumstances, so the documents that are drafted must be prepared correctly.

Sending an ex-husband to prison is unlikely to produce the money that an ex-wife needs, although the threat of imprisonment may do so. The order can be suspended if he undertakes to pay regular amounts off the arrears together with current maintenance; it can be reinstated if he fails to keep up the payments.

The court is likely to order the ex-husband to pay the costs of the application.

Disappearing ex-husband

If a woman does not know her ex-husband's address, it may be possible to get the DSS to disclose it to the court because his up-to-date address may be known to it through his National Insurance record. A form can be obtained from the court on which the ex-wife should give as much information as she can about his last-known address and employer, his date of birth and National Insurance number. The CSA too has powers to trace a missing parent for child support purposes but it cannot reveal his or her whereabouts unless he or she authorises it to do so. The same duty to keep the address confidential applies to the court.

Enforcement of lump-sum or property-transfer order

An unpaid lump sum may be enforced either by bankruptcy proceedings (unwise, except as a powerful threat) or by a court order that any property belonging to the person ordered to pay be sold to raise the sum. An order for such a sale (for example, of a house or stocks and shares) can be made when the lump sum is ordered. If it is not made then, the usual procedure is to apply for a charging order and then for an order for sale of the asset.

If the transfer of property order is not complied with, the district judge at the court can execute the relevant conveyance in place of the person who is refusing to do so. Application has to be made to the court with the relevant documents prepared for the district judge and an affidavit in support.

It is advisable to have a solicitor's help in such proceedings.

Enforcement in or via a magistrates' court

If an order made in the divorce court is registered in the FPP (magistrates' court), the court staff will summons the payer to appear in court if he or she defaults. The procedure is quicker and simpler than that in the county court.

If the payer is in arrears, the magistrates can order that a disclosure of means be made, and can make one of the following orders:

- attachment of earnings
- distraint on goods (seizure and sale)
- committal to prison (for not more than six weeks).

Changes in circumstances: variations

The capital parts of a final order cannot later be changed (varied) but maintenance provisions can be varied if a change in either spouse's circumstances justifies it.

Variations and the CSA

One potentially useful feature of child support worked out by the CSA's formula is that there is an automatic in-built review of the amount paid every two years, on the anniversary of the assessment. Fourteen days before the anniversary is due, the Agency will send out further forms asking the parents about any changes in circumstances. Once the forms are returned, it will recalculate the amount of maintenance.

As the present formula is based on income support rates, which go up every year, there is an element of inflation-proofing built into the system, although usually the amount of child support actually paid will increase only where the paying parent's income has gone up too. In recent years, given the rises in National Insurance contributions, the amount an absent parent has had to pay may have gone down unless he received a pay rise.

As well as the automatic review every two years, parents can ask the Agency for a change of circumstances review. There is no definition of a change of circumstances, so potentially any life or monetary change will be covered. One parent may, for example, gain or lose a job or go on to part-time working or have a baby. The Child Support Officer will review the case once a review has been asked for (either parent can request one) but the amount paid will change only if certain trigger points are reached. These are where the changes result in a difference (up or down) of:

- in most cases, at least £10 per week
- in cases where the absent parent comes under the protection of the protected income formula, at least £5 per week
- in cases where a qualifying child has left or joined a household of the person with care, at least £1.

In cases where the absent parent is on income support or is otherwise liable to pay the minimum payment (or exempted from paying this), a fresh assessment will be made straight away.

Variations and the courts

With a periodical payments order, even if a spouse had merely a nominal order of, say, 5p per year, which has not expired because of either remarriage or time limit, it is possible for either party to apply to the court to have the order varied – that is, for the amount payable to be increased or decreased, or even for the order to be brought to an end – if it can be shown that there has been a material change in the financial circumstances of either party. You can apply on your own behalf and/or on behalf of your children.

An application for a variation can be made at any time after the decree nisi, even many years later, provided that the recipient has not remarried. There is no limit on the number of variations that can be applied for. However, if the maintenance payable is only for a specified period – for five years for example, under the original order – a variation must be applied for well before the date the maintenance is due to expire.

The court can also vary any agreement that the couple made between themselves, even though they may have agreed not to refer the agreement to the court. In law, any term in an agreement that precludes one party from seeking the assistance of the courts is void.

What cannot be varied

A lump-sum or property-adjustment order cannot be varied, nor can someone go back to court to obtain another one, nor ask for one later if it had not been included in the original application. Although a lump-sum order cannot be varied, if the lump sum is being paid in instalments, the size and frequency of instalments can be varied, but not so as to alter the total of the lump sum originally awarded.

An order which was expressed to be 'final' cannot be varied, and a separation agreement so expressed is likely to be upheld.

If an application for maintenance made previously was formally dismissed by the court, the application cannot be revived later.

Applying for a variation

An application can be made at the divorce court where the order you want to vary was made. If that original court is now inconvenient or if it has not been designated a Family Hearing Centre (FHC), you should ask for the case to be transferred to an FHC more convenient for you. (If the order was registered in a magistrates' court you must apply to the FPP there, not to the court which originally made the order.)

The application should be made on the standard form of notice of application, available from the court office. If circumstances have changed, lodge the application as soon as possible so that any variation of periodical payments can be backdated to the date of the application. You do not have to file an affidavit with the application but you may need to do so in order to spur your ex-spouse into responding to the application. He or she then has to file an affidavit in reply within 28 days. Your affidavit should give up-to-date details of your financial position and why you feel a variation is (or is not) appropriate. The court fee is £80.

Reasons for an application

Major factors that are likely to affect financial orders made in the divorce court are:

- a change in financial circumstances of the payer or payee, including retirement
- remarriage of the payee (a periodical payments order ends automatically, so normally no application is necessary)
- cohabitation of the payee
- remarriage or cohabitation of the payer
- death of either
- either becoming disabled
- children having got significantly older
- length of time elapsed since the making of the last order.

If the court rejects the application for a variation, this does not preclude an application for a variation being made at some later stage if circumstances change again.

The court's approach

The court must consider all the circumstances of the case anew, as well as any change in them, giving first consideration to the welfare of any child of the family under 18. Where child maintenance is concerned, there are likely to be arguments that the amounts paid should increase to levels similar to those produced by the child support formula. The court must also consider whether given the circumstances it would be appropriate to vary an order so that the payments are for only as long as would be sufficient to enable the recipient to adjust without undue hardship to the termination of the payments, or to terminate the payments altogether – a clean break.

Marriage of ex-spouse

If she marries again, a former wife's right to maintenance for herself ceases immediately and cannot be revived against the ex-husband even if she finds herself on her own again – divorced, separated or widowed.

There is no formal requirement for the former wife to tell the previous husband that she has married again, but if she does not do so and he finds out, he can ask her to repay what he has paid her since her new marriage; if she does not pay up, he can sue her for the overpaid money as a debt.

Maintenance payments for children are not automatically affected by the mother's new marriage, but the remarriage of either parent may give rise to a situation in which a variation is justified.

An ex-wife's right to occupy what had been the matrimonial home may cease on remarriage. The terms of the court order may require the house or flat to be sold and the proceeds divided in the specified proportions.

If a man made a lump-sum payment of, say, £20,000, to his ex-wife and six months later heard that she had remarried, he cannot usually apply for a variation. Where a lump sum has been ordered to be paid in instalments and the recipient ex-spouse marries again, instalments have to be continued until the full amount is paid. (Very rarely an application to have the order set aside on the grounds of fraudulent non-disclosure of the intention to remarry may succeed.)

Cohabitation

When a man is paying his ex-spouse maintenance and she cohabits with another man, he may have grounds to apply to the court for a variation of the order. The courts will normally expect it to be proved that there is some permanence to the cohabitation and that it is reasonable to infer that the cohabitant is making some financial contribution. However, the courts are less likely to allow a variation for cohabitation because they are often reluctant to 'absolve' a former husband of his obligations to his ex-wife. If a former wife now has a partner, the court will not automatically assume that she is being completely supported by that partner. It will look at the actual payments that he makes – not at what he could make if he chose to.

If you are paying maintenance to your ex-spouse and children and you set up home with someone who already has children, which involves you in additional expenses, this does not mean that your obligations to your former spouse and children cease. If you apply for a variation, the court will take into account your new obligations even though you are not married, but these will normally be expected to take second place to your obligations to the children of your marriage.

Since the Child Support Act 1991 came into force, any assumed obligations to children who are not your own will in some circumstances be overridden by your obligations to pay child support for your natural children (whether born within or outside marriage).

Retirement

In the case of either the recipient's or the payer's retirement, an application should be made to vary the order by the party who is feeling the pinch. Usually, the court will look at the actual needs and resources of the parties and will be concerned to try to share out the more limited finances fairly. There are, however, extra tax allowances available for those over 65 which could help financially.

Variation of a magistrates' court order

Magistrates' court orders also can be varied, either upwards or downwards, where there has been a change in circumstances. Applications are dealt with by the FPP of the magistrates' courts.

If the couple subsequently divorces, this will not necessarily bring a magistrates' court order to an end. An order made during the marriage will end automatically only if the divorce court substitutes its own order. If not, the magistrates' court order will continue, and also the right to apply for a variation. The order will cease automatically on the recipient's remarriage or death. If the payer remarries, this does not affect the order but may provide grounds for variation.

In the case of a lump sum, the position is different to that in divorce proceedings: there is apparently no restriction on when or how often a lump sum may be applied for (subject to a £1,000 limit each time).

Registered order

If a divorce court order has been registered in the magistrates' court, an application for a variation has to be made to the FPP. The FPP cannot discharge a divorce court order but it can vary the amount of the order on application. No affidavits are required and the magistrates will not have before them the information and calculations on which the district judge at the divorce court based the original order. So, unless they are provided with full up-to-date information about the parties' finances, they may reduce the order unrealistically. A 1990 survey by the DSS showed that magistrates' courts made, on average, weekly maintenance orders of £15, as opposed to £20 by county courts.

When on income support

Maintenance paid by a husband counts in full as income for income support calculations. Unless the maintenance that the husband could pay is more than the total income support payable, there is little point in a woman seeking an increase in her maintenance because she will still only be topped up to the same 'needs' level by the DSS; if maintenance increases, therefore, income support decreases. Occasional presents to an ex-wife or children are not counted as income, so it might be better for the wife to concentrate on getting these, where possible. However, maintenance will be disregarded in calculating entitlement for the working families' tax credit, housing benefit and council tax benefit (as long as the claimant is not in receipt of income support).

Registration of a maintenance order in the FPP is useful when the amount of maintenance is equal to or less than the rate of any income support the recipient would be entitled to. When the order is registered, the payments due under the order can be assigned by the former wife to the DSS, which will then pay her the full amount of her income support entitlement, irrespective of whether any payments are made by the ex-husband or not. This saves anxiety and inconvenience if he does not pay up.

Where the amount of the order is greater than the income support entitlement, payments by the DSS will be limited to the amount of income support the woman is entitled to.

Death of a former spouse

When the recipient dies, the payer can immediately stop any maintenance payments. But any outstanding instalments of a lump sum become due to the deceased's estate, and an unfulfilled transfer of property order can be enforced by the estate.

If the person paying maintenance dies first, the maintenance order comes to an end (unless the order was for secured payments). The former spouse may be able to apply to the court under the Inheritance (Provision for Family and Dependants) Act 1975 (as amended by the Law Reform (Succession) Act 1995) for financial provision out of the deceased's estate (unless the court has previously ordered that such a claim shall not be made). An application can also be made by or on behalf of a child. The application must be made within six months of probate being granted – to be safe, make sure the application is lodged as soon as possible.

Other payment on death

Employers' schemes normally provide a lump-sum death benefit (of up to four times the member's pay) when the member of the scheme dies before retirement. After the divorce, it is likely that the ex-husband will have changed the name of the person he wishes to receive the money on his death, so that his ex-wife may not benefit. The decision whether to pay any sum to her used ultimately to rest with the trustees for the pension scheme and some schemes prohibit ex-wives from benefiting in any event. Since the Pensions Act 1995 was brought into force, the divorce court can order the husband to nominate the wife as his beneficiary for the lump-sum death-in-service benefit, and the trustees must accept this.

Chapter 13

Pensions and other money matters

The issue of the courts' new powers to deal with pensions has already been looked at in the previous chapter. In this chapter the different types of pensions, including state pensions, are examined in a little more detail. *The Which? Guide to Pensions* will give you a fuller picture.

Pensions can broadly be divided into state and private pensions (all non-state pensions, such as personal pensions and occupational schemes in the private and public sectors).

State pensions

The state retirement pension consists of two main components – the basic pension and an additional pension currently paid under the State Earnings-Related Pension Scheme (SERPS) which began in 1978 and is to be replaced, from 2002, by the State Second Pension. The rate of the additional pension is based on earnings between the lower and upper earnings limits for National Insurance (NI) contributions paid by class 1 (employed earners). At state pension age, earnings are re-valued in line with the growth in national average earnings.

The current state pension age for women is 60. However, women will be brought into line with men for a standard retirement age of 65 by the year 2020.

Since SERPS was introduced, employers have been able to contract out (that is, provide a pension to their employees in place of SERPS), provided certain conditions have been met. Employees must either participate in SERPS or be fully contracted out. If they are contracted out in a salary-related scheme, the pension payable in respect of periods up to April 1997 must not be less than an amount known as the guaranteed minimum pension (GMP). This is roughly equivalent to the SERPS provision which would have been earned had the employee not been contracted out. For benefits built up from 6 April 1997 onwards, there are no longer GMPs. Instead, the package of benefits from the scheme must, for at least nine members out of ten, be at least as good as the benefits from a 'reference scheme'.

The payment of the basic state retirement pension to a divorced woman depends on her age when she got divorced and on whether it is based on her own or her former husband's NI record (or a combination of both). (Note that the rules regarding basic retirement pension apply equally to men and women, but because women are most often the ones relying on a former spouse's record, the discussion below refers to women.)

A woman divorced when under the state pension age can have her former husband's contribution record added to her own record if that helps her qualify for a state basic retirement pension when the time comes, or gains her a larger pension. She has a choice of formulae to calculate her state retirement pension. Either her former husband's contribution years replace *all* her years up to the time of divorce, or the ex-husband's contribution years replace hers only for the years of the marriage. If, however, she marries again before she reaches the state pension age, she cannot make use of her previous husband's record: she has to rely on her new husband's record or on contributions she had made herself.

The accepted view is that if a woman who is approaching the state pension age can time the decree absolute to follow closely on her reaching that age, she may qualify for a state basic retirement pension immediately, without having to have contributed at all herself. If, however, the decree is made absolute before that birthday, she may have to pay contributions for the intervening period in order to be eligible for a full pension.

A woman divorcing when she is over the state pension age may qualify for a retirement pension immediately after the divorce is made absolute, even if her former husband has not yet retired. If she was already receiving the married woman's lower rate of pension, she may be entitled to have her pension increased to the full rate. The amount of pension she gets depends on the ex-husband's contribution record using the rules described above.

If a divorced woman marries again after the state pension age, any pension based on her previous husband's NI contributions will continue to be paid, despite her second marriage. But if her new husband's record would give her a higher pension, that may be used instead.

The Department of Social Security (DSS) publishes a leaflet (NP46) which gives very brief details of retirement pensions for people who are divorced, but the rules are complex, so ask for help from your local Benefits Agency.

The Pensions Act 1995 made changes in the way war widows are treated. Since October 1995 a war widow who has remarried and then later divorces (or is bereaved) will be entitled to re-claim the war widow's pension.

Private pensions

There are a number of different ways you and your spouse may have chosen to build up a pension. A spouse involved in a divorce may have a complex pension scheme history, and all of it may be relevant to the process of reallocation of pensions: a recent change of job, for example, may mean that there are substantial rights in past schemes but only small ones in the current one. The issue of pensions is too complex to explore at length here, but it is worthwhile knowing about the different types of arrangement available.

Salary-related schemes

This heading covers a number of different types of pensions, but the main feature of them is that the employee's pension is calculated according to a formula. The employer promises to pay the formula pension and must ensure that enough funds are in the scheme to meet the promise. The most common type of defined benefit scheme is the 'final salary scheme'. In such a scheme, the employee's pension is equal to one-sixtieth or one-eightieth of his or her pay at or near retirement multiplied by the number of years in the scheme.

Unfunded public-sector schemes

Most public-sector pension schemes are final salary schemes and work as described above. However, many are 'unfunded'. Instead of the pensions being paid out of a fund of money which has been built up by investing contributions from the employer and employees, in an unfunded scheme, pensions and other benefits are paid out of what-ever resources are available to the employer at the time payments fall due. In the UK, large unfunded schemes are offered only by the government and other public-sector bodies – they are able to do this because, if need be, taxes can be raised to meet the bill. However, private-sector employers sometimes offer unfunded schemes as a way of providing pensions additional to those from a main scheme, especially for higher-paid employees.

Defined contribution (money purchase) schemes

There are variations on the theme, but with all these schemes basically you build up your own pension fund. The amount of pension you eventually get depends on:

- the amount paid in through contributions made by your employer and usually you too
- how well the invested contributions grow – they are likely to be invested mainly on the stock market
- the charges deducted from your fund to cover administration and so on
- the 'annuity rate' at which you can convert the resulting pension fund into pension at the point of retirement.

Additional voluntary contribution arrangements

A member of a pension scheme can pay at least 15 per cent of his or her salary into a pension scheme, but most members' ordinary contribution rates are less. There is thus scope for employees topping up their contributions voluntarily. These additional voluntary contributions (AVCs) can either be paid into a scheme run by the employer or into a free-standing scheme (called an FSAVC scheme) which works broadly like a personal pension (see below). From April 2001, most members of employers' pension schemes earning less than a given amount (initially set at £30,000 a year) can also pay up to £3,600 a year into stakeholder schemes and personal pensions (see below).

Small self-administered schemes and executive pension plans

Normally there are only a few members of such schemes, typically the owners and share-holding directors of a family company. The maximum number of members of a small self-administered scheme is

12, but this limit is not treated as breached if including an ex-spouse under a pension-sharing arrangement takes the total above 12.

All the schemes and plans mentioned so far qualify for favourable tax treatment, but employees can also pay into unapproved pension arrangements which do not have any special tax benefits.

Personal pensions

Typically, these are used where there is no employer's pension scheme available – for example, because you are self-employed or your employer does not run a scheme. However, some employers offer group personal pension schemes (GPPS) through the workplace. These are the same as individual personal pensions, but your employer may have negotiated some special terms, for example, lower charges or more flexible contribution rules.

All personal pensions are money purchase arrangements (see above). Similar schemes, called retirement annuity contracts, could be taken out before July 1988 and many still remain in force. From April 2001, personal pensions, including those which qualify as stakeholder schemes (see below), can be taken out by people who are not working.

Stakeholder pension schemes

The term 'stakeholder' indicates a money purchase pension which meets given standards and conditions which include:

- charges of no more than 1 per cent a year of the value of the pension fund
- flexible contributions
- no extra charges on transfer to another scheme.

Stakeholder schemes go on sale from April 2001. Most will be personal pensions, but money purchase employer schemes can also apply to be registered as stakeholder schemes if they meet the conditions.

Pensions – more safeguards?

The Pensions Act 1995 not only changed the law on pensions in divorce, it also introduced a new regime with the aim of making employer pension schemes safer (reducing the likelihood of another

Maxwell-type pension fraud occurring) and better run. Some aspects of the new regime, together with many other changes affecting pensions, are causing a drift away from salary-related pension schemes towards money purchase arrangements. In general, this will not affect you if you are already in a salary-related scheme, but in many cases now the salary-related scheme is closed to new members and new employees are instead offered a money purchase arrangement.

The key issue to remember in pensions on divorce is that a proper valuation needs to take place so that all parties know the figure placed on the value of either or both spouses' pensions. Valuing pensions is not an exact science – pensions experts argue over which basis is best in different cases. The government has laid down that the 'cash equivalent transfer value' or CETV (that is, what a scheme would pay out to a member if he or she were leaving his or her employment or moving to another pension scheme) is the one to use in divorce. Some experts argue that this undershoots the true value of an occupational pension, particularly where there has been a long marriage, and that a better valuation would be one that is made on the basis that the employee is staying. However, the current position is that in dealing with pensions in divorce, the courts will look at the CETV to work out what the pension is worth. See Chapter 12 for more information about how to value the pension and how the courts deal with pensions on divorce under the new law.

Keeping tabs on an earmarked pension

If someone is awarded a share of a spouse's pension under an earmarking order (see Chapter 12), it is his or her responsibility – not the scheme's – to keep the scheme administrators up-to-date about changes of address. Ideally he or she should write annually to the scheme with a note of his or her address. If the scheme's administrators cannot find him or her, they can pay the earmarked share of the order to the member of the scheme him- or herself.

Pensions mis-selling – the impact on divorce

If someone was advised to transfer pension rights out of an employer's pension scheme and into a personal pension, or to start saving through a personal pension instead of joining an available employer's scheme during the period 29 April 1988 to 30 June 1994, he or she may have been the victim of pensions mis-selling.

The Financial Services Authority (FSA) is responsible for a personal pension review (originally started by the FSA's predecessor, the Securities and Investments Board, and handled by the Personal Investment Authority). The review aims to identify people who were mis-sold a personal pension and as a result have suffered loss. They are entitled to redress, which can take four forms:

- reinstatement in the original employer's scheme
- lump-sum compensation paid into the personal pension
- purchase of replacement benefits, such as life cover, which the employer's scheme provided but the personal pension does not
- an addition to your pension if the pension has already started to be paid.

The pensions review split claimants into two groups. In Phase 1, people who had already retired or were close to retirement were contacted – some 700,000 people in all. Of these, 400,000 have already been offered redress. Offers accepted so far amount to £3 billion. Phase 2 covers younger people. The closing date for applying for a review was 31 March 2000 and the FSA was expecting over 2 million cases. Compensation in each case could be around £4,000 or more.

The review started in late-1994 and the FSA has now put a target date on its completion of 30 June 2002. If, in the meantime, you are seeking a divorce from a spouse affected by the review and still awaiting settlement, make sure that any potential redress is taken into account when the pension rights are valued.

Marriage contracts

The term 'marriage contracts' actually covers two different types of agreement – pre-nuptial agreements, made before a couple marry; and contracts made during marriage, which can include arrangements for division of the property on separation or divorce.

The primary purpose behind both types is to clarify who will get what in the event of marriage breakdown (whether by separation, death or divorce), often by side-stepping or trying to override the courts' powers. The formats can be flexible enough to cover agreements about other areas of concern for a couple (for example, the time they want to start trying to conceive a baby).

The Family Law Committee of the Law Society (which is broadly in favour of marriage contracts) recommends that areas covered should include:

- ownership of income and assets acquired before the marriage and the possibility of making claims against that property whether on death or divorce
- ownership of income or assets acquired in contemplation of or since the marriage
- the form of ownership of assets – as joint tenants or as tenants in common (and if the latter in what proportions)
- the exclusion, if required, of assets below a certain value
- treatment of gifts or inheritance
- ownership of items for personal use, such as jewellery
- liability for tax and debts
- provisions relating to duration, variation, review
- which country's law will govern the agreement
- liabilities for costs and expenses in relation to drawing up the agreement and any ancillary documentation
- methods of resolution of disputes arising from the document
- any other issues of importance to the individual couple.

(Extracted from *Maintenance on Capital Provision on Divorce: Recommendations for Reform of the Law and Procedure made by the Family Law Committee*, May 1991.)

In fact, despite their media popularity, marriage contracts (and even cohabitation contracts) are fairly rare: they tend to be entered into more often by the super-rich. It is doubtful whether a contract will actually achieve a couple's aim of circumventing the courts, especially, say, if one separating spouse later chooses to try to challenge a contract's validity. English courts are resistant to the notion that their powers can be overridden. The following case, sometimes cited in support of the effectiveness of marriage contracts, certainly does not give a surefire answer.

> **Example**
>
> A husband and wife had, as is usual in Brazil, entered into a marriage contract. Could the wife subsequently obtain a divorce and claim for financial relief in England? Held: yes, she could claim. The marriage contract would be included as one of the factors which the court would consider in accordance with section 25 of the Matrimonial Causes Act 1973. (*Sabbagh v Sabbagh*, 1975)

Although this case related to a Brazilian marriage, it still has persuasive effect in the courts here. However, all it really says is that a divorce court is likely to look at the terms of any marriage contract but may not necessarily feel itself bound by them. In subsequent cases, the courts have noted the existence of marriage contracts, but have often by and large ignored them, and have certainly not wished to be bound conclusively by them. In essence a marriage contract will be one of the factors considered by the court but will rarely be the decisive one. If a marriage contract is proved to have been entered into because of fraud, duress or without each party having properly received legal advice, it is unlikely to be worth the paper it is written on.

Other matters to consider

During the course of divorce proceedings, or once these are finally over, you need to consider protecting your overall financial position in the areas of school fees, insurance and wills.

School fees

If your children are privately educated, the cost of funding their school fees will add to the overall juggling of finances on divorce. You may find that you can no longer afford to pay for private education and that the children will need to be moved to local state schools. Finding a new house in a catchment area for a good local state school may need to be a priority.

If you want to enquire about making provision by way of policies or investment schemes to fund the future cost of schooling, consider contacting an experienced broker. Alternatively you may find a local accountant who has experience of recommending tax-efficient funding schemes for parents (or even grandparents) to provide capital or income.

Life insurance

Because maintenance payments will cease when the payer dies, it may be advisable, on divorce, for the spouse who is going to be dependent on payments from the other to take out a life insurance policy on the payer's life.

You have to have an insurable interest in the life of anybody on whose life you wish to take out an insurance. An individual has an unlimited insurable interest in his or her own life and also in the life of his or her spouse, and can insure it for any amount he or she chooses. Apart from yourself and your spouse, you have an insurable interest in somebody only if his or her death would cause you financial loss. You can insure for the amount of money you would lose if he or she dies to provide for your future upkeep. This would apply to an ex-spouse who is receiving maintenance or an earmarked share of pension payments.

The parent who is not looking after the children may want to take out an insurance policy on the life of the parent who is, so that if that parent were to die while the children were still dependent, some money would become available towards the extra cost to the other parent of taking on responsibility for the children.

The policy can be a whole life policy whereby the sum assured is paid out on the death of the insured person. Alternatively, it can be a 'term' insurance which pays out a set sum on death within so many years, taken out for the period of likely dependence. Premiums for term policies are generally lower than for other types of insurance. There are some term insurance policies, called 'family income benefit' policies, where instead of one lump sum on the insured person's death, regular sums are paid (say, every quarter) for the balance of the insured period.

Endowment policies

Endowment policies are insurance policies with a surrender value, usually used as security for paying off a mortgage. Such policies usually provide for the payment of a fixed sum on death to clear the mortgage and for a minimum sum, plus bonuses, to be paid to the policy-holder at the end of the term. Such policies can often be surrendered, but their surrender value is tiny in comparison with the amount payable once the policy matures, and typically amounts to only the monthly sums paid in, less administration costs, and occasionally a bit extra.

The most sensible financial action is to hold on to your endowment policy after divorce until it matures – the cost of taking out a loan for the equivalent of the surrender value will often be cheaper than losing the benefits of the policy. If you really cannot afford to keep it on, enquire about selling the policy via a broker who will auction the policy (if it has about ten years or fewer still to run) and thus raise extra funds, typically adding approximately 50 to 70 per cent to the basic surrender value.

National Insurance

Divorce does not affect a man's NI contribution position. Nor does it affect that of a woman who is paying self-employed (class 2 and class 4) contributions or the standard rate of employed (class 1) contributions at the time. After divorce, each continues to pay as before.

It is not so straightforward for an employed woman who, before the divorce, had been paying the class 1 contributions at the married woman's reduced rate: she is treated as a single person from the date on which the decree is made absolute and therefore becomes liable to pay the full class 1 rate. She should get from her employer a 'certificate of reduced liability' or 'certificate of election' to send back to her local Benefits Agency. The full class 1 contributions will be deducted from her wages from then on. See leaflet CA10 (*National Insurance contributions for divorced women*) available from tax offices.

Anyone whose earnings are below a specified minimum (£67 a week for the 2000–1 tax year) or who is not earning at all, does not have to pay NI contributions, but can pay class 3 contributions voluntarily; these give a woman the right to claim retirement pension. The Inland Revenue's leaflet CA08 (*NIC voluntary contributions*) gives information about making voluntary contributions. (You cannot make voluntary contributions for periods when you were paying reduced-rate class 1 contributions.)

A woman over the age of 60 does not have to pay NI contributions.

There are various free leaflets explaining the position about contributions and benefits in specific circumstances. If you are at all unsure of your position, get advice about NI contributions from your local tax office. Your local Benefits Agency will be able to give you advice on benefits. Alternatively, a Citizens Advice Bureau may be able to help to clear up any queries. Detailed information about contributory benefits under the NI scheme is given in the *Rights Guide to Non-Means-Tested Benefits*, produced by the Child Poverty Action Group.*

Other insurance

You should check that your insurance cover is adequate for the change in your personal circumstances. When your finances are tight, it is tempting to stop paying premiums in order to reduce outgoings. However, this may be a short-term benefit and a long-term loss.

Buildings insurance is insurance against the destruction or damage of your privately owned freehold property. If you have a mortgage on your home, buildings insurance will usually have been arranged by your mortgagee. If you own a leasehold property, your landlord will normally have arranged the insurance, but you pay the proportional cost for your property by means of a service charge.

Contents insurance, which protects against the loss of, theft of, or damage to your belongings, may need to be adjusted after divorce if now you own much more (or much less) of household goods and other property than before.

Car insurance, either 'third party, fire and theft' (the statutory minimum) or 'comprehensive' (providing you with full cover in the event of an accident, however it is caused), may have to be transferred from one spouse to the other, depending on who now has the family car.

Wills

Wills will need reviewing on divorce to ensure that they cover your new circumstances (if you have not already made a will, now is the time to do so). Check whether your will is a 'mutual will' – in which case you need to change it fast. A mutual will is a legal term used to describe wills made by a husband and wife which complement each other and which are made on the basis that the first spouse to die binds the second spouse to make a will in the original agreed format – no changes will be allowed. Mutual wills are rare – they are not the same as the more common 'mirror wills', whereby both spouses agree to make similar wills, which can be changed whenever a spouse wants. If a mutual will is to be changed, it must be changed before the other spouse's death.

When making a will, remember that if you own any foreign property you may need to take specialist advice about the effect of an English will on the foreign property – and you may even need to make a will abroad. If you own property in Spain, for example, you will have only limited freedom in deciding who your estate should go to. A spouse and children have priority rights which, if not reflected in the will, open up the way for a challenge to the will. Spanish law will recognise an English will, although if it is not drawn up in terms acceptable under Spanish law, you could still have a legal headache. It is best, therefore, to check the local law.

A will made by either a husband or a wife is not automatically revoked on divorce (or even an annulment of the marriage), but is interpreted as if the ex-spouse had died on the date of the divorce (or annulment). So if the ex-spouse was named as an executor, that appointment will be ineffective, and the same applies to an appointment of an ex-spouse as guardian of the children – unless there is any contrary intention expressed in the will.

The gift in a will of any property to an ex-spouse will fail as well. As long as the will states that some other person should have the 'residue' – what is left after the payment of debts and expenses, and all the gifts – that person, known in legal jargon as the 'residuary beneficiary', will receive the ex-spouse's gift as well. If it was the ex-spouse who was the residuary beneficiary and there was no substitute beneficiary, the rest of the estate will be dealt with according to the intestacy rules – rules which apply to the sharing out of the estate of someone who died without making a will.

If there is no will and a divorced person's estate has to be dealt with under the intestacy rules, the former husband or wife will not be taken into account in the distribution of the estate. But any children remain eligible for their share of an inheritance.

Community Legal Service funding for making a will is now limited. You can now ask for advice under the Legal Help scheme for preparing your will only if you meet all the financial criteria listed in

Chapter 1 and are aged 70 or over, or are disabled, or if you have a child who is disabled. A single parent looking after a child and who wants to appoint a guardian for the child to act after death is also eligible. But you no longer need to appoint a guardian for your child after your death via a will as this can be done by deed or in writing. Make sure you check first with the person you wish to act as a guardian that he or she is willing to take on this important responsibility.

Part 3

Other legal problems

Chapter 14

Domestic violence

Domestic violence most commonly occurs within the confines of the home, behind closed doors, with no outsider witnessing the event. That is not to say that it is rare. A campaign to challenge the acceptance of violence against women, Zero Tolerance (launched in February 1994), reported that domestic violence accounts for one in four of all reported crimes. Domestic violence cuts across all classes of society. It is more likely to occur where a pattern of violence has already been formed, in the relationship between the man and the woman, or even have its roots in the childhood of either one. Frequently, violence is linked to substance abuse of some kind, whether of alcohol or drugs. The crisis of a separation or divorce can, in a few cases, be itself sufficient to spark off an incident of violence. In the great majority of cases, violence is inflicted by men upon women, so the violent partner is here referred to as 'he' and the victim as 'she'.

If you are the subject of violence, you need to take steps quickly to protect yourself. If you are behaving violently towards your partner, you too need to take fast preventive action, for example by leaving the home or seeking help by contacting an organisation such as Alcoholics Anonymous.★

You can get legal advice about domestic violence matters under the Legal Help scheme (see Chapter 1), if you are financially eligible. Community Legal Service funding is available (again subject to financial eligibility) for applications for an injunction (see below), and emergency certificates can be issued on the same day in extreme cases. (If you go to a solicitors' firm which has a legal franchise – or a contract as it is now known – it can make the decision as to whether an emergency certificate should be granted there and then.) In 1996 the Legal Aid Board (now the Legal Services Commission, LSC)★ issued guidance that emergency legal aid would be granted only if the applicant 'is in imminent danger of significant harm'. If you are not eligible for CLS funding, the cost of obtaining an injunction is likely to be some hundreds of pounds.

Contacting the police

In the past the police gained a reputation for failing to treat seriously incidents of domestic violence. The attitude is now changing. In London the Metropolitan Police have instructions to investigate and record every incident of domestic violence (which can provide useful corroborative evidence later in any proceedings). Some police authorities now have specific initiatives for tackling domestic violence, such as the Thames Valley Police, which not only monitors all domestic violence cases but offers help and support to victims too. It is wise to contact the police if violence is threatened. They can lower the heat of the situation by talking separately to each partner, or in certain circumstances by removing the threatening spouse from the home. If an assault has actually occurred, the police should consider whether criminal charges should be brought. Since June 1997, criminal prosecutions can also be taken to stop stalkers from harassing their victims (see *Stalking – new court powers*, below). Some police forces have a policy that if a crime has been committed, for example assault, they will prosecute. In other areas, prosecutions ensue only if the victim is prepared to give evidence. Studies abroad have shown that levels of violence can drop if police take a consistently strong line.

Leaving the home

In principle, and generally, it is tactically better to remain in the matrimonial home until either an agreement is reached or court proceedings have been finalised. But in an extreme emergency you may have no choice but to leave home.

If your physical and mental welfare are severely threatened, it may be safer to leave the home for a temporary period – but get legal advice as soon as possible about your rights in the situation. Take your children with you if at all possible. You may want to contact Women's Aid★ for advice.

Finding somewhere to stay

As long as you have not made yourself 'intentionally homeless', your local authority is under an obligation to provide accommodation for you if you have priority needs (for example, you have young children living with you), and have nowhere else to stay. Contact – by telephone, or in person if you can – the housing department of your local authority or the social services department. The accommodation they are most likely to offer will be basic bed and breakfast.

There are a number of women's refuges across England and Wales which provide a roof to sleep under for female victims of domestic violence and their children. Women's Aid can advise you about where to go. The contact numbers for refuges are closely guarded in order to ensure that victims of violence in refuges and their families are not harassed further by their violent partners or ex-partners.

Changing the locks

If you jointly own or rent the home with your partner, you have no instant right to lock him out. Until divorce proceedings have been concluded, both spouses have a legal right to continue to occupy the matrimonial home. If you do change the locks, your partner may be able to get a court order restoring him to the home. If your partner has been extremely violent, you can apply to the court for an injunction to force him out of the house. After he has been ordered to leave, you will be in a position legally to change the locks.

Children and violence

In some cases where a spouse is behaving violently towards his partner, the children suffer violence as well. It is extremely important for you to protect your children's interests if they are being physically attacked by your spouse. If you have to leave home, take them with you if at all possible. However, if you have to leave them, get immediate legal advice on what action to take to get them back with you. Some solicitors in different areas have joined together to run a domestic violence hotline to ensure that a victim of violence can get immediate access to a solicitor who specialises in dealing with these cases. The police or your local Citizens Advice Bureau should be able to give you more information.

Domestic violence and injunctions

The whole law covering domestic violence has changed since 1 October 1997 when a part of the new Family Law Act 1996, Part IV, was brought into force. This new law means that lots of confusing old laws have been scrapped and in their place one single statute, the Family Law Act, is now in force which covers all applications in all courts for domestic violence injunctions. The new law has opened up the categories of people who can apply to court for an injunction to protect them from domestic violence, so that cohabitants and ex-cohabitants, other family members and even people who have lived closely together in the same household can seek the courts' protection. As this book is written for people who are or were married, advice in this chapter will primarily be designed to cater for their needs.

There are now basically two types of court order which can be obtained, both of which are often termed 'injunction'. An injunction is an order by the court telling someone what he or she must or must not do; the penalty for disobedience can be imprisonment. The two types are:

- a non-molestation order
- an occupation order.

A non-molestation order orders the spouse not to assault, molest or otherwise interfere with you. Non-molestation orders can also be obtained for the protection of children. Molestation can include pestering, such as repeated telephone calls, or other forms of harassment.

An occupation order can require a violent spouse to leave the home and/or not come within a specified area around it (for example, 100 yards around the home). An occupation order can also allow a spouse back into the home if she has left it out of fear of violence and can require the violent spouse to let her back in (and possibly require him to leave too). Occasionally, the court may make an order confining one spouse to a defined part of the home, but this is rarely practicable.

When making an order, the courts have to weigh up the balance of harm as between the victim (and children if they are affected too) and the violent partner before deciding whether or not to make an occupation order. In some cases this will mean that the court will want to see whether the violent partner will have accommodation to go to if he is ousted from the family home.

Which court?

Before the new law came in, it had been thought that the government would restrict access to the courts for domestic violence injunctions to the family proceedings courts, but so far this has not been the case. All courts can make the orders: it will be up to you (after getting advice from your solicitor) to decide which. If you have already started off divorce proceedings, it is likely to be the court which is dealing with your divorce case that you will apply to – otherwise it will be the local county court or possibly the family proceedings court.

If you are financially eligible and want to make an application in the county court or divorce court, you should apply for CLS funding. If your solicitors' firm has got a legal aid franchise, they should be able to make a decision as to whether an emergency application should be granted there and then. If it is not an extreme emergency, there may be a few days' wait before the decision is made. Sometimes you will need to comply with a requirement from the LSC that a letter should be sent to the violent partner asking him to stop harassing the victim, before court proceedings are taken.

Obtaining an injunction to protect the children

In the rarer cases where it is the children, rather than a spouse, who are at risk, the courts can make an order stopping contact between the violent (or abusive) adult and the children. This can be done either under the courts' inherent jurisdiction or by an order under the Children Act 1989. Since Part IV of the Family Law Act has been in force, social services departments can also take action under an emergency protection order or an interim care order and can seek an occupation order to oust an abuser (say a stepparent) from the family home.

Ex parte or on notice?

In the case of a real emergency, it is possible to apply for an injunction *ex parte*, which means that the other spouse is not told of the hearing before it takes place. Courts are more ready to listen to an *ex parte* application and grant an injunction if the application is for a non-molestation order. For occupation orders, the situation needs to be fairly desperate before a court will order a spouse out of the home without giving him the opportunity of presenting his case to the court. If an order is obtained *ex parte*, this will usually be limited to a temporary period (of a week), and the respondent (the person against whom the order is obtained) has to be told of the resumed hearing, which may be as early as one week later although it could be anything up to two months later, and be given the opportunity to put his case before the court. By this time, having received the papers from the court, he will have had the chance of obtaining legal advice.

In all other cases where an injunction is applied for, this application will be 'on notice', that is the respondent will be told in advance of the hearing date. The application with accompanying papers must be served on the respondent at least two clear working days before the hearing date.

The documents that must be filed at court to start off the application are:

- an application, in duplicate, together with the court fee of £40
- a sworn statement in support, giving particulars of any children, of the accommodation and alternative accommodation available to each party, and of the conduct complained of and why an injunction is necessary.

In turn, the respondent should produce a sworn statement dealing with the allegations. He can suggest solutions, such as alternative accommodation, or explain the possibility of remaining in the same house.

Women who have been injured, or even just bruised, should go and see their doctor or the casualty department of the local hospital and make sure that a physical examination is carried out and the injuries noted on medical records. Such records can provide useful evidence in court proceedings. Indeed, a solicitor may ask the doctor concerned to prepare a report, for which a fee of about £40 will be charged. If anyone other than the two parties involved has witnessed the violence, that person should be asked if he or she would be willing to come forward to attend court, if need be, as a witness.

It may also be helpful to photograph injuries, to show the extent of bruising, for instance. Some solicitors keep a Polaroid camera for this purpose. Alternatively, depending on the location of the injury, you could use a photo booth.

An application 'on notice' for an injunction is usually heard very quickly – normally within a few days. In ex parte proceedings, the application may be heard on the same day as long as there is sufficient time to file a sworn statement. Before making an occupation order, the judge or court will want to be satisfied both that the circumstances warrant such an order and that there is no satisfactory alternative in the light of the spouse's conduct, the children's needs and the available accommodation. In one case in 1993, an ouster order (the old equivalent of an occupation order) was granted because of very serious dissension caused by the husband's 'jealous, argumentative and unyielding nature': the wife found it impossible to live with him. However, this case is very rare: usually the courts require evidence of fairly severe physical violence before an occupation order is granted. An occupation order is seen as a draconian remedy.

Injunctions can be limited to a specific period, for example three months, or in more severe cases they may have no time limit. If the parties are reconciled and resume cohabitation, the injunction can lapse.

Power of arrest

Where the court makes an occupation order or a non-molestation order and where the respondent (the violent partner) has 'used or threatened violence against the applicant or a relevant child' then the courts will nowadays attach a power of arrest to the order (unless the court is satisfied that the victim will be adequately protected without such a power of arrest). A power of arrest means that if, once the offending spouse has been served with the order, he breaches it, the police can be called to arrest the offender straight away without a warrant and take him before a magistrate. If a power of arrest is given, the applicant must take a copy of the order to the local police station straight after the court hearing, to put the police on notice. At the time when the power of arrest lapses, the police must also be notified.

A power of arrest normally lasts for a fixed period of three months. Under the new law it can last for the same length of time or a shorter period than the order itself. It is in practice the most effective preventive action that can be taken to curb future violent attacks. If, after violence has been threatened, the violent partner offers to give an undertaking at court not to be violent in the future, the court is likely to have to consider whether it is satisfied that the applicant (and/or relevant children) will be adequately protected – it looks as if the court cannot accept an undertaking at face value. In any event, as a power of arrest cannot be attached to the undertaking, a victim should think carefully before accepting an undertaking rather than asking the court for a formal court injunction.

In the past, courts frequently accepted undertakings when offered. However, when the new law was first introduced, many courts indicated that they would be likely to feel bound to make a preliminary legal finding as to whether or not violence or threats actually happened before accepting undertakings. This may mean in practice that the courts' time in dealing with domestic violence injunctions may have to rise significantly.

A note of warning

Injunction proceedings should be considered carefully before being commenced.

Bear in mind the consequences of seeking and obtaining an occupation order in terms of your future relationship. If that is the way your divorce proceedings begin, the prospect of negotiating reasonably and reaching a sensible agreement recedes dramatically. If, however, you have no alternative, you must take the best steps to protect your and your family's safety.

What to do if you have been served with an injunction

If you know that you are at risk of being violent towards your spouse, whether because you have been violent in the past or because you feel the tension in the house is becoming unbearable, you need to take steps to minimise the risk. Take responsible action, such as leaving the house for a cooling-off period.

If you are served with an injunction or injunction application, read it carefully, together with any other documents given to you, for example the sworn statement. See a solicitor as soon as possible and make an appointment with him or her as much in advance of the hearing date as you can. If you are financially eligible, you can get advice under the Legal Help scheme.

A few solicitors will not act for violent men, so check this in advance. The solicitor will take a statement from you and make this into a sworn statement to be lodged at the court. As an alternative to having an order made against you, you can offer the court an undertaking not to molest your partner. Breaking the terms of an undertaking can invoke just as serious a penalty as breaking the terms of a court order.

Unless you have real grounds to contest your partner's claim for a non-molestation order, you are unlikely to be able to obtain CLS funding to be represented in court, even if you would otherwise qualify on financial grounds.

Stalking – new court powers

Sometimes the stresses of separation and divorce can surface in obsessional behaviour from an ex-spouse or others and stalking can be the result. Another new Act, the Protection from Harassment Act 1997, which creates a new criminal offence of what is in effect stalking, was brought in to the law in June 1997, and gives courts extra powers for serious persistent harassment. Although stalking is not defined in the Act, it is well known as having come to mean open or unmistakable harassment, of which the victim is aware. The new law says that a person must not pursue a course of conduct

(a) which amounts to harassment of another; and
(b) which he knows or ought to know amounts to harassment of the other.

Two criminal offences have been created by the new Act (see box). The police can now take action to stop stalking – several cases have been brought against ex-partners, including against a 78-year-old man who stalked his ex-partner and her new lover, and against a woman who bombarded her former lover with up to four abusive letters a days after he ended their relationship. She moved to a home two doors away from him and broke into his home wielding two carving knives. The police can arrest someone who is stalking a victim. When the case comes to court, prison sentences can be ordered in very severe cases and the courts usually will order the stalker to cease having any contact whatsoever with the victim.

Stalking has also become, in lawyers' terms, a 'statutory civil tort', which means that a victim can claim money damages to compensate her (or him) for having been stalked, as long as a claim is made within six years of the conduct taking place. To try to avoid too much over-sophisticated legal argument about what the stalker intended, the new law says that these criminal offences are strict liability – that is, that the victim's lawyer does not have to prove that the stalker himself or herself had criminal intent. The only defences are (a) prevention of crime; (b) legal authority (for example where bailiffs have to enforce a judgement) or (c) that in the particular circumstances the conduct was reasonable.

New stalking offences

The Protection from Harassment Act 1997 creates two specific criminal offences:

the lesser: causing harassment or distress (sections 1 and 2). A summary-only offence to be dealt with by the magistrates' court

the greater: putting the victim in fear of violence (section 4). This is 'indictable' which means it is likely to be heard in the Crown Court.

Chapter 15

Child abduction

Child abduction is one of the most fraught areas of separation and divorce. Reunite★ (the National Council for Abducted Children) estimated in 1996 that about 1,000 children are abducted from the UK each year. Statistically this means that abduction happens only rarely, but when it does it tears the family apart as one parent faces the prospect of never seeing his or her child again.

Prevention is by far the most effective form of action. Many countries (including the UK) are signatories to the Hague Convention, under which they undertake to enforce other countries' custody orders about children (this will apply to residence orders under the Children Act 1989, too) and to return any abducted child to the country he or she was snatched from. However, many other countries have failed to sign the Convention, so in them it provides no recourse. Even if a child has been taken to one of the signatory states, the procedures for enforcement are at best time-consuming and at worst unsuccessful. In 1996 the Lord Chancellor's Department took the unusual step of naming the countries which were the worst offenders for harbouring children snatched by a parent. Germany came out worst (of the 17 cases in 1995 of children abducted from the UK and taken to Germany, none was handed over as a result of the legal process, although four were handed over voluntarily). The USA, Greece and Spain also came out poorly.

There are two areas of law which have a bearing on child abduction. The first is the criminal law: the Child Abduction Act 1984 made kidnapping a child a crime. Under that Act, a parent who takes a child out of the country without the prior written consent of the other, or permission of the court, may be committing a criminal offence.

Second, there are civil laws which prevent children from being abducted, but the position now is different from that before the Children Act 1989 was brought into force on 14 October 1991. Thus it is important to see when (and if) a court order was made over the children.

Before 14 October 1991

Whenever there were children in families in divorce proceedings, the court made an order not only for custody and care and control, but also that the children should not be taken out of the country without the consent of the other parent or the court. If such an order has been made, it will remain effective and enforceable after 14 October 1991.

After 14 October 1991

After that date, in the majority of divorces involving children, no court orders will be made, so there will usually be no civil order stopping the other parent from removing the child abroad. (An abducting parent may, however, still be committing a criminal offence under the Child Abduction Act.) If a residence order is made, it prevents the other parent from removing the child without consent, but the parent in whose favour it was made is allowed to take the child abroad for periods of up to one month at a time.

The purpose behind these changes was to emphasise that it is the parents' responsibility to agree on arrangements for the children wherever possible and to allow the parent with whom the child lives to take him or her abroad for a holiday. Obviously, if there are real grounds for suspecting that the other parent intends to take the child abroad permanently and not just for a holiday, then the circumstances are different and court action can and should be taken fast.

Worries about abduction

If you have fears that your child may be abducted by the other parent (if, for example, the other parent is a foreign national and there are grounds for believing that he or she plans to return to his or her home country with the child), you could ask the court to make a prohibited steps order to state that the other parent cannot take the child abroad without your prior consent or the court's permission. Alternatively, it might be in the child's best interests for a residence order to be made either on decree nisi or later on: this will automatically include an order that the child may not be removed abroad without the consent of the other parent or the court. Talk to your solicitor about the best course of action.

If your child has been or could be abducted

If you believe that your child is about to be abducted by the other parent you need to take action fast. The need for immediacy cannot be overemphasised: as Reunite points out, 'the longer a dispute goes on, the more difficult it becomes to repatriate a child'.

Contact your solicitor immediately. He or she can act to obtain an emergency court order preventing the child from being taken abroad, either via a residence order and/or a prohibited steps order, or by using the old remedy of making a child a ward of court (whereby the court becomes in law the parent of the child and no step affecting the child can be taken without the court's consent). The courts can make such orders even outside court hours: a duty judge should always be available. The order should be served on the potential abductor if his or her whereabouts are known.

Emergency Community Legal Service funding and Legal Help are available, subject to financial eligibility (see Chapter 1).

In addition to taking legal action, either you or your solicitor should contact the police and ask for a port alert to be carried out. Under this, if there is a real and imminent danger of the child being abducted ('real and imminent' means within the next 24 hours), the police are obliged to notify all airports and seaports of the danger of the child being taken out of the country.

In practice, it is often difficult for officials to recognise and intercept children at ports where there is heavy traffic, and the effectiveness of this action has been lessened since the reduction or near-disappearance of border controls between European Union countries since 1993. To maximise the usefulness of a port alert, provide as many details as you can of the potential abductor and the child, such as full names, addresses, dates of birth, personal descriptions, photographs and (best of all) details of the flight or sailing if you have them.

Once your child has been abducted and taken abroad, your remedies are fewer and harder to enforce, but you should still not give up hope. If the child has been taken to a country which is a signatory of the Hague Convention, you should be able to get the appropriate authority to act to get the child returned to you. Even if the child has been taken elsewhere, it may be possible to ask the court in England and Wales to sequester (that is, take away) the abducting parent's property if he or she has broken a court order. This can act as a lever to force the abducting parent to return the child (as in the 1993 Peter Malkin case). Ask your solicitor for more information.

Support for parents and families

For support and information for parents and families about child abduction, contact the parents' self-help group, Reunite.

A free booklet called *Child Abduction* is available from the Child Abduction Unit.★

Chapter 16

Stepfamilies

Stepfathers and stepmothers often occupy a distinctive place within a new family, having taken on the burdens (and joys) of an actual parent but without being recognised by the law as such. However, the greater flexibility of the courts' powers under section 8 of the Children Act 1989 can be helpful for stepfamilies.

Stepfamilies and children

Stepparents do not automatically have parental responsibility during a marriage (nor after divorce) for their stepchildren (for a further explanation of 'parental responsibility' see Chapter 4). Parental responsibility belongs automatically to both the natural father and mother of a child (if the parents were married at the time of the birth or later married each other) or to the mother alone if the parents were unmarried.

To become recognised by the law as having the role of a parent, stepparents can apply for a residence order under section 8 of the Children Act jointly with their new partner if the children are living with them. This indirectly gives them parental responsibility and puts them on an equal footing with anyone else who has parental responsibility – usually the parents. In this case the stepparents' parental responsibility lasts only as long as the residence order lasts, rather than until the child reaches 18.

As long as the stepparent is married to the parent of the child, he or she will not need the court's permission to make an application for an order under the Children Act for residence or contact. Other people who can apply to the court as of right are those:

- with whom the child has lived for at least three years

- who have the permission of everyone who has a residence order in their favour
- who have the consent of everyone with parental responsibility for the child
- if the child is in care, who have the consent of the local authority.

Anyone else can apply too, but the court will first have to give its permission before giving the application the go-ahead. The factors the court then considers are the type of application being made, the connection between the applicant and the child, and any risk the application might have of harmfully disrupting the child's life.

When the court considers an application for a residence order, it will have to consider whether making an order is better for the child than making no order at all. Very often this 'no-order' principle means that in practice a court is reluctant to make a residence order. The court's first and paramount consideration is the welfare of the child. The court may grant such an application in the joint favour of the parent and a concerned and involved stepparent, particularly if more certainty would benefit the new family (in particular the child) and if the absent natural parent takes little or no interest in the child. The court would want to be satisfied that the new family arrangement is stable.

Another option would be for the stepparent to apply jointly with his or her new spouse (that is, the child's natural mother or father) for an adoption order. Again the courts are not keen to grant this as they are unwilling to terminate all links with natural parents, which an adoption order necessarily does.

Stepfamilies and money

One situation which can generate considerable strain and even resentment for a new stepparent is the possibility of his or her partner's former spouse 'getting their hands on' the new couple's assets. Second wives or husbands can find it especially galling to feel that their own paypackets are being used to fund maintenance payments for their new partner's former spouse and family.

Since 1995 the formula used by the Child Support Agency (CSA)★ to calculate the amount that a parent or stepparent should pay as child support has taken into account the full housing costs for the second family but ignores debts and extra costs like child care. However, low earners should find themselves and their second families being cushioned from the harsher effects of the formula by the protected income formulae. First there is a 'cap' of 30 per cent of the absent parent's net income, which ensures that he (or she) has to pay no more than this. Second, a further calculation is made, designed to ensure that an absent parent's income does not sink below income support rates. The CSA will need to know the amount of a new partner's income to work out the level of protected income (see Chapter 6).

The courts will not approach the question of dividing up the family's assets by seeking to get their hands on the new partner's money. They will not formally take the individual income and assets of a new partner into account, but will look at them to the extent that the new partner's income and property increase the ex-spouse's ability to meet any financial order that may be made against him or her. So, if a man remarries and moves into his new wife's home, the bills for which are met out of her own earnings, the court will take into account the fact that his housing needs have been met without any great outlay, so he can possibly afford to make greater maintenance payments to an ex-wife. Conversely, if an ex-husband has to take on extra financial responsibility for a new family, the courts will also take that into account as limiting his ability to pay.

A new partner can refuse to disclose details of his or her income and assets. If the court feels that a new partner's means are relevant in the financial part of a divorce case, an 'inspection appointment' can be arranged. At this the spouse who wants information about the new partner's means can ask for some limited disclosure by the new partner of financial evidence. The court will not necessarily need to know what a new partner earns, but will want to know the extent to which she or he relieves the ex-spouse from having to provide for living accommodation, for example. Usually a summary of the new partner's financial position will do.

The courts draw a distinction between a woman cohabiting and remarrying. On remarriage, her former husband's financial obligations to maintain her (although not the children) end. However, if she chooses to cohabit with a new partner, although the ex-husband can apply for a reduction in her maintenance payments if her financial position has improved, the court will not transfer the ex-husband's duty to maintain her to her new live-in partner.

As a general rule, it is best to try to conclude arguments over money before remarriage (or even before permanent cohabitation) to ensure that problems of the earlier marriage do not become enmeshed in the creation of a new family relationship.

When the parent/partner dies

On the death of his or her partner, the stepparent has no automatic rights vis-à-vis the stepchildren. If the natural parents were married at the time of the birth, then the other parent (not the stepparent) should automatically take over responsibility for looking after the children and the stepparent would have no automatic legal rights. Moreover, the other parent may be unwilling to give contact in the future to the stepparent: if there is any conflict the stepparent could apply for a contact order under section 8 of the Children Act. If the stepparent wants to continue looking after the children, then again he or she will have to apply for a residence order.

To protect against a legal shutting-out of the stepparent, especially where the absent parent was uninterested in the children, the parent/partner can make a will or written appointment nominating the stepparent as a guardian of the child on his or her death. This would suffice if the mother of the children had not been married to the father at the time of the birth or had married him later. Otherwise, to make the position watertight, the stepparent and parent should apply jointly to the court for a residence order as otherwise the appointment as a guardian would not take effect until the death of the surviving natural parent (which defeats the object of an appointment).

Another problem that can arise on death (or even if the remarriage breaks up) is that of securing a family home for the children. If, following divorce, a parent purchases a property jointly with a new partner, perhaps with the aid of a capital sum paid via the divorce courts, he or she should be careful how the joint ownership of the new home is expressed.

If the new partners buy as joint tenants, the share of one would pass automatically to the surviving partner whatever his or her will might state. This could mean that if there were relationship problems later between the stepparent and the children, the stepparent would be within his or her legal rights to ask the children to leave the home and they might have no financial security. If, however, a new property were purchased expressly under a tenancy in common, both partners' property interests would be clearly defined and the parent could ensure that his or her share passed to the children by will. A joint tenancy can easily be converted to a tenancy in common by 'severing' it. A letter from one joint owner to the other stating that the writer is thereby severing the property will suffice (see Chapter 7) – ask a solicitor if you want to find out more.

A tenancy in common will be assumed to divide the ownership equally between the partners unless any other proportionate division is stated. So if the parent has provided most of the capital for the purchase and wants to ensure that the children are securely provided for in the event of death, the tenancy in common could be stated to be divided 75 per cent to the parent and 25 per cent to the stepparent. The parent should also execute a will leaving his or her share of the property to the children in trust until they reach the age of 18 (or some other later date). The parent should also think about whether he or she wants to make sure that the new spouse can remain in the property during the latter's lifetime. A deed of trust for the ownership of the property can also set out clearly what will happen if certain events occur: for example, if the parties split up, what are the agreements for one buying out the other.

A solicitor can advise further about ownership of the property, making a deed of trust and a will. Some of the costs may be offset by Community Legal Service funding, if you are financially eligible, although there are now restrictions on such funding for wills (see Chapter 14). Otherwise, if you are paying privately, the extra costs of preparing a deed of trust are likely to be £200 (plus VAT) upwards.

Making a will

Remarriage (as with marriage) automatically revokes any earlier will unless that will was specifically stated to be made in contemplation of the marriage. In any event, if there are children, making a will after a remarriage should be a priority. Otherwise, the rules of intestacy will automatically operate after your death, which may not accord with what you actually want to happen (see chart below). Although these rules differ depending on the circumstances, what they achieve in broad terms is to give a spouse the first £125,000 (plus chattels and a life interest in one-half of the estate over and above this sum) if there are children; or the first £200,000 (plus chattels and one-half of the remainder absolutely) where there are no children. The balance will be divided among the children, where there are surviving children, or among other relatives if there are none.

Making a will is not a watertight guarantee that a person's wishes will be carried out after his or her death – claims can be made against a deceased person's estate by his or her widow(er) or other members of their family or dependants under the Inheritance (Provision for Family and Dependants) Act 1975. For example, since 1 January 1996, under changes made by the Law Reform (Succession) Act 1995, claims can be made against a deceased person's estate by an unmarried cohabitant as long as she (or he) lived with the deceased as husband and wife for at least two years.

There are significant advantages to making a will. As long as you have made a will at least the rest of the world will know what you wanted to happen after your death. If your priority is to ensure that the children are cared for after your death, by making a will you can be reasonably certain that your wishes will be carried out. You may also appoint a guardian to care for your children after your death: the appointment will be effective immediately after your death if you have a residence order in your favour; otherwise the appointment is not effective until your surviving ex-spouse has died too.

Stepfamilies and divorce

If the stepfamily itself breaks up, broadly the advice contained within this book will apply. However, the question also arises whether a stepparent (more commonly the stepfather) may face claims for financial support for the children of his or her ex-partner.

If the children have been treated as 'children of the family' (this term generally covers any child who has been brought up in the same household), their details must be included on the statement of arrangements form and in the divorce petition itself. The divorce court will consider the arrangements made for them as well as for any natural children of the parties. If the stepparent wants to look after the children in the future, he or she will probably have to make an application for a residence order even if this proposal is agreed to by the natural parent. Without such an order, the stepparent's responsibilities will not be recognised in law. Usually, however, the court will be predisposed to the natural parent continuing to care for the children.

Intestacy flow chart: where will your estate go if you die without a will?

Do you have a wife or husband?

- **yes** → **Is your estate worth more than £125,000?**
  - **no** → Wife/husband gets everything
  - **yes** → **Do you have children?**
    - **yes** → Wife/husband gets first £125,000 plus life interest in half the rest: the balance goes to the children
    - **no** → **Do you have parents/brothers and sisters?**
      - **yes** → Wife/husband gets first £200,000 plus half the rest: the balance goes to parents, or brothers and sisters if your parents are dead
      - **no** → Wife/husband gets everything

- **no** →
  - **Do you have children?**
    - **yes** → Shared equally between the children
    - **no** → **Do you have parents?**
      - **yes** → Shared equally between the parents
      - **no** → **Do you have brothers and sisters?**
        - **yes** → Shared equally between brothers and sisters
        - **no** → **Do you have half-brothers or sisters?**
          - **yes** → Shared equally between the half-brothers and sisters
          - **no** → **Do you have grandparents?**
            - **yes** → Shared equally between grandparents
            - **no** → **Do you have uncles and aunts?**
              - **yes** → Shared equally between aunts and uncles
              - **no** → **Do you have half-uncles and aunts?**
                - **yes** → Shared equally between half-uncles and aunts
                - **no** → Everything goes to the Crown

Following the marriage of the stepparent to the natural parent, as the stepchildren would be 'children of the family', applications for maintenance (which could be secured), lump sums and transfers of settlement and of property could be made against the stepparent (although if the parties had never married and if the stepparent had not otherwise legally assumed financial responsibilities for the step-children, no such claims could be made). Applications will usually be limited to children aged up to 17, although they can be allowed after that age if the children are continuing in full-time education or train-ing. Child support applications cannot be made against a stepparent via the CSA unless he or she had legally adopted the child(ren).

The CSA seeks to trace the natural (or adoptive) parents for them to pay maintenance for their children: financial duties to one's own natural (or adopted) children will specifically override assumed obli-gations for the previous children of a new partner.

The courts will also expect the natural parents to fulfil their financial obligations towards their children first, so before a financial order was made against a stepparent, the court would want to ensure that exhaustive steps had been taken to track down the absent natural parent to make an order against him (or her) for the children.

Chapter 17

Unmarried families

Unmarried families break up in much the same way that married families do. However, although the emotional and practical problems may be the same, the legal framework is not. The law offers children of married and unmarried families virtually the same sorts of protection and court orders, but the adult partners are not treated in the same way. Unmarried women can find that they are particularly vulnerable at the time of breaking up.

The relevance of this book to unmarried couples

Many of the chapters of this book – with a little adaptation – will apply to you if you are unmarried.

Chapter 1 The costs of divorce

You may well need to use a solicitor if there is property or child support to sort out, so this chapter will apply to you as well. You can get Community Legal Service (CLS)★ funding to deal with the resolution of a property dispute, or to deal with money for the children if the Child Support Agency (CSA)★ does not have jurisdiction. The same rules about financial eligibility will apply.

The statutory charge can be postponed, as for matrimonial property, if you recover or preserve an interest in a house which is going to be a home for you and/or your children.

The £2,500 exemption to the statutory charge applies only to family cases. This means that it would apply if you were making an application under the Children Act 1989 for the children to have a share of the house, but would not apply if the only legal action were one between yourself and your partner to decide your shares in the house.

Chapter 2 Financial planning

The suggestions about how to work out and plan your finances apply just as much to you as to married couples. Department of Social Services (DSS) benefits are available to married and unmarried couples.

Chapter 3 Legal advice

Unmarried people need solicitors too and generally you will find that solicitors who deal with family law will deal with unmarried families as well as married ones, so this chapter is mostly relevant to you. As your legal situation can be trickier than that of a married couple (as described below) it makes sense to get some sensible legal advice, if only at the start, to make sure you understand your legal position.

Chapter 4 Your children

The early part of the chapter has as much relevance for unmarried families as married ones. The legal position is, however, different.

Parental responsibility

If a child is born to an unmarried couple, only the mother has parental responsibility – the bundle of rights and duties that go with parenthood. The fact that the father is registered on the baby's birth certificate does not alter the legal position.

The father can share parental responsibility with the mother if she agrees and they both complete a Parental Responsibility agreement which is then registered at the court. If you have done this before your relationship breaks up, the father's parental responsibility continues; only the court can take it away from him.

In the absence of such an agreement the father can apply to the court for an order that he be granted parental responsibility. If the court grants the application, the order would normally be that he would have parental responsibility in addition to the mother – it would be most unusual for the court to take it away from the mother and give it to the father. A father can couple the application with an application for a section 8 order for contact or residence (see Chapter 10).

Contact and residence

The rules about applying for contact are the same as described in Chapter 10. The court will treat married and unmarried families in the same way. However, if the relationship between the father and the mother has been short-lived, the father will probably have more difficulty than a married father in establishing his commitment to the child.

Chapter 5 Mediation

Mediation is available to unmarried families just as it is to married families and can be particularly helpful when the legal framework is less structured.

Mediators can help not only with issues surrounding the children, but financial matters as well. Because unmarried mothers are less protected by the law in financial matters it makes sense to try to agree a settlement based on as much mutual good will as you can salvage, and mediation can help you do this.

Chapter 6 Using the Child Support Agency

All of this chapter will be relevant to you as the CSA makes no distinction between children of married and unmarried couples. If the child has an absent parent who is his or her parent by blood or adoption, the absent parent will be liable.

It is possible that there may be more cases of disputed parentage in unmarried families, but the basic rules remain the same.

Chapter 7 Protecting your interest in the family home

This is an area of the law where the difference between married and unmarried couples is substantial and unmarried couples can be particularly vulnerable.

If you are a joint owner of the family home, your position and ownership of it is protected by the fact that your name will be on the deeds of the property. How you realise or increase that share is dealt with below.

If you are not a joint owner, you will have some additional protection in the law if you have been engaged to be married to your partner. This would bring you within the scope of the Married Women's Property Act 1882. Under this you can apply for a declaration of ownership in the family home and, if you have made a substantial contribution to the improvement of the property, you can seek a share or an enlarged share of the property because of that contribution.

If you were not engaged, your only remedy is to ask the court to declare that there is a resulting implied or constructive trust in your favour and you could then ask for a sale of the property under the Trusts of Land and Appointment of Trustees Act 1996. There is no automatic entitlement to such a trust being declared and each case will turn on its particular facts. Simply looking after the family and being a good 'wife' and mother will not be enough to gain you an interest in the property.

This makes it difficult to protect your interest if you have to move out of the home. You do not have 'rights of occupation' as a married person would, and cannot register them as described in Chapter 7. If you are starting legal proceedings, however, you can register the fact that there is a pending application over the property and this should warn any prospective purchaser of your interest in it.

This means that you will need to act quickly if you do have to move out. You will need to take some legal advice and decide whether and what action to take to protect your interest in the property.

You should read the section in Chapter 7 about severance if the property is in your joint names.

Chapters 8 to 13

These chapters of the book are not going to be much use to you because they deal with divorce law.

Chapter 14 Domestic violence

The Family Law Act applies to both married and unmarried families in the protection that it offers from domestic violence. You come within the scope of the Act if you are or have been cohabiting. There is a rather sinister provision in the Act that says that when dealing with unmarried partners the court is to 'have regard' to the fact that they have not ' given each other the commitment involved in marriage'. In practice, however, the courts have been concerned to protect people from domestic violence and have not drawn any significant distinction between married and unmarried couples.

Chapter 15 Child abduction
This chapter will apply to you.

Chapter 16 Stepfamilies
In the context of family law a stepfamily is recognised as such only where the parties are married. A married stepfather, for instance, can be ordered to maintain his stepchildren if they have been treated by him as 'children of the family', but an unmarried stepfather cannot.

Separation agreements

There is no reason why an unmarried couple cannot make a separation agreement between themselves and you may find it helpful to read the sections in Chapter 8 about this. The same observations about disclosure of your financial position and taking sensible legal advice apply. If you can negotiate matters satisfactorily between you, it is obviously going to be cheaper and better than going to court. If the document is drawn up as a deed, you can enforce it later if you need to by bringing an action for damages, as you can with any legal contract.

Financial obligations towards each other

You need to know what you can do to protect yourself and the children financially. The next section of this chapter is written on the assumption that you are the female partner, because in the vast majority of cases it is the female partner who needs to apply to the court. However, the law makes no distinction based on gender, so this chapter will equally apply to a male partner who needs support or who is not a co-owner of property.

Maintenance
There is no legal obligation for your former partner to maintain you, even if there are children of the relationship and you cannot work as a result. The only maintenance that you will be able to get will be for the children. This may mean that you will benefit indirectly, but the court does not have power to increase the children's maintenance with an element for you 'by the back door'.

Capital
The family home
Rented property In some ways you are better off if you have a tenancy because the court has the power to transfer a tenancy between cohabitants even if you are not joint owners. The court can make orders about tenancies if you are:

- protected or statutory tenants under the Rent Act 1977
- statutory tenants under the rent (Agriculture) Act 1976
- secure tenants under s.79 of the Housing Act 1985
- assured tenants or assured agricultural occupants under Part I of the Housing Act 1988.

The court can order one of you to have the right to occupy and if necessary have the tenancy transferred. An order can be made at any time after you have stopped living together as husband and wife.

The court has to consider:

- your individual housing needs and resources and those of the children (if any)
- your financial resources
- the likely effect of any order on your health, safety and well-being and that of the children (if any).

If only one of you is entitled to occupy the property because of the tenancy, the court must also consider:

- the nature of your relationship
- the length of time that you have lived together as husband and wife
- whether there are any children
- the length of time since you ceased to live together.

Owned property As indicated above, your entitlement to property if you are not married is worked out on the basis of ordinary property law. Broadly speaking, the fact that you have been living together does not make a difference to the shares in which you are entitled to hold the property.

If you own the property jointly, your shares will depend on what the deeds of the property say. The law will assume that you hold the property in equal shares unless there is a deed of trust that says otherwise and states the proportion in which you hold the property. When you bought the property together with your partner you should have been advised about the implications of joint ownership, particularly if you put unequal amounts into the purchase. (If you did not receive such advice, you should consult another solicitor about whether you were properly advised and whether you have a claim for negligent advice.)

If your partner owns the property in his sole name, you may find it very difficult to establish that you have any interest in the property. The courts will not give you an entitlement simply because you have lived together; you will have had to have made a substantial financial contribution, either in cash or improvements, to the purchase of the property or an increase in its value. Generally too, there will have had to be some sort of understanding between you that you were entitled to a share. If this not the case, then your only remedy – which will apply only if you have children – will be to apply on their behalf for a transfer of property order under the Children Act 1989.

The only exception to this is if you have been engaged. If you make the claim within three years of the engagement being broken off, you will fall within the scope of the Married Women's Property Act and this will give the court wider powers to declare your rights in the property.

Other property

If you have bought other things together, such as furniture or cars, again the law will apply strict property principles and divide them according to contributions.

The Married Women's Property Act will apply to other property if you have been engaged, as explained above.

Financial obligations towards the children

Maintenance
Maintenance where the CSA has jurisdiction

In most cases the CSA will have jurisdiction to deal with the children's maintenance (see Chapter 6 for details). You can still apply to the court for capital orders under the Children Act (see below).

Where the CSA does not have jurisdiction

The most likely situation in which the CSA has no jurisdiction is if the children's father is no longer in the UK. If the person that you want to maintain the children is not related to them by blood or adoption, the CSA will not be able to pursue him. There is also no liability in family law if you were not previously married to him, even if in the past he has helped to support the children.

If the CSA does not have jurisdiction, you can apply for an order under Schedule 1 of the Children Act 1989 for periodical payments.

Capital orders

You can also apply to the court for orders for a lump-sum payment to children, or a transfer of property order. Property can be ordered to be transferred to you, for the benefit of the child, or to the child him- or herself. Normally a court will prefer not to transfer the property direct to a child (it would have to be held by an adult on trust for the child until he or she gets to 18 in any event). Instead an order would be made transferring the property to you.

Procedure

To make the application to the court you have to fill in form C1, which is the general Children Act application form, together with form C10 (a supplemental form that sets out the financial orders that you are seeking) and C10A (a statement of your financial position).

The fee for the application is £80 (which will be waived if you are in receipt of Legal Help or on income support). You will need to file two copies at the court. The court then returns to you a stamped copy of the forms to serve on the father, together with form C6, which states when the first hearing will be, and C7, which is the form that he has to complete to show that he has received the papers. The court will also add a blank form C10 for the father to complete.

You have to send the papers to the father, or arrange for them to be served on him and prove that you have done this by filing form C9 at the court to say how service took place.

The first hearing will probably be one where the judge gives directions about evidence to be filed and will make an order only if you have agreed one or there is no dispute about your financial position. Although the procedure for financial relief in divorce cases has recently been altered and Children Act cases are not subject to the same procedural rules, similar methods of resolving the case may be used by the county courts, so read the relevant sections of Chapter 12.

Criteria

The court has to take the following matters into account when making orders:

- both your incomes, earning capacities, property and other financial resources, now and in the foreseeable future
- both your financial needs, obligations and responsibilities
- the children's financial needs
- the children's income, earning capacity, property and other resources (if applicable)
- any physical or mental disability of the children
- the manner in which the children were being, or expected to be, educated.

Financial obligations on death

Although this is really outside the scope of this book it is worth highlighting one of the key differences between married and unmarried families – their inheritance rights. If you split up, but nevertheless want to make sure that your partner is provided for on death, you need to think about making a will because your partner will not automatically inherit what you want him or her to inherit if you die 'intestate' (without making a will).

Whereas spouses automatically get a share of each other's estate if one dies intestate, cohabitants have no such rights. The only remedy that you would have would be to make a claim under the Inheritance (Provision for Family and Dependants) Act 1975. If you have been living together as husband and wife for a period of at least two years ending on the death of one partner, the other has a right to claim a share of the estate if he or she was dependent on the other. But if you have split up, this right will not apply. If you can establish a financial dependency, you may be able to make a claim, but you will get no special consideration from the court because of your former cohabitation.

Children, however, do have claims on both their parents' estates, whether their parents were married or not, and all children rank equally. The children should be provided for, especially if your partner marries after your relationship breaks up, as the new spouse will take priority in the division of the estate, and there may not be much left over for the children.

Appointing a guardian

If you have parental responsibility for a child, which you have automatically as a mother, you can appoint someone to be the child's guardian in the event of your death. The child's father will not automatically take over responsibility for the child unless he has acquired parental responsibility.

You can make the appointment in a will or simply in writing, in a document which needs to be dated and signed by you, but does not need any further formalities.

Part 4

Other parts of the UK

Chapter 18

Divorce in Scotland

Scottish family and divorce law is significantly different from that in England and Wales. You can bring divorce proceedings in Scotland if you or your spouse are domiciled in Scotland (that is, if Scotland is regarded as your permanent home) or if either of you were habitually resident in Scotland for at least a year immediately before starting proceedings.

Grounds for divorce

There is no minimum period you have to wait after marriage before you can bring divorce proceedings. The sole ground for divorce is irretrievable breakdown of the marriage; this can be established only by proof of one of the following:

- adultery
- unreasonable behaviour
- desertion for two or more years
- non-cohabitation for two or more years and your spouse consents to the divorce
- non-cohabitation for five or more years.

If your spouse has committed adultery you do not have to show you find it intolerable to live with him or her. You cannot base your case on adultery which you have condoned or connived at. Condonation means that you forgave your spouse by resuming married life for more than three months after you knew about the adultery. Connivance means active encouragement, such as participation in wife-swapping or sex parties.

Unreasonable behaviour includes being violent, nagging persistently, abusing the children and being financially irresponsible, as well as negative conduct such as ignoring your spouse or his or her emotional or sexual needs.

Non-cohabitation means not living together as any normal married couple would. You and your spouse may have to continue sharing the home after your marriage breaks down because neither of you can get anywhere else to live. You would have to have been living separate lives to get a divorce on grounds of non-cohabitation.

Most divorces are dealt with in the sheriff courts. These are local courts situated in most major towns throughout Scotland. You can bring proceedings in the court for the area in which you or your spouse have been living for the past 40 days; you would usually choose your own local court. Divorces are also heard in the Court of Session in Edinburgh. Legal aid is not available for a Court of Session divorce, unless the case is unusually complex or difficult.

There are no decrees nisi or absolute in Scotland. The court grants a single decree of divorce which is immediately effective, although a certain period (14 days in the sheriff court, 21 days in the Court of Session) is allowed for an appeal.

Getting a divorce

There are two types of procedure: the simplified procedure (usually called a d-i-y divorce), and the ordinary procedure.

D-i-y divorce can be used only where the ground for divorce is non-cohabitation for two or five years. In addition, there must be no children of the marriage under 16 years of age, no financial claims by you or your spouse and no other legal proceedings affecting your marriage waiting to be heard; the divorce must be uncontested, and you and your spouse must not be suffering from any mental disorder. As the name implies, you do not need a solicitor for a d-i-y divorce. Nevertheless, you should consider seeking legal advice before you start in order to make sure that you are fully aware of the consequences and are not giving up rights in ignorance.

Printed forms for the d-i-y procedure are available from the courts or Citizens Advice Bureaux (CABx). For a divorce by consent after two years of non-cohabitation, you fill out part 1 of the form, and send it to your spouse for completion of part 2 (for his or her consent to the divorce). On its return, you complete the affidavit in part 3, swearing it before a notary public or a justice of the peace. Most solicitors in Scotland are notaries public but they will charge for affidavits. Your local council will have a list of justices of the peace whose services are free. In the case of a divorce after five years of non-cohabitation, your spouse's consent is unnecessary. Part 2 of this form is the affidavit which is sworn as before.

You send the completed form (parts 1, 2 and 3 or parts 1 and 2) to the court with your marriage certificate (the original or an official copy, but not a photocopy) and the court dues (currently £57). You may have to pay another £30 if the form has to be served on your spouse in a manner other than by post. If you are on income support or are seeing a solicitor under the legal advice and assistance scheme (the 'pink form scheme') you will not have to pay these dues. The court takes all remaining steps and will tell you and your spouse when the divorce has been granted. This usually takes about two months.

If you cannot get a d–i–y divorce, you will have to use the 'ordinary procedure'. This is more complex and you are strongly advised to get a Scottish solicitor to act for you. Most divorces are heard in the sheriff courts, so only that procedure will be described here. The Court of Session procedure is slightly different.

Your friends may be able to recommend a solicitor if you do not already have one. Alternatively, your library or CAB should have lists showing which local solicitors undertake divorce work and whether they will act for clients on legal aid (most do). The Law Society of Scotland★ will also help you find a solicitor.

Divorce expenses and legal aid

In d–i–y divorces the pursuer (the spouse seeking the divorce) pays his or her own expenses (£57 plus more for service costs if necessary). The defender (the other spouse) usually has no expenses since the proceedings must be undefended and have no associated financial and other claims.

The procedure for an ordinary divorce, however, is not cheap. The average costs of an ordinary undefended divorce with financial and other claims will amount to about £900. Defended proceedings are much more expensive. It is sensible for couples to keep disputes and litigation to an absolute minimum. Your respective solicitors should be able to help you negotiate a fair settlement without having to fight it out in court. Mediation services are also available (see later in this chapter). You and your spouse should be flexible and not regard certain matters as points of principle. The more that goes in legal fees, the less there is for both of you and the children.

A negotiated settlement should deal with the divorce expenses. If there is no agreement as to expenses, the court will apportion them at the end of the proceedings. The main factors that influence the courts are which spouse won and whether each spouse conducted the proceedings in a responsible way. For example, if you make exaggerated claims or are uncooperative, thus forcing your spouse to litigate unnecessarily, you could end up paying most of your spouse's expenses as well as your own. Often no award is made, so each spouse is left to pay his or her own expenses. The courts are reluctant to order a legally aided spouse to pay the other's expenses. It is common for consent to be given to a two years' non-cohabitation divorce on condition that the consenting spouse will not be liable for the other's expenses, and this condition will be enforced.

For proceedings other than divorce proceedings the normal rule is that the loser pays the winner's expenses as well as his or her own.

Even if your spouse pays your expenses you will almost certainly be out of pocket. You will have to pay for consultations with your solicitor and other extras which your spouse is not required to pay for.

Legal advice and assistance are available to help you with preliminary advice and to find out whether grounds for divorce exist. It does not cover representation in court. Assistance by way of representation (ABWOR) is not available for family litigation in Scotland. Legal aid is available for court proceedings: divorce, financial claims and matters concerning the children or housing, whether with the divorce proceedings or separately. Your solicitor will help you apply for legal advice and assistance, or legal aid. The Scottish Legal Aid Board★ runs both schemes. Eligibility depends on your own income and savings (your spouse's income and savings are not considered together with yours where you are opponents or are living apart). For legal aid the Board has also to be satisfied that you have a reasonable case. The financial limits are the same as in England and Wales (see Chapter 1).

Legal aid does not mean you can indulge in expensive litigation without fear of the financial consequences. The Scottish Legal Aid Board deducts the amount of your expenses from money the court awards you, or property that the court orders to be transferred to you, if it cannot recover the sum in full from your contributions or from your opponent. However, no deduction is made from any aliment (money paid periodically for a person's support) or periodical allowance or the first £2,500 of any capital sum or transfer of property awarded.

Separation agreements

Instead of going to court a couple may enter into an agreement specifying aliment for the children, which parent they are going to live with, when the other parent can see them or have them to stay (contact), aliment for the wife (less commonly for the husband), and what is to happen to the family home for the period from separation to divorce. Separated couples may also enter into agreements as to how their property is to be divided. They can then rely on this agreement and need not apply to the divorce court for financial orders. An agreement may be an oral, written or formal one (i.e. one prepared after negotiations by the couple and their respective lawyers). The advantages of formal agreements are that they are clear, easily proven and readily enforceable.

An agreement cannot prevent later applications to the court relating to the residence of, and contact with, the children, or to the Child Support Agency (CSA)* for maintenance for the children, where one of the parents starts receiving certain state benefits, including income support and working families' tax credit. You have to take into consideration the amount likely to be fixed by the Agency, as the amount could make it difficult or unfair for you to fulfil other terms of the agreement which you may not be able to alter. Terms which affect only the spouses, however, are generally binding so you ought to obtain legal advice beforehand. The court can set them aside only if satisfied they were not fair and reasonable at the time the agreement was made. A common formula provides aliment for the wife at an agreed rate in return for which she gives up her right to apply to the court for aliment. The court can vary the amount in the agreement only if the circumstances have changed, and will take the agreed amount as the baseline.

Ordinary divorce procedure

Proceedings start with your solicitor lodging the initial writ in court. This document sets out briefly the facts of your case and details the orders you are asking the court to make. A copy of this writ is then served on your spouse. You are called the pursuer and he or she is the defender. A copy also has to be served on any person (a co-defender) with whom you aver your spouse has committed adultery. The children may be sent a notice telling them about the court proceedings (if a parental rights order is sought) unless the court considers it inappropriate because of the children's age and they will be invited to express their views either in person or in writing. In a divorce action based on either two or five years' non-cohabitation, your spouse is also sent a notice warning of the possible financial consequences of divorce (loss of pension or inheritance rights, for example). The notice alerts your spouse to the financial and other applications he or she can make to the court.

In your initial writ you can apply for various interim orders, or you can add them on later (which will incur extra court fees). Interim orders last until the divorce is granted, when the position is reviewed and fresh orders made. Examples of interim orders are:

- interim aliment for you. The CSA deals with maintenance for the children
- interim residence for and contact with the children
- an interim interdict (prohibition) against violent behaviour or disposal of assets
- an interdict against taking the children out of Scotland. Your application for this need not be intimated to your spouse so that he or she may get no warning at all
- an exclusion order excluding your spouse from the family home.

You can also apply for these remedies separately; they are not available only in divorce proceedings. If you cannot apply for a divorce as soon as you and your spouse split up, you may need to use separate proceedings.

Defences

A notice of intention to defend must be lodged within 21 days (42 if the defender is abroad). The court will then specify the date defences have to be lodged by and the date of the options hearing (see below). In your defences you can oppose your spouse's claims and/or make claims against your spouse. Each of you will then adjust your case to meet the other's. An options hearing will then be held during which the court will clarify the issues in dispute and decide how to proceed. You and your spouse and your respective solicitors are required to attend, but you or your spouse may be excused. Some courts involve the couple in the discussions, others listen only to the solicitors.

It is unusual for the divorce itself to be defended. More commonly your spouse will defend your application for financial orders or matters relating to the children or apply for similar orders. Where the divorce is defended, the case is heard in court with each side and their witnesses giving evidence. But where only financial aspects are at issue, the divorce itself is generally disposed of on the basis of sworn statements (affidavits) containing full information about your and your spouse's financial resources (income and capital) and needs.

Affidavits

An affidavit is accepted by the court as evidence of the facts contained in it. You, your spouse and others can give evidence by affidavits instead of attending court, but this is not advisable unless the action is undefended or the evidence is uncontroversial. Your solicitor will prepare your affidavit from the information you give, and you will then swear it before a notary public (who may be your own solicitor). The information must be up-to-date, complete and accurate; otherwise further affidavits or oral evidence will be called for. Deliberately concealing facts or making false statements is regarded as a very serious offence for which you could well be imprisoned.

Reconciliation

You and your spouse can still try to save your marriage even though divorce proceedings have started. The court will, if asked, stop proceedings for a reconciliation. If this does not work, you can ask the court to let the proceedings continue from where they were stopped.

The children

You should show that satisfactory arrangements have been made for any children of the marriage who are under 16. Most couples reach agreement about who is to look after the children. Your or your spouse's affidavit will state who is going to look after the children, how they are going to be looked after, and what accommodation will be available for them. In addition, the court requires an affidavit from a relative or a person (such as a neighbour) who knows the children well. If these affidavits are satisfactory, the court will accept the arrangements without interviewing the couple or the children.

If you or your spouse apply for an order in relation to the children, a child welfare hearing will be fixed. This hearing takes place on the first convenient date three weeks after lodging the notice of intention to defend. You and your spouse will be expected to attend; the children may attend and may be given an opportunity to make their views known. The court may decide the matter there and then, it may refer you both to mediation (see overleaf) or it may postpone the matter to a later date for more thorough consideration. If the outcome is the last of these, the court may ask an independent person to prepare a report. The reporter is often an advocate or solicitor, but sometimes a social worker is used. The court will consider this report along with all the evidence from witnesses and other sources before deciding what would be best for the children's welfare.

Joint minute

If you and your spouse can agree on the financial aspects and future arrangements for the children before proceedings start, you can ask the court simply to make the appropriate orders and your spouse need not defend. An alternative, which is sometimes adopted, is for a formal enforceable agreement to be prepared covering these matters (this is similar to a separation agreement). Then the court is applied to only for the divorce; even a d-i-y divorce may be possible. In many cases, however, agreement is reached only after proceedings have started, as a result of negotiation or mediation. You and your spouse will then arrange for your respective solicitors to submit a joint minute to the court. This minute either sets out the orders that you and your spouse request the court to grant, or requests the court to make no orders because the matters are to be covered by a written agreement. The terms of the joint minute should be checked very carefully. Once it has been lodged in court it is normally impossible to change your mind and ask the court to do something different.

Where the proceedings are undefended or a joint minute is submitted, the court will normally grant the orders sought without further enquiry. The court may, however, demand further information in matters affecting the children.

Decree

A decree is a formal document containing the orders made by the court. The financial orders are usually granted at the same time as the divorce, although it is possible to have these left over for a later hearing if disagreement on this front is holding up the divorce.

The court will notify you that decree has been granted and also notify your spouse if his or her address is known. There is a 14-day period allowed for appeal (21 days in the Court of Session). After that, an extract (certified copy) of the decree can be obtained from the court which details the orders the court made. You will need an extract to show that you are divorced if you plan to marry again and also to enforce the orders if your spouse refuses to pay.

Mediation

There are two kinds of mediation services for family breakdown problems. They can be used at any time: before, during or after legal proceedings. You can either contact the service directly or ask your solicitor to make the arrangements.

Local mediation services affiliated to Family Mediation Scotland★ generally help couples resolve disputes relating to the children. Some services may also offer mediation on financial issues. Mediation is free but donations are most welcome. Information about local services in your area can be obtained from a CAB or from Family Mediation Scotland. When you and your spouse are engaged in legal proceedings relating to the children the court may refer you to mediation if it thinks that might resolve the dispute. The court can refer couples to a local service affiliated to Family Mediation Scotland without their consent.

Members of Comprehensive Accredited Lawyer Mediators (CALM)★ deal with the financial aspects of splitting up as well as matters affecting the children. The mediators are all family lawyers accredited as mediators by the Law Society of Scotland. Mediation sessions are generally taken by two lawyers (one male and one female if possible). The fee charged to the couple is £94 per hour, and generally two to three sessions of about one-and-a-half hours each are needed. If either of the spouses is legally aided, his or her share of these fees will be paid for. People entering into this type of mediation are encouraged to have their own solicitors because the outcome will be proposals which are worked up into a formal agreement by the spouses and their solicitors.

The home

Before divorce

Most couples now own their home together as co-owners. This means that both of them are equally entitled to live there and occupy it and are equally liable for the outgoings. Both have to consent to any sale or other disposal, although the court will order a sale against the wishes of one co-owner unless a sale is undesirable. A sale will not usually be ordered while the divorce proceedings are pending if the home is at issue. On sale, the proceeds of sale are divided equally between the couple unless the title deeds specify a different proportion. Each co-owner's share of the proceeds increases his or her capital which the court can reallocate on divorce.

The Matrimonial Homes (Family Protection) (Scotland) Act 1981 gives you certain rights if you do not own the home and your spouse is the sole owner. You are entitled to continue to occupy and live in the home. Moreover, your consent is required for any sale or other disposal, although the court can dispense with your consent if it is being withheld unreasonably. These rights are automatic: you do not have to register them in the Land Register for Scotland or the Register of Sasines (public registers of property and its owners).

Married co-tenants and spouses of sole tenants have similar protection against the tenancy of the home being given up.

You can renounce your occupancy rights but it is seldom in your interest to do so. A renunciation must be in writing and signed and declared before a notary public.

Exclusion orders

You can apply to the court for an order excluding your spouse from the family home and immediate vicinity if he or she behaves violently towards you or the children. This order is called an exclusion order and even a sole owner or tenant can be excluded. You can apply separately or as part of your divorce proceedings. An exclusion order will, if defended, take many weeks to obtain. You may apply for your spouse to be excluded during this period by means of an interim exclusion order. In many cases an interim order suffices, since it or an exclusion order lasts only until divorce.

The court has to be satisfied, first, that the (interim) exclusion order is necessary to protect you and/or the children from your spouse's violent behaviour or threats and, second, that it is reasonable for him or her to be excluded. Your spouse must be sent a copy of your application for an (interim) exclusion order and given an opportunity to oppose it. You will have to back up your claim with as much evidence as you can, such as affidavits from your doctor or neighbours about your health and past incidents of violence, reports by the police if they have been involved, and evidence of your need for the home and the unsuitable nature of your present temporary accommodation if you have been forced to leave home.

Interdicts

Another way of protecting yourself from violence or molestation by your spouse is to apply for a court order (called an interdict) prohibiting such conduct. Interdicts can be obtained extremely quickly, within a day if necessary. You can apply separately or as part of your divorce proceedings. Interdicts last until the court recalls them. Behaviour contrary to the interdict (a breach of interdict) is treated seriously. Your spouse can be fined or imprisoned, but is usually given a warning for the first breach.

It is possible to have a power of arrest added to your interdict. The advantage of this is that once you have sent a copy of the interdict and power of arrest to the police you can ask the police to arrest your spouse for breaching the interdict. Also, the police will generally respond more quickly to your call for assistance if you have a power of arrest. The drawback is that if you want a power of arrest added, your spouse has to be given notice of your application for the interdict and an opportunity to oppose it. Courts usually require evidence of one or more past violent incidents before a power of arrest is added. The power of arrest lapses on divorce.

Orders called non-harassment orders (NHO) might also be available to prevent undesirable conduct. Breach of an NHO is punishable as a criminal offence.

On divorce

Orders regarding the home are part of the overall financial settlement (see *Financial orders*, below). The court on granting divorce may:

- make no order and allow the home to be sold; the proceeds will have been taken into account in any lump-sum award made
- transfer the ownership (or tenancy) of the home or a share of it from one spouse to the other. The date of transfer can be deferred, but delays of more than a few months to allow time for the legal documents to be prepared are not common
- regulate who is to occupy the home after divorce. This is not often done, but it might be used to allow a wife and children to continue to occupy the home owned by her husband until she can get a job and afford somewhere else. An express exclusion of her husband from the home might be necessary if he was likely to interfere with her occupation of the home. The wife's occupancy rights prevent the home being sold without her consent, prior to divorce.

The children

You and your spouse have to decide what is to happen to the children after divorce. Talk things over with them, explain what is going on and what is going to happen to them and, if they are old enough, take account of their views as well as your own. You and your spouse should make every effort to reach agreement over the children. A mediation service is available to help divorcing couples resolve their disputes about the children.

The Children Act 1989 does not apply to Scotland; the legislation applicable is the Children (Scotland) Act 1995. In Scotland parents have various legal responsibilities towards their children, such as safeguarding them, advising them and acting on their behalf in legal transactions; and various rights, such as deciding where they are to live, controlling their upbringing and having contact with them. These responsibilities and rights cease when the children reach 16. The children can then live where they like, look after their own money and generally make their own decisions. A child under 16 can consent to medical treatment if the doctor thinks that he or she can understand what the proposed treatment involves, and in such a case the parents cannot overrule the child.

While the parents live together they share the parental responsibilities and rights. Each can act alone, neither can veto the other's actions, and any irreconcilable disputes have to be resolved by the courts. On divorce the court may, on application, reallocate these responsibilities and rights. Orders may be unnecessary if the parents are going to cooperate or if the absent parent will not interfere with the day-to-day decisions of the parent looking after the children. Otherwise the parent who is going to be looking after the children may need to apply for a residence order, which will give him or her the right to have the children living with him or her in addition to the other responsibilities and rights. The other parent retains these except in relation to the children's residence.

If the parents cannot agree which of them the children are to live with, the court will decide on welfare grounds, taking any views expressed by the children into account. Children of 12 and over are presumed able to form a view, and courts rarely go against firm views of 14- or 15-year-olds. Children below 12 can also give the court their views, which will be taken into account.

Arrangements for contact are best worked out on the basis of what is mutually acceptable. The parent with the children should allow the other reasonable contact and, indeed, encourage the children to keep up links. If these informal arrangements break down, the court will regulate contact – for example, allow the other parent to see the children for a certain number of hours every weekend or to have them to stay for part of the school holidays. Only in exceptional circumstances will the court refuse contact to a parent who has been previously involved with the children.

A woman may want to change her children's surname to that of her new husband. She should think carefully about this because their father (and perhaps the children too) may resent a change. The court probably has no power to allow or prohibit changes of name.

Child abduction

The Scottish provisions of the Child Abduction Act 1984 are different from those for England and Wales. A parent commits a criminal offence by taking a child out of the UK only if:

- the other parent (or someone else) has been awarded custody or has a residence order and has not agreed to the child's removal, *or*
- the court has interdicted removal.

If your spouse is likely to take the children abroad you should apply for a residence order or an interdict at once. You can do so even without applying for divorce but if you have started divorce proceedings the application has to be made in the context of those proceedings. Children cannot be made wards of court in Scotland. In an emergency you can obtain an interdict at any hour of the day or night. Once you have an interdict or a residence order you can ask the police and sheriff officers to trace the children and prevent their removal from the country.

If your child is abducted abroad see your solicitor immediately. Most European and Commonwealth countries and states in the USA are in the Hague Convention, which obliges the foreign country to trace the children and secure their return.

Financial orders

Many couples negotiate a financial settlement instead of litigating. Such an agreement is binding and will be set aside only if the court is satisfied that it was not fair and reasonable at the time it was entered into. The court will not look at, still less vet, the agreement unless an application is made to set it aside. A bad bargain is not enough to make an agreement unfair, so you ought to get legal assistance in negotiating.

The negotiations will obviously be influenced by the financial orders the court is likely to make in the absence of any agreement. The principles in the Family Law (Scotland) Act 1985 make it fairly easy to predict what the court is likely to do. If negotiations lead to an agreement the couple can lodge a joint minute setting out the orders they wish or asking for no financial orders to be made at all, leaving the agreement to regulate matters.

The main financial orders the court can make on divorce are:

- ordering one spouse to pay a lump sum (a 'capital' sum) to the other; *and/or*
- ordering one spouse to pay the other a periodical allowance – a regular sum each week or month; *and/or*
- ordering a spouse to pay aliment for the children of the marriage but only if the CSA cannot assess maintenance; *and/or*
- transferring the ownership of property from one spouse to the other.

It is possible, but unusual, for the court to grant a divorce and postpone the financial orders to a later date if disagreement is holding up the divorce.

The court can also order the house to be sold immediately or at a later date and/or say who is to occupy it and to have use of the contents. Where the house is rented, the court can transfer the tenancy from one spouse to the other.

Either the pursuer or the defender can apply for financial orders. You have to state in your initial writ or defences exactly what orders you seek from the court and give evidence of your and your spouse's needs and resources to demonstrate that they are reasonable claims. The court also needs to know the amount of aliment currently being paid. Making exaggerated claims is a bad tactic as it will merely get your spouse's back up and may result in you having to pay your spouse's legal costs. Almost inevitably a couple's living standards drop after divorce. A fair settlement should result in this drop being shared between the spouses.

A claim for a lump sum or transfer of property must be made before the divorce is granted. You can claim periodical allowance afterwards but you are very unlikely to get it then, because the principles required to justify an award (principles 3 to 5 below) generally speaking apply to your situation at the time of divorce. You cannot claim periodical allowance later if you and your spouse at the time of divorce made a formal agreement that you would not claim.

The Family Law (Scotland) Act 1985 sets out a series of principles to guide the court in making financial orders, as follows.

1. **Sharing matrimonial assets** The home and its contents, savings, investments and other assets which you or your spouse own and which were acquired between the date of marriage and the date of final separation are matrimonial assets. The home and contents are also counted as matrimonial assets if they were acquired before marriage as a family home for the couple. Assets given to you or inherited by you are not regarded as matrimonial assets. Matrimonial assets are to be shared equally unless there is a good reason for unequal division, which might be ordered where, say, your parents helped you buy the home or where you run a business that cannot be divided. An important matrimonial asset, especially for older couples, is the lump sum and pension payable on retirement

under a superannuation scheme. This can now be divided between the spouses. Alternatively, its value can be taken into account in calculating each spouse's share of the total matrimonial assets. From 1 December 2000 it is possible for the first time to 'split' pension schemes to allow spouses to share in the value (see Chapter 13 for details).

2. **Balancing economic advantages and disadvantages** The court has to take account of your financial and non-financial contributions to your spouse's wealth – and the other way round. Examples include helping with the running costs of the home, sacrificing a career to look after the children or working in your spouse's business at an artificially low wage. Courts tend not to use this principle to any great extent.

3. **Sharing childcare** Future childcare costs are to be shared. These include your loss of earnings while looking after the children and the expense of keeping up a larger and more expensive house than you would need if you were living on your own. If maintenance for the children is assessed by the CSA it includes an amount for childcare costs; the court will then take account of this principle only for extra costs.

4. **Financial dependency** Under this principle you are entitled to support for up to three years after divorce to enable you to become self-supporting if you were financially dependent upon your spouse during the marriage.

5. **Severe financial hardship** If you are unlikely to be self-supporting after divorce (too old or ill, for example), you may need support for many years (the rest of your life, perhaps) to avoid severe financial hardship.

Court orders

Principles 1 and 2 can be satisfied only by the award of a lump sum and/ or a transfer of property. The lump sum may be payable all at once, shortly after divorce or at a specified later date, or by instalments. Principles 3 to 5 should be satisfied by a lump sum or transfer of property if possible, otherwise by a periodical allowance. Wives who are looking after young children ought to get a periodical allowance under principle 3 as compensation for loss of earnings or the childcare costs if they work. Women tend not to ask for a periodical allowance as they do not wish to have continued financial links with their ex-husbands.

If a periodical allowance at the time of divorce cannot be justified by principles 3, 4 or 5 a spouse will not be awarded one. The court will not award a nominal periodical allowance on divorce with the intention that it could be increased later if the recipient's financial circumstances get worse.

Aliment for the children

The CSA now assesses maintenance for children up to and including 18 years of age who are still in secondary education. The courts have no power to deal with claims for aliment made for these children.

Certain categories of children are not within the Agency's remit and can still be awarded aliment by the courts. The most important of these categories are:

- children aged 19 to 24 who are undergoing further educational training at a university, college, apprenticeship or so on. Children have to look after themselves once they reach 25 as the parental obligation of aliment ceases then
- a child who has been accepted by you or your spouse as a child of the family. The accepting spouse will have an obligation of aliment. The usual example is a stepfather accepting his wife's children by her former marriage. The CSA will assess the children's father for payment, but if this is not feasible (father dead, untraceable or no money) aliment can be claimed via the courts against the stepfather
- where the parent due to pay aliment is abroad.

The CSA will refuse to assess if the parties have entered into a formal written registered agreement about aliment, unless one of the parties starts claiming state benefits (including income support). This is because a registered agreement, unlike in England, has the same effect as a court order. The courts may retain the power to alter aliment up or down where the CSA cannot make an assessment.

The amount of aliment awarded depends on what the person paying it can afford and what the child needs. The previous level of support the child enjoyed is also important.

A child over 11 can apply to the CSA for an assessment of his or her own maintenance. Children over 18 who wish aliment via the courts must claim themselves. Below that age a parent may claim on their behalf.

Change in circumstances

After divorce your or your ex-spouse's financial circumstances may change. You may be able to go back to court to get your orders changed, depending on the type of order involved.

Lump-sum order

You cannot apply for a lump-sum order after divorce. If you were awarded a lump sum on divorce the court cannot generally change the amount payable. There are two rare exceptions. First, if the true facts were concealed from the court or lies were told to obtain the original order, the court will make a new order. Second, if your ex-spouse became bankrupt within five years and the order resulted in his or her debts exceeding assets, then the court can order you to repay all or part of the lump sum. Apart from these two exceptional cases, all the court can do is to alter the way in which the lump sum is paid, perhaps by ordering payment by instalments or giving more time to pay.

Property-transfer orders

You cannot apply for a transfer of property order after divorce. If you were awarded a transfer on divorce the court cannot alter the property to be transferred except in the two rare cases mentioned above. All it can do is to alter the date set for transfer.

Periodical allowance

You can apply for a periodical allowance after divorce but it would be awarded only in unusual circumstances. You cannot apply if you agreed not to do so as part of the divorce settlement.

You or your ex-spouse can apply to the court for the amount to be increased, decreased, terminated or made payable only for a certain number of years more. For example, if you lose your job or now work part-time your allowance could be increased. If your ex-spouse's business is not doing so well, your allowance could be decreased or even terminated. Your allowance, which was awarded on grounds of severe financial hardship, could have a time limit put on it if you were offered a re-training course with a job at the end. If you were awarded an allowance on financial dependency grounds (principle 4) it cannot be extended beyond three years after divorce.

You cannot expect your allowance to be increased simply because of inflation. After all, inflation may be affecting your ex-spouse just as much as you.

Your remarriage terminates your allowance automatically. A woman's allowance is usually terminated by the court if she lives with another man even if he is not supporting her, but not all courts take this attitude. Your ex-spouse's remarriage will result in your allowance being reduced or terminated if the court thinks his or her commitments have increased. Your allowance should not be reduced if your ex-spouse lives with another partner. But if they have children the court will take these new liabilities into account.

When you die, your allowance comes to an end automatically. But the death of your ex-spouse does not mean that your allowance comes to an end automatically. The executors have to apply to the court for it to be terminated. Occasionally the court will then order payment at a reduced rate or set a time limit on the allowance, rather than terminate it.

Any variation the court awards can be backdated to the date of the application, or to the date when the circumstances changed, as long as there was a good reason for the delay in applying for the variation.

Another variation the court can be asked to make is to substitute a lump sum (payable by instalments perhaps) for a periodical allowance. You and your ex-spouse should weigh up the advantages and disadvantages carefully because once the substitution order is made it cannot be reversed.

Old orders

There are some special rules for periodical allowance awarded in divorce proceedings started before 1 September 1986 (when the Family Law (Scotland) Act 1985 came into force). First, the court cannot substitute a lump sum for your allowance. You or your ex-spouse could, of course, agree to do this without going to court. Second, the court cannot backdate a variation of the allowance.

Aliment

The CSA now deals with the assessment of most children's maintenance. The assessed amount depends on the financial circumstances of each parent and also on the age of the child. Application may be made to the Agency for variation of the assessment.

In exceptional cases (see *Aliment for the children*) the courts may still award aliment and can vary the amount awarded subsequently. Apart from these cases, if aliment is payable under a court order which was made in proceedings commenced, or a written agreement entered into, before April 1993, the courts retain power to vary the amount. A variation of aliment can be applied for if the circumstances of the child or the paying parent change. The amount of aliment is not reduced merely because the paying parent or the parent looking after the children remarries or cohabits. Aliment ceases automatically when either the paying parent or the child dies.

Enforcing maintenance

A great number of people who have a court order for their own aliment or periodical allowance or for aliment for the children never get paid regularly. The longer the time over which the arrears have built up, the less likely it is that you will be paid.

If informal demands for regular payments do not produce the required results, you will have to use legal enforcement methods (called diligence). You do not have to go back to the court but you will need a solicitor's help. The legal aid certificate for your divorce covers the cost of diligence for up to 12 months later. After a year, or if you are applying for your ex-spouse to be imprisoned for failure to pay, you will have to apply for legal aid or legal advice and assistance.

Where your ex-spouse is employed, the best diligence to use is a *current maintenance arrestment*. You (or your solicitor) send a copy of the court order to your ex-spouse, and if, not less than four weeks later, three or more instalments are in arrears, a current maintenance arrestment can be served by a sheriff officer on your ex-spouse's employer. The employer thereafter automatically deducts every payday the maintenance due to you for the period since the last payday and sends it to you or your solicitor. A current maintenance arrestment does not enforce arrears but you can use an earnings arrestment or another diligence at the same time to recover the arrears.

The following diligences enforce arrears only, although the threat of repeating them may make your ex-spouse keep up regular payments in future:

- **Earnings arrestment**: a sheriff officer serves a notice on your ex-spouse's employer who deducts every pay-day an amount which varies with the earnings payable then. The deductions are sent to you or your solicitor and stop when the arrears are paid off.

- **Arrestment of a bank or building society account**: a sheriff officer serves a notice which freezes the money in your ex-spouse's account. You then have to apply to the court for an order requiring the bank or building society to pay you, unless your ex-spouse agrees to release the money.

- **Poinding and sale of goods**: a sheriff officer goes to your ex-spouse's home or business premises and makes a list of his or her goods and their value. The court can then order these 'poinded' goods to be auctioned to pay the arrears.

- **Imprisonment**: if the court is satisfied that your ex-spouse's failure to pay was wilful, he or she can be imprisoned for up to six weeks. Only a handful of people are actually sent to prison each year, but the threat usually works wonders. Imprisonment is available only for failure to pay aliment; you cannot use it to enforce your periodical allowance.

The CSA will collect and if necessary enforce child maintenance on request and will always do so if the parent looking after the children is on benefit. If your ex-spouse is employed, the CSA will use a deduction from earnings order (very like an earnings arrestment). If not, it will have to go to court to get a liability order for the arrears and then use the diligences of bank arrestment, poinding or imprisonment.

Effect of divorce on your inheritance rights

After divorce, you have no rights to your ex-spouse's estate if he or she dies without a will or leaves you nothing. The Inheritance (Provision for Family and Dependants) Act 1975 does not apply to Scotland.

Legacies or other provisions for you in your ex-spouse's will are not cancelled by divorce after the date of the will. Generally speaking, you are entitled to take them unless the will makes it clear that you are not. Your ex-spouse's will is not cancelled by his or her subsequent remarriage.

After divorce, you and your ex-spouse should review any existing will. You will probably want to cancel any bequest to your ex-spouse, but other changes may also be desirable. Most married couples who own their home together have in the title deeds that the property will go to the survivor when one of them dies. This is another thing that ought to be changed on or before divorce. A solicitor's help will be needed to change the title deeds.

Judicial separation

Instead of a divorce, you can apply for a judicial separation. The grounds are the same as for divorce. The court granting a judicial separation has no power to award a capital sum or order a transfer of property: it can only award aliment for you. You and your spouse remain married to each other so neither of you can remarry. There is limited legal point in getting a judicial separation because now you can get aliment from the court without asking for separation, but a few couples still opt for a judicial separation for religious reasons.

A husband does not inherit any of the property the wife acquired after separation if she dies without having made a will. There is no equivalent rule disinheriting a separated wife.

Stepfamilies

A stepparent has, despite being married to the child's parent, few legal rights and responsibilities towards the child. He or she cannot act as the child's legal representative and does not have the right to say where the child is to live, unless the court grants such rights or appoints the stepparent as guardian.

A stepparent can obtain all the rights of a parent by adopting the child. The child then becomes in law a child of the marriage of the stepparent and the natural parent (the stepparent's spouse). Adoption by a stepparent is becoming less common because many consider that the legal relationship with the other natural parent (and his or her relatives) should not be terminated. Some stepparents apply instead for some of the parental responsibilities and rights, or for guardianship, which confers them all. The welfare of the child is the paramount consideration and the court will not grant an adoption application unless satisfied that to do so would be in the long-term interests of the child and that there is no better practicable alternative.

A stepparent becomes liable to aliment for a stepchild if he or she accepts the child as a child of his or her family. This liability can be enforced by an application to the court by, or on behalf of, the child either in connection with the divorce proceedings between the stepparent and the child's parent or in separate proceedings. While the child's father is alive and able to afford aliment he is regarded as primarily liable to pay. The CSA will make a maintenance assessment against the child's absent father. It will not deal with aliment due from stepparents.

On the breakdown of the marriage between a child's stepparent and parent the court hearing the divorce must be satisfied that the future arrangements for the children of both the parties' first and second marriages are suitable.

As mentioned before, a person's will is not revoked by his or her subsequent marriage or divorce. If the stepparent is not mentioned in his or her spouse's will, a claim for legal rights could be made. Legal rights amount to one-half or one-third of the spouse's property other than land or buildings. The higher fraction applies if the spouse leaves no surviving children.

The title to the 'stepfamily home' may be taken simply in the name of the spouse and the stepparent. Each person then owns an equal share (unless the title deeds specify a different proportion) and on his or her death that share is dealt with by his or her will (or the rules of intestacy). Where the title is taken in the name of the spouse, the stepparent and the survivor of them, the home will belong entirely to the survivor. If you are remarrying you should think carefully about your will and whether to use a survivorship title.

The child's parent may by will appoint the stepparent to be the child's guardian after his or her death. The stepparent will then share parental responsibilities and rights with the other parent if he or she is still alive. Any disputes between them would have to be resolved by the court.

Chapter 19

Divorce in Northern Ireland

To a large extent divorce in Northern Ireland mirrors divorce in England and Wales. This chapter should not, therefore, be read in isolation. Much of what has been written in the preceding chapters regarding children, the Child Support Agency (CSA),★ financial issues and child abduction is relevant to readers contemplating divorce in Northern Ireland. However, the process in Northern Ireland is different in some ways from that in England and Wales. The most important differences – although not all – are highlighted in this chapter.

The High Court and county courts in Northern Ireland have jurisdiction to hear a petition for divorce or judicial separation if either of the parties is domiciled in Northern Ireland when the proceedings are begun. Divorce proceedings cannot be brought within the first two years of marriage.

A petition can be brought for judicial separation instead of divorce where one or both of the parties have religious objections to divorce. The main difference between divorce and judicial separation is that a decree of judicial separation does not formally end the marriage but simply brings to an end the couple's duty to live together. Neither of the parties is free to remarry following a decree of judicial separation. However, each party is still free to petition for divorce at a future date. The most obvious difference to a petitioner (that is, the spouse initiating the divorce) in Northern Ireland is that he or she is required to give oral evidence in court regardless of the ground for divorce upon which he or she seeks to rely. The 'special procedure', which deals with undefended divorces, does not apply to Northern Ireland. There is provision under the Family Law (Northern Ireland) Order 1993 to dispense with oral testimony in cases where a petitioner alleges two years' separation and the respondent (i.e. the other spouse) consents to a decree being granted, or in cases where a petitioner is alleging five years' separation, but this has still not come into force.

A petitioner will be required to appear in person before a judge and formally prove the ground upon which the petition is based, whether in the county court or the High Court. The judge will hear the petitioner's evidence in private (known as 'in chambers'), and most undefended divorce hearings are relatively brief (about ten minutes).

After hearing the petitioner's evidence, the judge, if satisfied that the marriage has broken down irretrievably and that one of the five facts outlined below has been proved, will grant a decree nisi. Six weeks from that date the petitioner can apply to have the decree made absolute, thereby ending the marriage and leaving each party free to remarry. Divorce, judicial separation, or even the drawing up of a separation agreement may affect inheritance rights and it is advisable for the parties involved to discuss this with a solicitor at the earliest opportunity.

Which court?

In Northern Ireland divorces can be brought in either a county court or the High Court. There is at least one county court for each of the six counties in Northern Ireland, including Recorder's Courts in Londonderry and Belfast. The High Court is situated in Belfast. Whether the divorce petition is to be heard in a county court or the High Court is a decision for the petitioner's solicitor. By and large, for petitions that are likely to be defended or in which there are sizeable assets to be taken into account the High Court is considered the more appropriate venue. However, as more and more divorces are being heard in county courts, it is likely that fewer divorces will be heard in the High Court. In any event at present most financial matters are still transferred from the county courts to the High Court.

Stamp duty payable on a divorce petition is £135 in a county court and £150 in the High Court.

The petitioner must complete and include with the petition a form entitled 'Statement as to Arrangements for Children', outlining the proposed future arrangements for the children. The petitioner should try to agree the arrangements with the respondent in advance of lodging the form with the court, and should obtain the latter's signature on the form to show his or her consent to the arrangements. Obviously this depends on the cooperation and goodwill of the respondent, and given the animosity which often surrounds divorce, this may not always be forthcoming. In such a case it would be sufficient for a petitioner to show that he or she had done everything possible to obtain the respondent's consent. The petitioner can sign the form him- or herself and lodge it with the divorce petition. The respondent still has the option of filing a statement of his or her own. If the court is not satisfied with the arrangements for the children, it can request Social Services to prepare a welfare report to aid it in reaching a decision.

A social worker interviews both parents and completes a form provided by the court which gives details of income, living conditions and proposed arrangements for the children. Occasionally the social worker may be asked to provide further details, but normally a standard report is completed and forwarded to the court, where it is read by the judge before any order in relation to the children is made.

Proceedings can be adjourned by the court at any stage if there appears to be a reasonable prospect of a reconciliation between the parties. Counselling is offered to married, divorcing or divorced couples by RELATE.★

Legal aid

Full legal aid can be applied for to bring divorce proceedings in either the county court or the High Court. A solicitor should be able to give advice about legal aid eligibility at the initial interview if the petitioner outlines his or her earnings and savings. Only those on income support or very low incomes will be entitled to full legal aid, but a contribution system is still in operation in Northern Ireland whereby the petitioner makes a financial contribution to the costs of obtaining the divorce by paying in 12 monthly instalments an amount set by the Legal Aid Department.★ The amount set will depend on the means of the applicant.

Divorce petitions – irretrievable breakdown

The Family Law Act 1996, which has led to extensive changes to divorce law being debated in England and Wales, does not extend to Northern Ireland. However, consultation is ongoing to see whether any of the provisions in the Act should be enacted in Northern Ireland. So far, one consultation paper has been drawn up by the Office of Law Reform, entitled *A Better Way Forward*. At present, one or more of the 'five facts' set out in the Matrimonial Causes (Northern Ireland) Order 1978 must be proved by the petitioner so that the court can find that the marriage has 'irretrievably broken down'. Put very simply the five facts are:

- the respondent has committed adultery
- the respondent has behaved unreasonably
- the respondent has deserted the petitioner for a continuous period of at least two years
- the parties have lived apart for a period of two years and the respondent consents to a decree being granted
- the parties have lived apart for a continuous period of at least five years, provided that admission of this fact will not result in grave financial or other hardship to the respondent.

The first three facts – adultery, unreasonable behaviour and desertion – are immediate grounds for bringing divorce proceedings. As mentioned above, it is intended at present that these grounds, known as 'fault' grounds, will remain in Northern Ireland.

However, there can often be difficulties in proving any of the three fault-based grounds. Obtaining evidence of adultery by the respondent, which the court will need, can be expensive. As regards behaviour, the court will not only look at the behaviour of the respondent that has been complained of, but also the character and personality of the petitioner. The courts are mindful that because fault grounds are immediate grounds for bringing divorce proceedings they are open to abuse. The judge will therefore study closely the type of behaviour being complained about. Desertion, while perhaps easier to prove on the facts, may be problematical if the respondent shows that a reasonable offer to return was made but was not accepted by the petitioner.

It is open to the respondent to defend any of the fault-based grounds. Defended petitions, although few in number, can be very costly, so a petitioner who wishes to allege the fault grounds for the sake of convenience and time should be extremely wary.

The most common ground for divorce is where the petitioner and respondent have lived apart for a continuous period of at least two years and the respondent consents to a decree being granted. This is quite rightly viewed as the most amicable basis for obtaining a divorce. It usually allows the matter of finances to be dealt with before the petition is issued (see below). An initial refusal by the respondent to consent to a divorce being granted on this ground can very often be reversed by the petitioner agreeing to bear the costs of obtaining the divorce.

Separation agreements

Unfortunately legal aid is not available for people wishing to enter into a separation agreement with their spouse. Separation agreements are, however, the preferred route for parties wishing to end their marriage as amicably as possible. This is particularly relevant where there are children, as a petition based on one of the fault grounds inevitably leaves a bad after-taste and often bitterness on the part of at least one of the spouses.

In essence, by entering into a separation agreement, the parties decide to deal with the financial matters relating to their separation before divorce proceedings are issued. The parties agree in advance that they will live apart for a period of two years and the respondent will consent to a decree being granted after the two-year period has passed. Both parties are under a duty to make full disclosure of their assets; they should, with their legal advisers, attempt to agree the financial separation. The terms of the separation agreement can be as simple or complex as the case requires and can include a clean break by way of a lump sum, or ongoing maintenance, or the transfer of the matrimonial home or the realisation of part or all of the house's equity. The separation agreement should state the date upon which either party can issue the divorce petition on the two-years' ground and that the other party consents. It should also deal with the costs of bringing the divorce petition. Should the parties wish to make the agreement an order of court, they can do so when the divorce petition is issued.

Although a court will be mindful of the terms of the separation agreement when dealing with the divorce petition, it will not allow an agreement to tie its hands. It is not necessarily bound by the agreement, particularly if one of the parties has attempted to conceal relevant information.

Money matters – ancillary relief

Ancillary relief is the legal term for applications to the courts for financial relief, and includes maintenance pending suit (that is, maintenance from the date the petition is issued to the granting of the decree absolute), financial provision (maintenance) and property adjustment. In cases other than the ones involving a separation agreement, when a decree nisi has been granted the court will deal with the financial position between the parties. As with the separation agreement, full disclosure of assets and liabilities will be required by both parties. What type of financial settlement the court orders will very much depend on the circumstances of the parties. Clearly most cases will involve some sort of financial provision to be paid by one party to the other. This can very often take the form of a lump sum payment to one party so as to attempt what is still termed a clean break. It is intended that this one-off payment will end any financial responsibility the paying party has to the other. However, since the creation of the CSA and in the light of the new legislation regarding pensions (see below) this has not always been the case. The courts may now prefer to order that one party make periodical payments (normally monthly) for the benefit of the other party or the children, for a term of years specified by them.

It is often the case that the only real asset the parties have is the former matrimonial home. This poses difficulties for the courts as clearly the parent with care of the children must have a roof over their heads, but also the other parent must have some means to access his (or, rarely, her) contribution to the home's worth. With this in mind the courts can alter the legal ownership of the matrimonial home (or other properties) by way of a property adjustment order.

Just because a spouse's name is not on the title deeds does not mean that he or she has no rights with respect to what is done about the house. The court may decide that the spouse has an 'equitable' interest in the property if it can be proved that he or she contributed to the family home by either direct or indirect financial contributions.

The Department of Social Security (DSS) may be able to help a divorcing spouse by providing information concerning financial help with housing and welfare benefit, and Benefits Agencies should have details of benefits which can be claimed. Information about help with rent and/or rates can also be obtained from the Northern Ireland Housing Executive.*

The Child Support Agency

The workings of the CSA in Northern Ireland mirror that in England and Wales. Under the Child Support (Northern Ireland) Order 1991 a child 'qualifies' under the scheme if either parent is an 'absent parent'. Article 5 (1) of the order states that each parent is responsible for maintaining a qualifying child and the duty to maintain shall be deemed to have been met where an absent parent makes the payments of maintenance determined by the CSA.

The CSA will be responsible for child maintenance in all cases where there is no existing court order. It is also intended that it will gradually become responsible for cases where there is an existing court order. The Agency will be automatically involved in cases where the parent who is looking after the child is in receipt of state benefits.

The 1991 order provides for considerable powers of enforcement and the Agency may use DSS or Inland Revenue records to trace absent parents. Also, if a parent with care refuses to cooperate by naming the child's father, she may incur a deduction in benefit.

The Children (Northern Ireland) Order 1995

Until 4 November 1996 Northern Ireland did not have any legislation in place equivalent to the Children's Act 1989. However, the 1995 order brings legislation relating to children in line with the rest of the UK and creates a new concept of 'parental responsibility'. Where parents are divorcing and there are children of the marriage the courts in Northern Ireland will no longer make custody or access orders but will make what are termed 'article 8' orders, most important of which are residence and contact orders.

A residence order, as the name suggests, settles the issue of which parent the children of the family are to live with. Normally the other parent will be given a contact order, which will allow the children to visit or stay with him or her. Residence and contact orders will usually remain in force until the child reaches the age of 16, and parents who were married when the child was born will continue to have parental responsibility for their children even when they are no longer living with them.

It is important to note that the 1995 Children Order explicitly states, as does its counterpart in England and Wales, that when deciding where a child should live and who should have contact with the child the courts will consider the child's welfare to be of paramount importance.

Pensions

Since 1996, courts must take pension rights into account when considering financial settlements. There are several ways they may do this including, for example, offsetting the pension rights against other assets (see Chapter 14), or earmarking lump sums or pension. In addition, the new pension-sharing rules described in Chapter 13 which apply to England and Wales are also extended to Northern Ireland under parallel statutory rules. Pension-sharing is optional and can be used in divorces started from 1 December 2000 onwards.

Domestic violence

In Northern Ireland a spouse or a cohabitant can apply under the Family Homes and Domestic Violence (Northern Ireland) Order 1998 to a court for protection.

The protection can take the form of a non-molestation order – that is, an order prohibiting the respondent from molesting a certain adult or child. Molestation is not confined to violence or the threat of violence, but can apply to conduct which the court deems amounts to harassment. In deciding whether to make a non-molestation order, the judge is required to take into account all the circumstances of the case, including the need to secure the health, safety and wellbeing of the applicant and any person in favour of whom the order is being made or any relevant child.

The court also has the power to make an occupation order. This can be used to:

- enforce the applicant's entitlement to remain in occupation
- require the respondent to permit the applicant to enter the property
- require the respondent to give the applicant peaceful use and enjoyment of the property
- regulate the occupation and use of the property

- prohibit, suspend or restrict the respondent's right to occupy the property
- restrict or terminate the respondent's matrimonial home rights on application by the spouse who owns the property
- require the respondent to leave the property
- provide for the respondent to remove specified personal effects, furniture, etc.
- exclude the respondent from a defined area in which the house is situated, any other defined area or other premises
- restrain the respondent from disposing of any estate in the property
- declare a proprietary interest or matrimonial home rights
- on application during the marriage, provide that the matrimonial home rights will not terminate on death or termination of the marriage.

When considering whether to make an occupation order, the court will consider all the circumstances of the case, including:

- the housing needs and resources of the parties and any relevant child
- the financial resources of the parties
- the likely effect of any order or failure to make an order on the health, safety and wellbeing of the parties and any child
- the conduct of the parties in relation to each other.

A person subject to domestic violence can, after seeing a solicitor, apply to the court for immediate relief. The court will require a written statement to be filed and he or she will usually have to give oral evidence.

If a person breaches either a non-molestation order or an occupation order, the police have the powers to arrest him or her without a warrant.

Appendix I

Which court? (England and Wales)

Before divorce

Applying for spousal maintenance or for maintenance for any children not covered by the Child Support Agency

Applying for a Children Act order

Applying for domestic violence injunction

Make application to:
1. Family Proceedings Panel (FPP) of local magistrates' court, or
2. Family Hearing Centre (FHC) (county court), or
3. If case is especially complex, the High Court

Make application to:
1. FPP
2. County court or FHC

Starting divorce proceedings

Make application to divorce county court (DCC) or FHC.

DCC will deal with administrative paperwork of divorce only; contested applications (e.g. for finance, about the children) will be transferred to FHC. If divorce becomes defended or is especially complex, DCC or FHC will transfer case to the High Court.

Once divorce is under way

Applying for ancillary (financial) relief and/ or applying for a Children Act order and/or applying for domestic violence injunction

Make application to court dealing with divorce. If this is only a DCC, case will be transferred to FHC (see above).

Appendix II

Code of practice for SFLA members

All members of the Solicitors Family Law Association (SFLA) have to follow a code of practice, which is designed to promote a conciliatory atmosphere in which matters are dealt with in a sensitive, constructive and cost-effective way.

General

1. At an early stage, you should explain to your client the approach you adopt in family law work.
2. You should encourage your client to see the advantages to the family of a constructive and non-confrontational approach as a way of resolving differences. You should advise, negotiate and conduct matters so as to help the family members settle their differences as quickly as possible and reach agreement, while allowing them time to reflect, consider and come to terms with their new situation.
3. You should make sure that your client understands that the best interests of the child should be put first. You should explain that where a child is involved, your client's attitude to the other family members will affect the family as a whole and the child's relationship with his or her parents.
4. You should encourage the attitude that a family dispute is not a contest in which there is a winner and a loser, but rather that it is a search for fair solutions. You should avoid using words or phrases that suggest or cause a dispute when there is no serious dispute.
5. Emotions are often intense in family disputes. You should avoid inflaming them in any way.

6. You should take great care when considering the effect your correspondence could have on other family members and your own client. Your letters should be clearly understandable and free of jargon. Remember that clients may see assertive letters between solicitors as aggressive declarations of war. Your correspondence should aim to resolve issues and to settle the matter, not to further inflame emotions or to antagonise.

7. You should stress the need for your client to be open and honest in all aspects of the case. You must explain what could happen if your client is not open and honest.

Relationship with a client

8. You should make sure that you are objective and do not allow your own emotions or personal opinions to influence your advice.

9. You must give advice and explain all options to your client. The client must understand the consequences of any decisions that he or she may have to make. The decision is to be made by your client, you cannot decide for your client.

10. You must make your client aware of the legal costs at all stages. The benefits and merits of any step must be balanced against the costs.

11. You should make sure that your client knows about other available services (such as mediation and counselling) which may bring about a settlement, help your client and other family members, or both. You should explore, with your client, the possibility of reconciliation and, where appropriate, give every encouragement.

Dealing with other solicitors

12. In all dealings with other solicitors, you should show courtesy and try to maintain a good working relationship.

13. You should try to avoid criticising the other solicitors involved in a case.

Dealing with a person who does not have a solicitor

14. When you are dealing with someone who is not represented by a

solicitor, you should take even greater care to communicate clearly and try to avoid any technical language or jargon, which is not easily understood.

15. You should strongly recommend an unrepresented person to consult an SFLA solicitor in the interests of the family.

Court proceedings

16. When taking any step in the proceedings, the long-term effect on your client and other family members must be balanced with the likely short-term benefit to the case.

17. If the purpose of taking a particular step in proceedings may be misunderstood or appear hostile, you should consider explaining it, as soon as possible, to the others involved in the case.

18. Before filing a petition, you and your client should consider whether the other party or his or her solicitor should be contacted in advance about the petition the 'facts' on which the petition is to be based and the particulars, with a view to coming to an agreement and minimising misunderstandings.

19. When you or your client receive a Petition or Statement of Arrangements for approval, unless there are exceptional circumstances, you should advise your client not to start their own proceedings without giving the other party at least 7 days' notice, in writing, of the intention to do so.

20. You should discourage your client from naming a co-respondent unless there are very good reasons to do so.

Children

21. You should encourage both your client and other family members to put the child(ren)'s welfare first.

22. You should encourage parents to co-operate when making decisions concerning the child, and advise parents that it is often better to make arrangements for the child between themselves, through their solicitors or through a mediator rather than through a court hearing.

23. In any letters you write, you should keep disputes about arrangements for the child separate from disputes about money. They should usually be referred to in separate letters.

24. You must remember that the interests of the child may not reflect

those of either parent. In exceptional cases it may be appropriate for the child to be represented separately by the Official Solicitor, a panel guardian (in specified proceedings) or, in the case of a 'mature' child, by another solicitor.

When the client is a child

25. You should only accept instructions from a child if you have the necessary training and expertise in this field.
26. You must continually assess the child's ability to give instructions.
27. You should make sure that the child has enough information to make informed decisions. The solicitor should advise and give information in a clear and understandable way and be aware that certain information may be harmful to the child.
28. You should not show favour towards either parent, the local authority or any other person involved in the court proceedings.
29. Detailed guidelines for solicitors acting for children have been drawn up by the SFLA. You can write to the SFLA to get a copy.

Glossary

absent parent A term invented by the Child Support Act 1991 to mean the parent not living in the same household with the qualifying child (q.v.)

access See contact

acknowledgement of service Form sent by the court to the respondent (and co-respondent, if any) with the petition, with questions about his or her intentions and wishes in response to the petition; its return to the court establishes service of the petition

adultery Sexual intercourse by a husband or wife with someone of the opposite sex at any time before a decree absolute

affidavit A statement in writing containing a person's evidence, on oath or by affirmation. The evidence in the affidavit need not be expressed in any formal way but should be set out in numbered paragraphs in the first person. If the person making the affidavit wishes to refer to any document, this document should be attached ('exhibited') to the affidavit

ancillary relief General term for the financial or property adjustment orders that the court can be asked to make 'ancillary' to a petition for divorce or judicial separation

annuity Money investment designed to produce regular fixed amounts of income, either for a fixed period or until death

answer The defence to a divorce petition, denying the allegations in the petition or cross-petition; strict time limits apply for filing an answer

application A document giving details, in broad terms, of the order sought from the court. All applications within divorce proceedings are started by filing a notice of application. Standard forms are available at divorce court offices; they include a space for the place, date and time of the hearing of the application, to be completed by the court office

Calderbank letter Where a husband knows he will be ordered to make payment if the case goes to hearing, his solicitor can write a 'without prejudice' letter making an offer of settlement; if the wife rejects the offer and at the hearing is awarded the same or less, she risks having to pay the husband's costs incurred after the date of the offer as well as her own; a wife can, similarly, make a Calderbank offer

care and attention   A term used to describe an uplift (increase) in a solicitor's legal bill which some solicitors apply if a case has been complex or has had to be dealt with especially quickly

care and control   An old order pre-dating the Children Act 1989 – care and control orders are no longer made. It means the responsibility for looking after and making everyday decisions about a child and providing the child's main home base

in chambers   When the district judge or judge considers an application in private rather than in open court; the proceedings tend to be less formal than normal court hearings and members of the public are not admitted

charge (on property)   Security entitling the holder of the charge to be paid out of the proceeds of sale when the house (or other property) is eventually sold

chattels   An old-fashioned legal term used for personal effects, usually of a house, like furniture, paintings, jewellery and ornaments

child of the family   Any child of both the parties and any child who has at any time been treated by both the parties as if a child of their own (but not foster-children); has to be listed in the petition irrespective of age. 'Family' in this context means married family

Community Legal Service (CLS) The new name for legal aid (q.v.)

clean break   A once-and-for-all order that deals with all financial issues between spouses, provides for the dismissal of maintenance claims and is not capable of subsequent variations even if circumstances change

conciliation   A process of non-partisan mediation to help a couple reach agreement on issues flowing from divorce; more usually about the arrangements for children than about comprehensive financial issues. Conciliation can be 'in-court' as part of the court process to try to help parties settle their differences over the children, or 'voluntary', i.e. provided by an independent service, for which fees may be payable (see Mediation)

conflict of interest(s)   Where a solicitor cannot act for a potential client because he or she would be unable to discharge his or her duty to the client because of a pre-existing professional relationship to another client or a duty owed to another

consent order   Order made by a court in terms agreed by both parties

contact (formerly termed access)   An order under the Children Act for the child to visit or stay with the parent with whom the child is not living or exchange letters, cards or telephone calls; contact orders may also be made in favour of non-parents, e.g. grandparents (the obligation to provide contact is on the parent with whom the child lives)

co-respondent The person with whom the respondent has committed adultery

counsel Barrister

cross-decrees When a petitioner is granted a decree on the basis of the petition and the respondent on the basis of the answer

cross-petition When the respondent puts forward different reasons for the breakdown of the marriage from the petitioner's, and seeks a divorce on those facts

custody An out-of-date term meaning the right formerly granted by a court for one parent (or both) to make major decisions for a child, such as education and upbringing, change of religion (subject to the non-custodial parent's right to ask the court to review any such decision). Custody orders are no longer made

decree absolute At present the final order dissolving the marriage

decree nisi Document issued once the court is satisfied that the grounds for divorce are established, allowing the petitioner to apply to have the decree made absolute after a further six weeks and one day. It does not end the marriage

directions for trial The stage of divorce proceedings when the district judge considers the petition and affidavit in support, and requests further information if required, before giving his or her certificate for a decree nisi to be pronounced by the judge; financial proceedings and applications about the children also have a directions for trial stage, when the district judge considers what further evidence will be required and makes orders accordingly

disclosure Full information about all matters relevant to any financial application; each spouse has a duty to give full and frank disclosure which, if they fail to abide by, may render a later court order invalid

discovery Procedure by which each party supplies to the other a list of documents relevant to an application and permits the other to inspect them

district judge Judicial officer appointed by the Lord Chancellor; responsible for dealing with most applications to a divorce court (used to be called a registrar)

divorce court Any county court designated by the Lord Chancellor as a court where divorce proceedings can be heard; the Divorce Registry in London serves as a divorce court. Divorce county courts not designated Family Hearing Centres (FHCs; q.v.) can deal only with the administrative process of divorces; any contested applications will be referred to an FHC

domicile Legal concept, not necessarily related to residence: domicile of origin is normally determined by the place where a person was born and is retained unless a new domicile – a domicile of choice – is adopted by a conscious decision to take up permanent residence in, and actually moving to, another country

equity (of a property)   The net value of house or flat after mortgage debts are discharged and expenses of sale met

exhibit   Document referred to in, sworn with, and attached to an affidavit; usually identified by initials and number

ex parte   An application made directly to the court without prior notification to the party or parties

Family Hearing Centre   A county court with the power to deal with the administrative process of divorce and any contested applications under the Children Act or for financial relief

filing   Leaving documents – petition and accompanying documents, affidavits, notices of application, for example – with the court office for sealing, and subsequent service

green form   Popular term for legal aid scheme under which a limited amount of legal advice and assistance is given

hearsay evidence   A fact reported to a witness, as opposed to being known by the witness; second-hand knowledge; hearsay evidence can be accepted by a court in family proceedings

injunction   Order by the court telling someone what he or she must do or must refrain from doing; the penalty for disobedience can be imprisonment

intestacy   Dying without a valid will

legal aid   Government-funded scheme administered by the Legal Aid Board based on financial eligibility and merits of case, now replaced by Community Legal Service funding

liable relative proceedings   Proceedings taken by the Department of Social Security against a person legally responsible for maintaining wife or husband and/or children who has failed to do so; usually predate Child Support Act 1991

Maintenance Application Form and Maintenance Enquiry Form   Standard forms sent out by the Child Support Agency to parents with care and absent parents respectively asking them about their means and circumstances

matrimonial home rights   Rights of occupation of a family home (or a home intended to be occupied as a family home) which last until decree absolute

MacKenzie friend A lay helper who can accompany a litigator in person in the court room, even in a closed hearing, but who cannot address the court or examine witnesses

mediation   An alternative form of dispute resolution over issues arising in the wake of separation or divorce. Comprehensive (or 'all issues') mediation covers problems over both the children and finances; other mediation (or conciliation, the terms are sometimes used interchangeably) services may deal with child-related disputes alone. Mediation may be offered by lawyer mediators or family mediators alone or both together

minutes of order Draft terms of agreement placed before the court with a request that a consent order be made in those terms

mortgagee The building society, bank or other corporate lender, or individual lending money on the security of a house or flat

mortgagor The person who borrows money on mortgage usually to enable him or her to buy a house or flat

nominal order An order for a nominal amount of maintenance (for example, 5p a year) made if, at the time an order for maintenance was made, payment could not be made or was not needed. This is done so that, if circumstances change, there is an order on the court's file which can be reviewed and increased

non-molestation Order to prohibit one person from assaulting, harassing or interfering with another

non-resident parent This term replaces 'absent parent' in the new CSA legislation and has the same meaning

notice of application Form on which applications to the court are made, beginning with the words 'Take notice that . . .' and containing full details of what is applied for

ouster Order excluding one spouse from the matrimonial home (or from a part of it)

parental responsibility The bundle of rights and duties that parents have towards their children; mothers and married fathers have parental responsibility automatically, while non-married fathers may acquire it by formal Parental Responsibility agreement or court order; others (e.g. guardians, a person with a residence order in his or her favour, a local authority) can acquire parental responsibility too

parent with care A term invented by the Child Support Act 1991 to mean the parent with whom the child has his or her home and who usually provides day-to-day care for the child

penal notice A warning endorsed on a court order, notifying the recipient that he or she is liable to committal to prison for breach of the order

pending suit While the divorce is still continuing (i.e. before decree absolute)

petitioner The person who initiates divorce proceedings by filing the petition

pleadings Formal statements or documents containing a summary of the issues in a case

prayer Formal request in the petition, or answer, for the court orders which the petitioner or respondent seeks; for example, dissolution of the marriage, orders under the Children Act, costs, ancillary relief

prohibited steps order Court order under the Children Act restricting a person's exercise of parental responsibility (e.g. preventing a parent from removing a child from the country without the other parent's consent or court permission)

qualifying child A term invented by the Child Support Act 1991 to mean a child under 16 or under 19 and in full-time non-advanced education – one of his or her parents must be an 'absent parent' (q.v.)

questionnaire List of questions delivered by one spouse to the other requiring further information and/or documentation about finances, in accordance with that person's duty of disclosure; also referred to as 'request under Rule 2.63', the rule of court permitting such a questionnaire

recovered or preserved Gained or retained (money or property) in the course of legal proceedings

relevant child Child of the family under 16 years of age at the date of the decree nisi or between 16 and 18 years of age and receiving instruction at an educational establishment or undergoing training for a trade, profession or vocation (or up to any age, if disabled and dependent)

reply Document filed by the petitioner in response to an answer and/or a cross-petition from the respondent, containing the petitioner's defence

reserved costs When decision on amount of costs to be awarded is deferred until later hearing

residence order An order under the Children Act which settles the arrangements about with whom a child will live; residence orders can be split between parents (or others) or shared, e.g. in favour of a parent and stepparent

respondent The spouse who is not the petitioner or the applicant

Rule 2.63 The rule of court relating to the statement of information which has to be supplied to the court for a financial consent order to be made

sealing by the court The court's stamping of a document when it is filed at the court office or of an order or decree when it is issued

Section 41 appointment Or 'children's appointment' – this was a short hearing before a judge for certificate of satisfaction in respect of arrangements for any relevant children before decree nisi could be pronounced. Section 41 appointments are no longer made since the Children Act came into force

secured provision When some income-producing asset of the payer is put under the control of trustees and, if necessary, the income diverted to the payee to provide the maintenance

separation order   A new order to be introduced by the Family Law Act 1996 which will provide for the formal legal separation of the spouses

SERPS   The earnings part of state retirement pension based on National Insurance contributions paid by an employee on earnings between the lower and upper earnings limits

service   The method by which the petition, notices of application, orders and decrees are supplied to the parties concerned; certain documents need to be served personally, others are served through the post, some by or on behalf of the person issuing them and some by the court

special procedure   In an undefended divorce, the decree can be issued without either petitioner or respondent having to appear (or be represented) at the court: the facts submitted by the petitioner in the petition and verified on affidavit are considered by the district judge. When he or she is satisfied that the facts in the petition are proved and that ground for a divorce exists, he or she issues a certificate to that effect and fixes a date for the formal pronouncement of the decree nisi by the judge. A copy of the decree is sent through the post to both husband and wife by the court office

specific issue order   An order under the Children Act resolving some particular dispute (e.g. schooling) about the children's upbringing

statement of arrangements   Form which has to be filed with petition if there are relevant children of the family, setting out arrangements proposed for them in the future; this should be agreed with the respondent and countersigned if possible before the divorce is started

statutory charge   The amount payable by legally aided person out of any property or cash that was recovered or preserved in the proceedings, where contributions to legal aid fund not sufficient to meet the legal costs of the case (in matrimonial proceedings, maintenance and a lump sum of £2,500 are currently exempt but this may change)

summons   Demand issued by a court for a person against whom a claim or complaint has been made to appear at the court at a specified time

undefended divorce   Where the dissolution of the marriage and how it is to be achieved are not disputed (even if there is dispute about ancillary matters such as the children or finances)

undertaking   Promise to the court to do or not do something which is outside the court's powers to order but is incorporated within a court order so that it is enforceable; the court has no power of its own to vary an undertaking

unfunded scheme   A pension scheme where the employee has a right or expectation to a pension benefit secured only by an undertaking from the employer, for example in a contract of employment; no advance financial provision is made via a trust fund or other insurance contract

without prejudice Phrase used to prevent communications in the negotiation process being made known to the court at the final hearing if those negotiations fail to produce agreement; however, Calderbank offers and responses to them can be disclosed to the court in evidence over costs

Addresses and web sites

Alcoholics Anonymous
Head office, tel: (01904) 644026
London helpline, tel: 020–7833 0022
Web site: www.alcoholics-anonymous.org.uk

Asian Family Counselling Service
76 Church Road
Hanwell
London W7 1LB
Tel/Fax: 020–8567 5616

Association for Shared Parenting
PO Box 2000
Dudley
West Midlands DY1 1YZ
Tel: (01789) 751157
Web site:
www.sharedparenting.org.uk

Association of Consulting Actuaries
1 Wardrobe Place
London EC4V 5AG
Tel: 020–7248 3163
Fax: 020–7236 1889
Email: acahelp@aca.org.uk
Web site: www.aca.org.uk

Bar Council
Complaints Department
Northumberland House
303–306 High Holborn
London WC1V 7JZ
Tel: 020–7440 4000 *(for advice and a complaints form)*
or
3 Bedford Row
London WC1R 4DB
Tel: 020–7242 0082 *(for advice and to obtain publications/leaflets)*
Fax: 020–7831 9217

Bar Council's Pro-Bono Unit
7 Grays Inn Square
London WC1R 5AZ
Tel: 020–7831 9711
Fax: 020–7831 9733
Web site: www.barprobono.org.uk
Applications for assistance in writing only.

Both Parents Forever
39 Cloonmore Avenue
Orpington
Kent BR6 9LE
Tel: (01689) 854343
*Provides help and advice to all parents
and grandparents involved in divorce,
separation or care proceedings*

**British Association of Lawyer
Mediators (BALM)**
The Shooting Lodge
Guildford Road
Sutton Green
Guildford
Surrey GU4 7PZ
Tel: (01483) 236237
Fax: (01483) 237004
Web site: www.balm.org.uk

**Cambridge Family and Divorce
Centre**
Essex House
71 Regent Street
Cambridge CB2 1AB
Tel: (01223) 576308
Fax: (01223) 576309

Child Abduction Unit
Official Solicitor's Department
4th Floor
81 Chancery Lane
London WC2A 1DD
Tel: 020-7911 7045/7047
Fax: 020-7911 7248

Childline
Helpline, tel: (0800) 1111
Web site: www.childline.org.uk
*A confidential listening and advisory
service*

Child Poverty Action Group
94 White Lion Street
London N1 9PF
Tel: 020-7837 7979
Fax: 020-7837 6414
Web site: www.cpag.org.uk

Children's Legal Centre
University of Essex
Wivenhoe Park
Colchester
Essex CO4 3SQ
Helpline, tel: (01206) 873820
(weekdays 10–12.30, 2–4.30)
Fax: (01206) 874026
Web site: www2.essex.ac.uk/clc
*National organisation aiming to improve
the law and policy affecting children in
England and Wales. Advice by
telephone or letter for children with legal
problems; service also available for adults*

Child Support Agency
Enquiry line, tel: (0345) 133133
Web site: www.dss.org.uk

Child Support Practitioners' Group
c/o James Pirrie
The Family Law Consortium
2 Henrietta Street
London WC2E 8PS
Email: jp@tflc.co.uk
*A group of about 200 solicitors with
experience in legal problems relating to
the Child Support Agency. Will
supply, where possible, names and
addresses of local solicitor members*

Community Legal Service
Selborne House
54–60 Victoria Street
London SW1A 6QW
Directory line: (08456) 081122
Web site: www.justask.org.uk

Comprehensive Accredited Lawyer Mediators (CALM)
Caroline Graham
MacLeod & MacCallum
PO Box 4
28 Queens Gate
Inverness IV1 1YN
Tel: (01463) 239393
Fax: (01463) 222879
Members are available to mediate all issues arising from breakdown of relationships

Council of Mortgage Lenders
3 Savile Row
London W1X 1AF
Information line: 020-7440 2255
Web site: www.cml.org.uk
Provides a useful free factsheet called 'Assistance with Mortgage Payments'

Dawn Project
South Yorkshire Surviving
  Separation and Divorce
95–99 Effingham Street
Rotherham S65 1BL
Tel: (01709) 512436

Department of Social Security (DSS)
Public enquiry office
Tel: 020-7712 2171
Fax: 020-7712 2386
Web site: www.dss.gov.uk
For general enquiries contact your local office

Disability Working Allowance Unit
The Inland Revenue
PO Box 178
Preston PR1 0YY
Tel: (08456) 055858
Fax: (01772) 239794
Minicom: (08456) 088844

The Divorce Corporation
187 Baslow Road
Totley
Sheffield S17 4DG
Tel: 0114-262 0616
Fax: 0114-235 0878

Divorce Registry
First Avenue House
42–49 High Holborn
London WC1V 6NP
Tel: 020-7947 6000

Families Need Fathers
134 Curtain Road
London EC2A 3AR
Tel: 020-7613 5060
Web site: www.fnf.org.uk

Family Credit Unit
Tel: (01253) 500050

Family Law Consortium
2 Henrietta Street
London WC2E 8PS
Tel: 020-7420 5000
Fax: 020-7420 5005
Email: flc@tflc.co.uk
Web site: www.tflc.co.uk

Family Mediation Scotland
127 Rose Street
South Lane
Edinburgh EH2 4BB
Tel: 0131-220 1610
Fax: 0131-220 6895

Family Mediation Service
76 Dublin Road
Belfast BT2 7HP
Tel: 028-9032 2914
Fax: 028-9031 5298

Family Mediators Association
46 Grosvenor Gardens
London SW1W 0EB
Tel: 020-7881 9400
Fax: 020-7881 9401
Web site:
www.familymediators.co.uk

Family Records Centre
Public Search Room
1 Myddelton Street
London EC1R 1UW
(personal visits only)
Recorded information line: 0151-471 4816
Certificate enquiries, tel: 0151-471 4800
General enquiries, tel: 020-8392 5300
Fax: 020-8392 5307
Web site: www.pro.gov.uk

Family Welfare Association
501-505 Kingsland Road
London E8 4AU
Tel: 020-7254 6251

General Register Office
PO Box 2
Southport PR8 2DJ
Tel: 0151-471 4830

Gingerbread
7 Sovereign Court
Sovereign Close
London E1W 3HW
Tel: 020-7488 9300
Fax: 020-7488 9333
Web site: www.gingerbread.org.uk
A support organisation for lone parents and their families, with around 200 groups in England and Wales. Also publishes advice and information leaflets

Grandparents Federation
Moot House
The Stow
Harlow
Essex CM20 3AG
Advice line: (01279) 444964
(weekdays)
Gives advice, information and support to grandparents of children affected by a divorce, separation or loss of contact for any other reason

Institute of Legal Executives
Kempston Manor
Kempston
Bedford MK42 7AB
Tel: (01234) 841000
Fax: (01234) 840373
Email: jburns@ilex.org.uk
Web site: www.ilex.org.uk

Jewish Marriage Council
23 Ravenshurst Avenue
London NW4 4EL
Counselling line, tel: 020-8203 6311
Fax: 020-8203 8727
Get advisory service, tel: 020-8203
6314
Crisis helplines, tel: (08457) 581999,
020-8203 6211

Land Charges Department
Land Registry Plymouth
Drakes Hill Court
Burrington Way
Plymouth PL5 3LP
Tel: (01752) 635600
Telephone searches: (01752) 635635
Fax: (01752) 766666

HM Land Registry
32 Lincoln's Inn Fields
London WC2A 3PH
Tel: 020-7917 8888
Fax: 020-7955 0110
Web site: www.landreg.gov.uk

LawGroup UK
85 Croydon Road
Caterham
Surrey CR3 6PD
Tel: (01883) 370000
Fax: (01883) 370066
Web site: www.lawgroup.co.uk

LawNet
Ince House
60 Kenilworth Road
Leamington Spa
Warwickshire CV32 6JY
Tel: (01926) 886990
Fax: (01926) 886553
Web site: www.lawnet.co.uk/
law.epoch

Law Society of England and Wales
113 Chancery Lane
London WC2A 1PL
Tel: 020-7242 1222
Web site: www.lawsociety.org.uk
Provides names and addresses of
solicitors. Not an advisory service

Law Society of Northern Ireland
Law Society House
90 Victoria Street
Belfast BT1 3GN
Tel: 028-9023 1614
Fax: 028-9023 2606
Web site: www.lawsoc-ni.org

Law Society of Scotland
26 Drumsheugh Gardens
Edinburgh EH3 7RN
Tel: 0131-226 7411
Fax: 0131-225 2934
Web site: www.lawscot.org.uk

Legal Aid Board for Scotland
see Scottish Legal Aid Board

Legal Aid Department
Bedford House
16/22 Bedford Street
Belfast BT2 7EG
Tel: 028-9024 6441

Legal Services Commission
85 Grays Inn Road
London WC1X 8TP
Tel: 020-7759 0000
Web site:
www.legalservices.gov.uk

Legal Services Ombudsman
22 Oxford Court
Oxford Street
Manchester M2 3WQ
Tel: (08456) 010794
Fax: 0161-236 2651
Web site: www.olso.org

**London Lesbian and Gay
Switchboard**
Tel: 020-7837 7324 (24 hours)

London Women's Aid
PO Box 391
Bristol BS99 7WS
National helpline, tel: (08457)
023468 (weekdays 10–5)

Lord Chancellor's Department
54 Victoria Street
London SW1E 6QW
Tel: 020-7210 8500
Fax: 020-7210 8740
Email:
general.enquiries@lcdhq.gsi.gov.uk
Web site: www.open.gov.uk/lcd

Marriage Care
Clitheroe House
1 Blythe Mews
Blythe Road
London W14 0HW
Tel: 020-7371 1341
Fax: 020-7371 4921
Email: marriagecare@btinternet.com

Marriage Care (for Scotland)
see Scottish Marriage Care

Marriage Counselling Scotland
40 North Castle Street
Edinburgh EH2 3BN
Tel: 0131-225 5006
Fax: 0131-220 0639

National Children's Bureau
8 Wakley Street
London EC1V 7QE
Tel: 020-7843 6000
Fax: 020-7278 9512
Web site: www.ncb.org.uk

**National Council for the Divorced
and Separated**
National Secretary
3 Selby Close
Epworth
Doncaster
DN9 1GH
Tel: (07041) 478120
Fax: (01427) 872 443
Web site: www.ncds.org.uk
*Has about 70 branches throughout the
UK which provide a venue where people
with similar experiences and problems
can meet and develop new interests*

**National Council for One Parent
Families**
255 Kentish Town Road
London NW5 2LX
Tel: 020-7428 5400, (08000) 185026
Fax: 020-7482 4851
Web site: www.ncopf.org.uk

National Debtline
The Birmingham Settlement
318 Summer Lane
Birmingham B19 3RL
Tel: 0121-359 8501 *(Mon, Thur 10–
4; Tue, Wed 10–7; Fri 10–12)*
Advice line, tel: (0645) 500511

National Family Mediation
9 Tavistock Place
London WC1H 9SN
Tel: 020-7383 5993
Fax: 020-7383 5994

National Housing Federation
175 Grays Inn Road
London WC1X 8UP
Tel: 020-7278 6571
Fax: 020-7833 1823
National Stepfamily Association
see Parentline Plus

Northern Ireland Housing Executive
Head Office
2 The Housing Centre
Adelaide Street
Belfast BT2 7BA
Tel: 028-9024 0588

**Northern Ireland Women's Aid
Federation**
129 University Street
Belfast BT7 1HP
Tel: 028-9024 9358
Helpline, tel: 028-9033 1818 (24
hours)

Office of Fair Trading
PO Box 366
Hayes UB3 1XB
Tel: (0870) 606 0321
Fax: (0870) 607 0321
*Produces a number of free publications
about personal finance, e.g. 'Debt – A
Survival Guide' and 'No Credit'*

Office for National Statistics
General Register Office
Smedley Hydro
Trafalgar Road
Southport
Merseyside PR8 2HH
Certificate enquiries, tel: 0151–471
4800
Web site: www.ons.gov.uk

**Office for the Supervision of
Solicitors**
Victoria Court
8 Dormer Place
Leamington Spa
Warwickshire CV32 5AE
Helpline: (08456) 086 6565
Enquiry desk, tel: (01926) 820082

One Parent Families Scotland
13 Gayfield Square
Edinburgh EH1 3NX
Tel: 0131-556 3899/4563
Fax: 0131-557 9650
Web site: www.gn.apc.org/opfs

Parentline Plus
520 Highgate Studios
53–79 Highgate Road
Kentish Town
London NW5 1TL
Tel: (0808) 800 2222
Web site: www.parentline.co.uk

RELATE National Marriage Guidance Council
Herbert Gray College
Little Church Street
Rugby
Warwickshire CV21 3AP
Tel: (01788) 573241
Web site: www.relate.org.uk
Telephone numbers of local branches are listed in the telephone directory under RELATE

RELATE
76 Dublin Road
Belfast BT2 7HP
Tel: 028-90 323454
Fax: 028-90 375298

Reunite (National Council for Abducted Children)
PO Box 24875
London E1 6FR
Tel: 020-7375 3440/3441
Fax: 020-7375 3442
Email: reunite@bircom.co.uk
A self-help network for parents whose children have been abducted

Scottish Legal Aid Board
44 Drumsheugh Gardens
Edinburgh EH3 7SW
Tel: 0131-226 7061
Fax: 0131-220 4878

Scottish Marriage Care
132 Huntly Street
Aberdeen AB1 1SU
Tel: (01224) 643174

Scottish Women's Aid
Norton Park
Edinburgh EH7 5QY
Tel: 0131-475 2372
Fax: 0131-475 2384

Shelter National Campaign for the Homeless
88 Old Street
London EC1V 9HU
Helpline, tel: (0808) 800 4444 (24 hours)
Web site: www.shelter.org.uk

Shelter Scottish Campaign for Homeless People
47 Belmont Street
Aberdeen
Tel: (01224) 645586
Fax: (01224) 632466

Society of Pension Consultants
St Bartholomew House
92 Fleet Street
London EC4Y 1DH
Fax: 020-7353 9396
Letters only

Solicitors Family Law Association
366 Crofton Road
Farnborough
Orpington
Kent BR6 8NN
Tel: (01689) 850227
Fax: (01689) 855833
Web site: www.sfla.co.uk

UK College of Family Mediators
24–32 Stephenson Way
London NW1 2HX
Tel: 020-7391 9162
Fax: 020-7391 9165
Web site: www.ukcfm.co.uk

Women's Aid (for London)
see London Women's Aid

Women's Aid Federation for England
PO Box 391
Bristol BS99 7WS
National helpline, tel: 0117-977 1888 (weekdays 10–5)

Women's Aid (for Northern Ireland)
see Northern Ireland Women's Aid Federation

Women's Aid (for Scotland)
see Scottish Women's Aid

Web sites
www.courtservice.gov.uk
www.divorce.co.uk
www.divorce.net
www.inlandrevenue.gov.uk

1. What is liability for the mortgage in Acton

2. What is position before divorce thru.

3 K's liabilities – joint responsibility

4

Bibliography

The following is a list of books that you and your children may find helpful in getting you through divorce and separation.[1] RELATE★ has a good selection of titles on divorce and other family issues.

General reading on divorce
Ahrons, C. 1995. *The Good Divorce*. Bloomsbury
Basciano, C. *Relationship Breakdown*. Ward Lock
Fisher, T. 1997. *National Family Mediation Guide to Separation and Divorce*. Vermilion
Peiffer, V. 1991. *How to Cope with Splitting Up*. Sheldon Press

Issues to do with divorce
Cockett, M., Tripp, J. 1994. *The Exeter Family Study*. Family Policy Studies Centre
Cox, K., Desforges, M. 1987. *Divorce and the School*. Routledge
Forster, G. *Healing Love's Wounds*. Marshall Pickering
Henshall, S. A. 1994. *Is this a Daddy Sunday?* Monarch
MacLean, M. 1991. *Surviving Divorce*. Palgrave
Wallerstein, J. *Second Chances*. Ticknor & Fields
Wallerstein, J. 1996. *Surviving the Breakup*. Basic Books

Women's issues
Franks, H. *Mummy Doesn't Live Here Anymore*. Doubleday
Keene, J., Jenson, I. 1995. *Women Alone*. Hay House
Sugarbaker, G. 1992. *Nice Women Get Divorced*. Fairview Press

---

[1] This list is based on the bibliography put together by the Dawn Project★ in South Yorkshire.

Single parenting

Lilley, M. 1996. *Successful Single Parenting*. How to Books

Slipman, S. 1993. *Essential Lone Parent Survival Guide*. Kenneth Mason

Worth, J., Tufnell, C. 1997. *A Journey through Single Parenting*. Hodder & Stoughton

Children's issues

Jewett, C. 1994. *Helping Children Cope with Separation and Loss*. Free Association Books

Kroll, B. 1994. *Chasing Rainbows*. Russell House

Mitchell, A. K. 1995. *Children in the Middle*. Routledge

Swan-Jackson, A. 1999. *Caught in the Middle*. Piccadilly Press

Wells, R. 1997. *Helping Children Cope With Divorce*. Sheldon Press

Relationships and recovery

Hay, L. L. 1995. *You Can Heal Your Life*. Eden Grove

Jeffers, S. 1997. *Feel the Fear and Do It Anyway*. Rider

Jeffers, S. 1998. *Losing a Love, Finding a Life*. Piatkus

Lee, S. 1996. *All by Myself*. Orion

Litvinoff, S. 2001. *Relate: Starting Again*. Vermilion

Therapies

Cooper, J., Lewis, J. 1995. *Who Can I Talk To?* Headway

Knight, L. 1995. *Talking to a Stranger*. Hodder & Stoughton

Stepfamilies

Collins, S. 1988. *Step-parents and their Children*. Souvenir Press

Coverley, B. 1996. *Successful Step-parenting*. Bloomsbury

Eckler, J. D. 1993. *Step by Step-parenting*. Betterway Books

Hayman, S. 2001. *The Relate Guide to Step Families*. Vermilion

Adult fiction

Cheek, M. 1996. *Dog Days*. Sceptre

Cheek, M. 2000. *Mrs Fytton's 'Country Life'*. Faber

Cowie, V. *Unsentimental Journey*. Mandarin Fiction

Trollope, J. 1998. *Other People's Children*. Bloomsbury

Older children: non-fiction

Stones, R. 1994. *It's Not Your Fault*. Piccadilly Press

Older children: fiction

Bailey, A. 1994. *Breaking Point*. Faber & Faber

Blume, J. 1989. *It's Not the End of the World*. Macmillan

Danziger, P. 1995. *The Divorce Express*. Mammoth

Fine, A. 1994. *Flour Babies*. Puffin

Fine, A. 2000. *Goggle-eyes*. Puffin

Fine, A. 1998. *Madame Doubtfire*. Puffin

Fine, A. 1996. *Step by Wicked Step*. Puffin

Hardcastle, M. 1996. *Please Come Home*. Faber & Faber

Harding, C. 1994. *Stepping Out*. Macmillan

Murphy, J. 1996. *Worlds Apart*. Walker

Pilling, A. 1998. *Henry's Leg*. Puffin

Storr, C. 2000. *The Mirror Image Ghost*. Faber & Faber

Wilson, J. 1993. *The Suitcase Kid*. Yearling Books

Young children: non-fiction

Batey, B. *Me in My Changing Family*. Scottish Family Conciliation

Brown, L. 1988. *Dinosaurs Divorce*. Little, Brown

Haycock, K. 1995. *Dealing With Family Break-up*. Hodder Wayland

Thomas, P. 1999. My Family's Changing. Hodder Wayland

Young children: fiction

Abercrombie, B., Graham, M. 1990. *Charlie Anderson*. Atheneum

Ackerman, M. J. 1997. '*Does Wednesday Mean Mom's House or Dad's?*' John Wiley & Sons

Ahlberg, A. 1996. *Mrs Vole the Vet*. Puffin

Ahlberg, A. 1997. *Ms Cliff the Climber*. Puffin

Ahlberg, A. 1996. *Miss Dirt the Dustman's Daughter*. Puffin

Bryant-Mole, K. 1995. *What's Happening?: Splitting Up*. Hodder Wayland

Cole, B. 2000. *Two of Everything*. Red Fox

Cole, J. 1997. *My Parents' Divorce*. Franklin Watts

Hoffman, M. 1997. *Grace and Family*. Frances Lincoln

Johnson, J. 1997. *My Stepfamily*. Franklin Watts

Nystrom, C. 1994. *Mike's Lonely Summer*. Lion Publishing

Index

abduction of children 174, 271–4, 307–8

'absent parent' 97, 98

abuse, child 85, 168, 263, 265

ABWOR (assistance by way of representation) 298

access 172
  see also contact

accountants 194

adopted children 98, 148, 285, 316

adoption order 276

adultery 128, 138, 143–4, 151, 152
  affidavit 156
  attempted reconciliation after 146–7
  co-respondent 138, 143, 144, 148, 151, 155, 156
  confession statement 144
  evidence 144, 156
  as grounds for divorce 135, 143
  and Scottish law 295, 300

advice and help 74
  free legal advice 70, 71
  see also mediation; solicitors

affidavits 139, 155–6
  exhibits 156
  fees 156, 158
  of maintenance arrears 235
  of means 218–19, 220, 240
  in Scotland 301–2

special procedure affidavit 155–8
  swearing 139, 158

agreed arrangements 126–8
  formal separation agreements 127–8
  informal 126–7

Alcoholics Anonymous 261

alcoholism 144, 168

aliment 299, 300, 311, 313–14, 316–17

ancillary relief 147
  in Northern Ireland 323–4
  pilot scheme 36
  see also lump-sum payment orders; periodical-payment orders; property-adjustment orders

appeals against court orders 171, 232

Approved Family Help
  applications for 24, 26–7
  certificate 27
  contribution towards costs 24, 26–7, 30
  General Family Help 22, 24, 25–6, 28–9
  Help with Mediation 22, 23, 95

arrestment of bank/building society account 315

assessment of costs 32–3
  challenging the bill 32, 33
  CLS-funded cases 32
  drawing up the bill 32